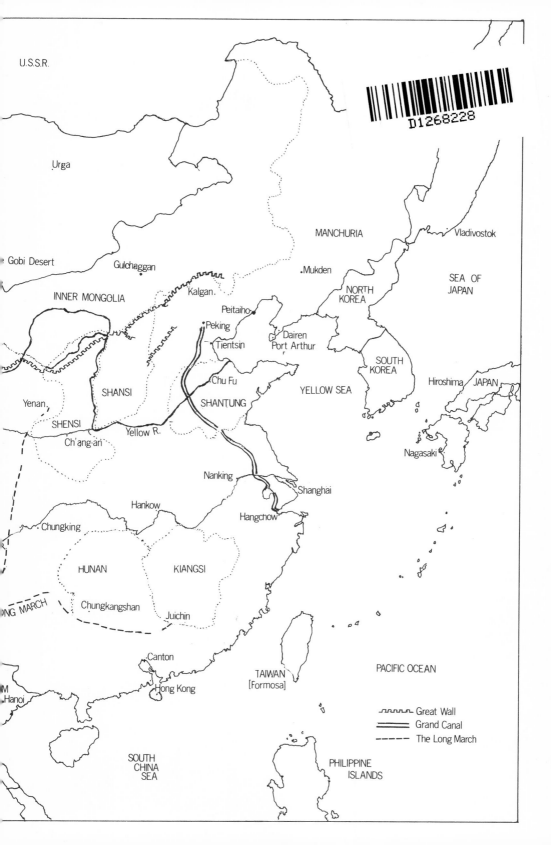

U.S.S.R.

Urga

Gobi Desert   Gulchaggan

INNER MONGOLIA

MANCHURIA

Vladivostok

.Mukden

NORTH
KOREA

SEA OF
JAPAN

Kalgan.

Peitaiho.
.Peking
Tientsin

Dairen
Port Arthur

SOUTH
KOREA

Hiroshima   JAPAN

SHANSI

.Chu Fu

SHANTUNG

YELLOW SEA

Yenan.

SHENSI

Yellow R.

Ch'ang·ari

Nagasaki

Nanking

Hankow

Shanghai

Hangchow

.Chungking

HUNAN   KIANGSI

NG MARCH   Chungkangshan

Juichin

PACIFIC OCEAN

.Canton

Hong Kong

TAIWAN
[Formosa]

M
Hanoi

Great Wall

Grand Canal

The Long March

SOUTH
CHINA
SEA

PHILIPPINE
ISLANDS

D1268228

The Footprints of the Pheasant
in the Snow

Note on the title

Just before I left Peking, a Chinese friend asked me for the negatives of my favorite Chinese pictures. These she had enlarged and put in a book with two sandalwood covers. On the top cover were four Chinese characters delicately carved. When she presented the book to me she said, "Here are some memories of your life in my country." She explained that the characters which she had chosen for the cover meant "the footprints of the pheasant in the snow"—for her Chinese words which meant memories.

The Footprints of the Pheasant
in the Snow

BY

ALNAH JAMES JOHNSTON

THE ENTRANCE TO YENCHING

PORTLAND, MAINE ❧ MCMLXXVII

First printing, October 1976
Second printing, February 1977

ACKNOWLEDGMENTS

Because this book spans many years of my life, it is impossible to acknowledge my indebtedness to all the writers—Chinese, English, and Americans—whose thoughts I have assimilated. How can one ever measure the debt one owes to the teachers and thinkers who have shaped one's life?

But a number of people, in addition to members of my family, have been most kind in encouraging me and in making helpful suggestions after reading parts of my book: Mildred Grimes and Dorothy Stanley, former colleagues at Dana Hall School, Elizabeth Ring, and Agusto Santos who read the entire manuscript. Dr. William Hung and Ling Jui T'ang, old China friends, kindly checked historic facts and specific details of Chinese life.

I am most grateful to Pearl Lester who deciphered my handwriting and typed and retyped my manuscript, to Harry Milliken of The Anthoensen Press for his patience and helpful suggestions regarding the making of a book, and to the Inness Photo Company who took my fifty-year-old negatives and made most of the pictures in this book.

PRINTED IN THE UNITED STATES OF AMERICA

BY THE ANTHOENSEN PRESS, PORTLAND, MAINE

TO GEORGE

remembering all that his understanding
and wisdom have meant to me
through the years.

Contents

CHRONOLOGICAL CHART

	DYNASTIES	WESTERN AND OTHERS
B.C.	HSIA	Greatness of Egypt Crete First Dynasty of Babylon
1766?	SHANG Earliest writing Emergence of cities Silk Culture flourishes Ancestor Worship	Moses Siege of Troy Homer
1122	CHOU (Feudal States) China's Classical Age Confucius Lao Tze Chuang-Tzu Advance in astronomy	Classical Age of Greece Sophocles Socrates and Plato Buddha Cyrus the Great of Persia Alexander the Great Asoka
221	CHIN 1st Emperor, Shih Huang-Ti The Great Wall	Hannibal crosses the Alps
207 **A.D.**	HAN Expansion under Wu Ti Historical Records Paper is made	Rome at its height Julius Caesar Jesus
222	"SIX DYNASTY" PERIOD Buddhism firmly established	Fall of Rome Silk worm introduced in Europe
589	SUI	Mohammed
618	T'ANG Capital at Ch'ang-an The Golden Age of Poetry Li Po and Fu Fu Examination system Porcelain—Tea Classic	Charlemagne

	DYNASTIES	WESTERN AND OTHERS
907	**SUNG** Great Age of Painting Hangchow at its height Printing Compass and gunpowder	The Crusades
1127	**SOUTHERN SUNG**	
1279	**YUAN** Kublai Khan Rise of the theater Marco Polo in China Christianity Islam	Moscow founded Magna Carta Paper made in Europe Mongol Invasion of Europe
1368	**MING** Yung Lo, Peking Architect Color in porcelain Portuguese traders Jesuit Matteo Ricci in Peking	Renaissance Gutenberg Prince Henry the Navigator Columbus Martin Luther Galileo Shakespeare
1644	**CH'ING (MANCHUS)** Ch'ien-lung era The Opium Wars Hongkong ceded to Britain China opened to West Empress-Dowager Tzu Hsi Boxer Rebellion Sun Yat Sen's Revolution	George III of England George Washington Napoleon Industrial Revolution Public libraries Mass education
1912	**THE CHINESE REPUBLIC** The Warlord era Chiang breaks with Communists Mao at Chingkangshan The Long March Sino-Japanese War Chiang withdraws to Formosa	Two World Wars Archeology flourishes Lindberg's flight across the ocean
1949	**THE PEOPLE'S REPUBLIC OF CHINA**	

PROLOGUE

The Dream

Often I think of the beautiful town
That is seated by the sea;
Often in thought go up and down
The pleasant streets of that dear old town,
And my youth comes back to me.

LONGFELLOW

MY PATERNAL GRANDFATHER was a ship builder and lived with his family in a little New England village at the edge of the sea near Portland, Maine. My grandmother always said that he died of a broken heart when his last ship, into which he had put his fortune, foundered in a winter storm on its maiden voyage. My father married soon after and took his bride to live in my grandmother's house. This is where I was born and where I spent my early childhood.

Although we moved to Portland when I was only six, I have vivid memories of that peaceful village with its elm-shaded streets and warm-hearted seafaring people. We were all like one large family. Village life centered around the community church; and the suppers there with an abundance of home cooked food were gala occasions. There were never any strangers that I can remember, although occasionally a tramp would knock at our kitchen door and ask for food. No questions were ever asked and after he had eaten he would go away as mysteriously as he had come.

In those days there was nothing for me to be afraid of—nothing except the dark. If ever I woke up in the night, I would jump out of bed and crawl in with my grandmother. As soon as I sank into the soft down of her feather bed I was off to sleep again. My grandmother was the delight of my life. I loved her dearly and felt closer to her than to my mother whose time was taken up with babies and the activities of a busy household. In the spring, it was my grandmother who taught me to love the delicate fragrance of our lilacs, the syringa, and lilies-of-the-valley and the bluebirds and robins that hopped about in our back yard; who took me into our Maine woods where pink lady's slippers grew and the delicate little pink and white arbutus we called mayflowers. "For lo," she would say, "the winter is past.... The flow-

3

ers appear on the earth and the time of the singing of birds has come."
(She knew the Bible almost by heart and went into her closet to pray,
as the Bible told her to do.) But I loved the winter as well as the spring
when our house, half buried in snow, was snug and warm. On cold
winter days, one of the joys of my childhood was to sit in her lap
before the big iron stove in our kitchen listening to the stories she told
me over and over again. My favorite stories told of the launching of
my grandfather's ships as they slid down the way, the hoisting of the
sails when they were ready to start on their voyages across the sea, and
of the thrilling days when the ships returned safely home, laden with
strange and wonderful things.

Our house was only a stone's throw from where my grandfather's
shipyard had been. Although it had disappeared long before I was
born, I was taken there often and to the promenade where I could see
the coastal islands and watch the five- and six-masted schooners sailing gracefully into Portland Harbor. Often at night, after I had been
put to bed, I would look out of my window toward the ships at anchor.
Then I would dream that someday I would sail far away to the Orient
where Uncle Heyward lived. Each summer he and his beautiful wife
came from Bangkok to visit us always bringing gifts: sapphires and
other jewels to my mother, meerschaum pipes with carved bowls
which delighted my father, and curious coins for all of us children.
I still treasure the coins and trinkets he brought to me.

Uncle Heyward was the physician to the King of Siam and I remember him as one of the most fascinating and charming men I have
ever known. (The Heyward Hayes Memorial Library in Bangkok is
a memorial to him.) He had been adopted by my grandmother when
he was an orphan boy, had gone to the nearby U.S. Marine Hospital
to train as a doctor, and as a young man had decided to board one of
the ships in Portland Harbor bound for the Orient. His first port of
call had been Bangkok, a city which so enthralled him that he left the
ship to seek his fortune there. His fabulous stories held our whole
family spellbound as he described his life in that picturesque, colorful
land and told of his visits to the palace of King Chulalongkorn of
The King and I fame. As I listened, the Orient with its palaces and
temples came alive to me; I thought it must be the most enchanting
place in all the world.

So it was really a childhood dream come true when years later, in the summer of 1923, I set sail from Seattle for Peking.

*   *   *

THE SETTING. Life was a blend of two worlds when I was growing up in Portland, Maine. In New England we were just emerging from an era of leisurely living. A few five and six-masted schooners were left to sail into Portland Harbor. In the city there were blacksmith shops and livery stables because people were still riding in their carriages. Trolley cars were the chief means of transportation and for five cents we would ride in all directions—for ten cents, to the end of the line. But most people walked. Children walked a good mile to school in all kinds of weather. I thought nothing of walking the three miles to my grandfather's house on the edge of the city—a spacious, rambling yellow house surrounded by meadows full of wild flowers. (Today the house has been replaced by a supermarket and the meadows are filled with busy streets.)

It was a place I loved dearly. In the winter when the curving rivulets in the meadows had frozen over, I would skate there all by myself, weaving in and out, invigorated by the cold crisp air. Then when the winter storms had covered the ground with drifts of snow, I would snowshoe softly over this beautiful white world—a world that was all my own for the meadows stretched for miles without a house or a person in sight. Like Thoreau, I grew in those days like corn in the night.

In the spring, in apple blossom time, my grandfather sometimes took me with him when he walked through the orchards or pasture land. Often he would exclaim about the beauty of the blossoms and stop to drink in the delicate fragrance of the air. He was gentle and kind; I loved him very much. It was from him that I learned how my mother and I got our odd name—a name I never liked as a child. My mother had come prematurely when my grandparents were visiting at the home of friends in Canada. Because of their kindness at the time of the birth, it was decided to name this first child after them. His name was Albert and her name, Hannah; so they combined the two to make Alnah. He told me about his name, John Proctor. It was the name of an ancestor who had lived in the Salem witchcraft days and who had tried to persuade the authorities that the whole business was a terrible hoax. But, instead, he was himself accused of witchcraft and was one of the nineteen persons hanged on Gallows Hill. Arthur Miller tells his tragic story in the play *The Crucible*.

In those days Portland was far from a provincial city. There were concerts with world-renowned artists and great theater. I can remember the night when my parents went to see the great Sarah Bernhardt at the Jefferson theater—a beautiful little theater named after the Shakespearian actor, Joseph Jefferson. I can remember Maud Adams, Ethel Barrymore, Robert Mantell, and other great artists who appeared on the Jefferson stage.

My family for generations had attended the First Parish Unitarian Church where the Longfellow family worshipped. A member of the family still occupied the Longfellow pew when I was a child. Henry Wadsworth Longfellow was born and brought up in Portland and was educated at nearby Bowdoin College. Not only was he a great poet, but as a young teacher at Harvard he was one of the first professors of modern languages in the country, and for many years the only American honored at Westminster Abbey in London. Thomas Brackett Reed, Speaker of the House who dominated the Republican Party in the late 1890s, lived near us. I heard much about him from my grandparents who named one of their seven children for him.

This was a time when it was still an adventure to take the train to Boston or New York, riding in the comfortable parlor cars and eating a delicious lunch beautifully served in the swaying dining cars. The only way to cross the country then was by train, a journey of five days; and of course the only way to cross the ocean was by ship.

But the pace of life was beginning to quicken. A few adventurous people were riding in their automobiles. They wore "dusters" and tied down their hats, for the first cars were open and went fifteen or twenty miles an hour—a good speed in those days. Many of the roads were still unpaved and dusty. Charles Lindberg had bought a single-engine airplane for five hundred dollars and within a few years was to make his solo flight across the Atlantic in thirty-three hours. (Forty years later, men were to walk on the moon.)

*   *   *

Try, if you can, to imagine what life was like without radio or television. During World War I, which ended when I was in college, we had to walk to the office of the local newspaper and read the bulletin board to get the latest news of the front. Although the war was not fought on our soil it brought profound changes. It made us, as a people, aware for the first time of the world around us. Europe became very much a reality when our fathers, brothers, and friends were fighting there. The Russian Revolution of 1917 made the world of Tolstoy and Dostoevski seem less remote. Our fleet in the Pacific made us conscious of the Orient in quite a different way from the days of the clipper ships.

The war also served as a catalyst for the first women's liberation movement. Many women served as volunteers at home and abroad. Life for them took on a new dimension; and before long, walls began to come down that had kept women in their homes. I can remember the day in 1916 when twenty-five thousand women marched down Fifth Avenue demanding the vote. A shudder went through many American homes. But in 1920 the Nineteenth Amendment was added to our constitution and the United States became the sixteenth nation to give women the vote.

By the end of the war, we had come to realize that our country was a World Power. We had won glory abroad by turning the tide of battle in Europe and moral stature by supporting (through Woodrow Wilson) the League of Nations. For the moment the world looked bright and the future seemed full of hope. We believed that we had fought the war to end war, to make the world safe for democracy, to make possible a World of Brotherhood. My father uttered a word of caution about all this optimism; but for those of us who were young it was an exciting time, a time of great promise and idealism.

On the other side of the world, it was also a moment of great promise and idealism. China was having a renaissance. The Revolution of 1911 had brought to an end not only the decadent Manchu dynasty but the empire which had existed since the third century B.C. Sun Yat-sen, the great revolutionary leader, had proclaimed his "Three Principles—Nationalism, Democracy, and the People's Livelihood," based on Abraham Lincoln's "Of the People, By the People,

and For the People." Under these principles he hoped to establish a
republic based on the United States Constitution, and strong enough
to be independent of the foreign powers which had exploited and
dominated China for more than a hundred years.

Young Chinese believed that the time had come to modernize and
unite their country. They flocked abroad, thousands to Japan which
had already become a modern nation, hundreds to the United States,
England, Scotland, and France. Mai-ling Soong (Madam Chiang Kai-
shek) came to the United States and was graduated from Wellesley
College in 1917. Chou En-lai joined a group of students who went to
France on a work-study program. Most of these students returned to
China convinced that science and democracy accounted for the
strength of the Western Powers and must be adapted to their country.

Hu Shih, who had studied at Cornell and Columbia and had become a disciple of John Dewey, led a movement to modernize the
written language by replacing the classical language with *pai-hua,* the
vernacular. Until 1917 the classical language was the only written
language China had. It was as if, in an American college, all the books
in the library and all the textbooks were in Latin. The success of this
movement was considered the most important single factor in mod-
ernizing the country for it spread literacy to the common people.
Literature and textbooks were now written in *pai-hua.* Modern newspapers and magazines became available. Within the decade (1910–
1920), the telephone, the moving picture, the widespread use of electric lights, the railway and automobile all joined to revolutionize
society. Education for the first time became coeducational, a National
Students' Union was organized and the National Peking University
became the center for a cultural revolution where old customs and
institutions were being revalued.

This ferment and spirit of excitement were contagious and spread
abroad. China became very much in the minds and hearts of the
American people. More churches supported missionaries in China.
Colleges and universities "adopted" Chinese institutions. There was a
Yale-in-China, a Princeton-in-China; Smith College adopted Ginling
in Nanking, Wellesley adopted Yenching in Peking. There was to be
a Harvard-Yenching Institute. The Rockefeller Foundation made possible the Peking Union Medical College which became the best

equipped hospital in the Orient, with a medical school that compared favorably with many medical schools in Europe and America. When Charles William Elliott retired as president of Harvard College, it was to China that he went.

How did it happen that I, brought up in a conservative New England family, was drawn into this exciting world? It happened quite by chance. A New York train, an hour late, changed the course of my life.

On the Way

There is a divinity that shapes our ends,
Rough hew them as we will.

SHAKESPEARE

AT THE EVENING WEDDING of my college roomate in Cleveland, I met Reginald Wheeler, a young man working with Dr. Henry Luce (father of the founder of *Time* magazine) to raise money for Yenching College in Peking which had recently been founded by Americans. He and I were the only guests returning to New York that night, so we left the reception early and drove together to the station only to find the train an hour late. But there was much for us to talk about. He had just returned from Peking and was filled with excitement not only about that fascinating city but about Yenching with its distinguished faculty drawn from all over the world.

I was excited, too, about my first job teaching literature at the Bennett School in Millbrook, New York. Charles Rann Kennedy, author of *The Servant in the House* and a distinguished Greek scholar, together with his beautiful wife, Edith Wynne Matheson (former leading lady of Sir Henry Irving), had organized a drama department which had gained renown because of its Greek plays. As a young teacher I was thrilled to be asked to take part in plays by Synge, Shaw, Shakespeare, and Sophocles. Reginald Wheeler listened to my enthusiasm about all this, and then said quietly "There is an opening in the English Department of Yenching's Women's College which I think would interest you. The salary is to be paid by your college, Wellesley." As the train pulled into the station he wrote on a slip of paper the name of Mrs. John H. Finley, wife of the editor of the *New York Times,* and told me she was the chairman of the Yenching College Committee which would make the appointment. "Apply for the position," he said, "it is worth trying for."

At first I did not take seriously this idea of going to live on the other side of the world. But the more I thought about it, the more intriguing the idea became. I did apply; but there was no reply to my letter after a month, after two months, nor after six.

A year later, when I had almost forgotten about Yenching University, I received a letter from Mrs. Finley inviting me to tea at her home in Washington Square to discuss the position in China. My heart skipped a beat—and I paused for a moment. Then I quickly accepted her invitation. It was a delightful experience to meet this distinguished woman. She must have seen the light that came into my eyes as she pictured what it would mean to live in one of the great cities of the world, teaching Chinese students, and working with an exciting international faculty. As we said good-bye, she handed me an application blank; her smile encouraged me.

I returned the application promptly, yet not without ambivalent feelings. At the time, I was involved in a production of *Antigone* to be given at the Ethel Barrymore Theater in New York as part of a revival of classical drama. I was playing the role of Haemon in a scene with Charles Rann Kennedy. Because I was the only amateur in the cast Mr. Kennedy had coached me until every gesture and every intonation of my voice were just as he would have them. Then came the performance and my moment on stage to feel the thrill of moving and holding an audience. To my great surprise the *New York Times* review of my performance was considered good enough to serve as an introduction to any producer on Broadway. Was it to be China then, or possibly a career in the theater?

Although Mrs. Finley had received a wholehearted endorsement of my application from President Ellen Fitz Pendleton of Wellesley College, she told me very frankly that she was troubled to find that I was a Unitarian. The obstacle might be surmounted, however, if I would have an interview at the Riverside Church in New York with Harry Emerson Fosdick, a member of the Presbyterian Board who would have to approve my appointment. I welcomed this opportunity, for of all the great preachers who spoke at our Wellesley College Chapel, he was the one who had meant the most to me. I found him, of course, a warm and understanding human being. It was sometime before he approached the subject of religion; then he said, half smiling, "so you are a heretic." When I made no reply he said quietly, "and so am I. But as a Unitarian," he continued, "you deny the divinity of Jesus." My reply was spontaneous. "I do not deny the divinity of Jesus; I affirm the divinity of man." After a moment's silence he said thought-

fully, "I have tried all my life to be like Jesus, but I have not succeeded." In spite of his reservation about my theology, he evidently ap-
proved my application for a three-year appointment was immediately
forthcoming.

It was not difficult to make my decision. In a letter to my parents I
wrote:

March 10, 1923

When I was home at Christmas time, I revealed to you the deep hope
I had of going to China. At that time I was really doubtful as to whether
I would receive the appointment at Yenching; for that reason I left a great
many things unsaid. But now the appointment has been confirmed.

I know this will be a shock to you at first, just as it was to me, when I
realized all that the next three years would mean to me in the way of
separation. Yet I have come to realize that love and friendship are things
of the spirit; they are as real in one place as in another.

The people whom I have met in connection with this new position have
all been interesting and charming people. They are the kind with whom
I can work to best advantage for they enable me to express some of the
feelings and thoughts which, up to now, I have kept mostly to myself. I
believe there is nothing that could possibly contribute more to my life than
three years in Peking. There I will come in contact with the oldest existing
civilization in the world, a civilization totally different from anything I
have ever known. That in itself is bound to stimulate and teach me as no
other experience could. I shall have the opportunity to study the philosophy
and literature of a great people who are just beginning to take their place
in world affairs. Besides this, it will give me an opportunity to travel, an
opportunity which I am sure I could have in no other way.

Please look upon the situation as I do. If you can, it will make it easier
for me to go, and it will make me happy in my work."

When President Pendleton heard that I had accepted the position at
Yenching, she invited me to be her guest at the college. She could not
have been more cordial. She told me with enthusiasm of her four
months' trip in 1919 to China and Japan to report on women's institutions and women's work in both of these countries. As chairman of
the Commission on Collegiate Education for Women, she had visited
Yenching. When we said good-bye, she embraced me and said, "You
are doing exactly what I would do if I were your age." Another mem-

ber of the Wellesley College faculty who rejoiced at my decision was Seal Thompson, that remarkable diminutive Quaker who brought great distinction to the Bible Department of the college and who was one of the great inspirations of my life. She had already spent a year at Yenching.

A party early in August given by my brother at our island summer home in Casco Bay will always remain vivid in my mind. The Chinese and American flags were crossed at the entrance to our huge porch; a special island steamer brought friends and relatives from Portland; and an orchestra was imported for dancing on the porch. The gaiety of the evening, the many speeches of farewell, and the presentation of a beautiful platinum bracelet were for me "a little bit of heaven." My brother had been a naval officer in World War I and had served in the Pacific. He had been to Hongkong and had visited Uncle Heyward in Bangkok. He was delighted that I was going to the Orient.

Throughout the evening much was said in a light-hearted way about the queer Chinese customs: men had pigtails and wore long gowns, women wore trousers and had bound feet, white was for mourning and red for weddings, soup was served at the end of a meal, books were read from right to left. These were the days of Dr. Fu Manchu. One of the last guests to depart was Scott Wilson, Judge of the U.S. Court of Appeals, who had a summer home nearby and with whom I enjoyed playing tennis. He came up to me with a twinkle in his eye and said, "So you're going to China where they eat rats. I understand they eat rice for breakfast, drink water for lunch, and let it swell for dinner." I knew better and so did he. After all Mai-ling Soong was at Wellesley College when I was there. But all of this was typical of the folklore about China in the 1920s. (It is significant that Wellesley College did not offer a course in Far Eastern history until 1927. A history survey course which I took did not ever mention the Orient. Civilization in those days meant Western civilization only. How different today when students are as familiar with Iran, Syria, and Ethiopia as we were with England, France, and Germany. Now there is a professorship in Asian Studies at Wellesley which is one of the College's strongest fields of study.)

At the railroad station the next day, the reality of the parting that would last for three years descended on all of us. My mother wished that I did not have peacock feathers curled around the brim of my hat—they were not known for good luck. As she kissed me good-bye, I am sure she thought she would never see me again. Tears mingled with smiles as the train started me on my way to Canada and across the continent.

*　　*　　*

The day finally came when I was on board ship, when the gang-plank of the steamship *President Madison* was lifted, the orchestra struck up the "Star Spangled Banner," and the ship slowly began to move on its month-long voyage across the Pacific. For me the voyage was my introduction to a world of romance: a cabin full of fruit and flowers; letters and telegrams from a host of friends; dancing every night; my first cocktail in the captain's cabin with new acquaintances. (I wondered what my parents would have thought as I sipped an "orange blossom" and had my first cigarette—girls brought up as I had been did not smoke; Wellesley College expelled girls for smoking.) There were moonlight nights on deck with friends, still nights alone under the stars, and the feeling deep in my heart that I was embarking on a thrilling adventure.

At my table in the dining saloon was another teacher on her way to Yenching, Alice Boring, a graduate of Bryn Mawr College who had been a professor of biology at the University of Maine and Wellesley College. Also at the table was a lively and attractive girl on her way to Peking to visit one of the daughters of Jacob Gould Schurman, the United States Minister to China. Through her I was to meet the "legation set" and share in the gay social life of Peking which was more sophisticated than anything I had ever known in America.

As days went by I came to know most of the passengers on board and discovered two people who were to reveal to me wonders of this earth of which I had never dreamed. One was Hiram Bingham, a professor of South American history at Yale University who, within the year, was to be elected governor of Connecticut and later U.S. senator. As we stood together one evening leaning against the railing of the deck watching a magnificent sunset, he told me in his quiet way of his explorations in South America and of his discovery of the royal city of the Incas hidden for centuries on top of a steep precipice in the most inaccessible part of the Andes. He named the city Machu Picchu because it lay in the shadow of the great mountain by that name. I listened spellbound as he told me of the last of the Incas who had lived there four hundred years ago hidden from the Spanish conquerors by enormous precipices, mountain passes miles high, and canyons more than a mile deep. He said there was nothing in the whole Western Hemisphere to compare to the marvel of the sight and the wonders and mystery of its construction. It was not until years later when I had read about Machu Picchu and saw pictures of its restoration that I fully appreciated his extraordinary discovery. Many years later he was invited to inaugurate the Hiram Bingham Highway that now makes the formidable climb to this "sanctuary in the sky."

But for me, the most interesting and impressive person on board was Henry Fairchild Osborn. He and his wife were a devoted couple who had taken me under their wings and for whom I had unbounded admiration. He was president of the American Museum of National History, a professor at Columbia University, and the inspiration for the Central Asiatic Expedition which had been working in Mongolia in the Gobi desert for more than a year. He was filled with excitement about the findings of the expedition because they had proved what he had long believed that "Asia is the mother of the continents." One day as we were sitting in our deck chairs I asked him about the expedition. I had studied zoology at college and had written a paper on evolution. The story he told and his enthusiasm in telling it left an indelible impression on my mind.

The expedition, consisting of geologists, zoologists, archaeologists, palaeontologists, and a topographer started off with a warning that they would find plenty of rock and sand in Mongolia but probably very few fossils. Three great explorers had crossed the desert before them but only one had found even the slightest evidence of extinct animals. Therefore it came as a great surprise when even before their first season in Mongolia had ended, it was evident that they had discovered one of the richest and most important fossil fields in all the world. Soon after they had passed the Mongolian frontier they came upon a fossil bed with the scattered bones and skull of the giant extinct rhinoceros of Central Asia, the largest mammal ever to appear on earth. The skull was five feet long and the bones enormous, one bone as large as the body of a man. It took four days to work the skull out of the earth and when it arrived at the museum it was in 360 pieces. Eventually the museum made a complete restoration of the animal and exhibited it in a case to show how it appeared on earth 30,000,000 years ago. The creature stood thirteen feet at the shoulders and had a reach of some eighteen feet when feeding.

This discovery was only the beginning. When the expedition moved on and reached the middle of the desert, an enormous "bad land" basin was discovered filled with the skulls, bones, and skeletons of all kinds of dinosaurs. In this same fossil bed were found hundreds of eggs. The stratum in which some of them were found was estimated to be 95,000,000 years old. Some of the eggs were whole, some were empty shells, but two were broken in half showing the delicate bones of embryonic dinosaurs. These were the first dinosaur eggs ever seen by human eyes.

Professor Osborn considered that the most brilliant discovery to date was a small skull eight inches long which none of the scientists could identify. At the museum it was found to belong to a small land reptile, the ancient long-sought ancestor of the fossil giant-horned dinosaur found years before in Montana. When he told me that this was a new species, a new genus, he quoted Darwin's words about "that mystery of mysteries—the first appearance of new beings on earth."

About the time when this little dinosaur was living, Professor Osborn believed one of the most important events in the history of the earth took place. Central Asia emerged from the sea and became a continent. The geologists of the expedition had learned from their study of the rocks that Mongolia was indeed "the roof of the world," the oldest continually dry land known to science. In 150,000,000 years it had never been submerged nor had it ever been covered with glacial ice. For millions of years Mongolia had evidently been a veritable Garden of Eden, one of the most genial and attractive centers of life on earth where vegetation and open spaces made evolution possible.

After hundreds of thousands of generations, when reptiles and mammals grew in size and number, some of them had evidently wandered into Siberia and across the landbridge eastward to North America and westward to Europe. Asia had evidently been a dispersal center, a migration route between these distant places accounting for a fact which had puzzled scientists for years that similar fossil dino-saurs had been discovered in the Rocky Mountain section of North America and in Western Europe without a trace of them in the 10,000 miles between.

Professor Osborn's enthusiasm was contagious, and I began to won-der how far Mongolia was from Peking. "Just think," he said, "we have penetrated the homeland of the reptiles. Before this expedition has ended I predict we shall discover that we have also penetrated the homeland of primitive man." Before the expedition had ended in 1925 this prediction had come true. In 1926 while I was still in Peking, research at the Peking Union Medical College on a fossil tooth found at Chou Kou Tien, west of Peking, identified a distinct genus of *hominid*. Later at the same site was found the skull of the famous "Peking Man," about 500,000 years old. (Since then, human fossils much older have been found. I thought of Henry Fairfield Osborn last year when the news came from Ethopia that an American an-thropologist from Cleveland and a French scientist had discovered the world's oldest human fossils believed to be more than 3 million years old. There were jaws like ours, and teeth and human tools. I could hear him say "Just think, if the jaws were like ours 3 million years ago, one thing is certain—so were the stars and the moon that went by overhead. Our Christian era has not yet reached the year 2000. It was only 8,000 years ago that the first human societies we call civilizations appeared—a moment's tick out of the long history of this solitary little planet drifting amid our galaxy. Only now are we beginning to sense the extraordinary drama that has been taking place on the face of our earth.")

Although it was fifty years ago that I met Professor Osborn on the *President Madison,* he is still vivid in my mind. He was in his late sixties at the time but because of his youthful spirit, his energy and vitality, it did not surprise me to learn that he was on his way to the Gobi desert to join the expedition and share with Roy Chapman An-drews and the other scientists, the joy of their discoveries. It was while he was with the expedition, that a tiny skull no bigger than that of a rat was found. It proved to belong to a small mammal that had lived at the end of the Age of Reptiles. As the reptiles were dying out, nature was trying to establish the warm-blooded mammals that now dominate the earth. This was her first attempt. Only one other such skull had ever been found. This was discovered in South Africa and placed in the British Museum where it was considered one of the world's greatest paleontological treasures.

*   *   *

This long voyage came to an end as we approached the coast of Japan. Yokohama was to be the first port of call. Life on board ship had offered many new experiences. For me there had been no time nor desire for little intimacies. I had resolved what I wanted my life to be, and from this voyage which had been a kind of testing ground, I knew that I held the controls. As I look back now I realize how incredibly naive and idealistic I was. Most of us growing up in the 1920s lived in a kind of age of innocence. Society protected us from the temptations and difficult choices facing young people today. The temptations were all there but they were kept under cover. Somehow we knew about them dimly and suspected the people involved with them, but they were only whispered about, never condoned nor respected.

We were taught to look forward to marriage and the joys of making a home. At the moment, life was far too exciting for me to think of marriage. I wanted to see the world, to taste of life before I settled down. Already I felt liberated from much of the provincialism of New England, but the values implanted in me there held firm: integrity, decency, and self respect. I felt ready for anything life had in store for me. What life had in store was a marriage that grew stronger over the years, but there was never to be any "settling down." Love for me was to grow out of an ideal companionship, out of sharing with my husband the joys as well as the sorrows of life, out of facing difficult problems and solving them together, out of mutual respect, loyalty, and warm affection; perhaps above all out of the desire for each other's fulfillment. This marriage was to come before I left the Orient.

The air tingled with excitement as we entered Yokohama harbor and the *President Madison* eased into the wharf swarming with Oriental life.

Our first glimpse of the Orient.

Professor and Mrs. Osborn as we
sighted land.

The great Daibutsu at Kamakura.

Japan and the Earthquake

MOST OF THE PASSENGERS left the ship at Yokohama in order to go overland to Kobe where we were to pick up the ship again. This stop made possible for me and a group of friends an opportunity to see the great Daibutsu at Kamakura and to visit the imperial city of Kyoto. The following are excerpts from a letter to my family written on delicate Japanese rice paper:

August 30, 1923

At the Kamakura hotel we left our bags and went to a Buddhist temple built on a hill overlooking the little village nestled near the sea. As we ascended the huge flight of stone steps, the bell begun to sound calling the people to worship—a beautiful sound that blended with the singing cicadas. It was interesting to watch the Japanese families assemble for the service; the dainty women in their picturesque kimonas, the men looking strange in less colorful ones, and the darling little boys and girls cuddling close to their mothers. As I watched their reverence, I felt sure that it mattered little what their religion might be.

From the temple we went to see the great Daibutsu. Just as we approached the Buddha, the last bit of color left the sky and a few stars began to peep through the pine trees. Everything was still. All of nature seemed to share the mood of the great pensive figure. I was deeply moved as I sat quietly looking into that face so calm and contemplative. One could not help being moved, too, by the beauty with which the Japanese have surrounded this great Buddha.

August 31, 1923

We left Kamakura this morning and rode all day over exquisitely beautiful country with fields of rice and lotus plants, tiny picturesque villages, and unusual mountain formations. We went very close to the base of Fujiyama, the highest peak in Japan, and had a wonderful view of it.

At seven-thirty we arrived here in Kyoto and drove immediately to this fascinating inn. On entering we had to take off our shoes, leave them by the door, and put on Japanese slippers. We found these terribly difficult to manage and were all greatly amused as we tried to climb the stairs. We were taken to two large rooms where beautiful white silk pillows were brought for us to sit on. Then tea was served. Little Japanese maids brought in something that looked like two tea cups, one on top of the other, together with a little glass of tea. The two cups proved to be a cup of water and a cuspidor so that we could rinse our mouths before drinking the tea. None of us liked it but the little cakes served with it were delicious. As we sat drinking and eating, the manager came to announce that our bath was ready. The men went to one room to undress and left the two rooms for us. Then Japanese maids brought each of us little baskets for our trinkets, hairpins, and underclothes.

Finally our kimonas were brought and we were ushered downstairs to the public bath. At first I suffered from embarrassment because men and women were there together, but it is surprising how quickly one can adapt to foreign customs. We each took a small pail of water and washed ourselves before stepping into the bath which all use together. The tub looks like a big trough and is brimming over with hot water. It was all a lark— a very refreshing one. Then upstairs again—still in our kimonas—for more tea, fruit, and other drinks.

As I write the maids are making up our beds by putting two white silk mattresses on top of one another on the floor. Over these come sheets and then an exquisite blue silk cover. The pillows are quite high and held in by ruffled slips. All the windows have been shut, for the Japanese never leave anything open at night. We are all tired, so now for a night's sleep in a bed of silk.

It was at the Imperial Temple the next day that we felt the earth move and shake. In the streets the wires and buildings swayed. Everyone recognized at once the tremor of an earthquake. Not until we boarded the ship again at Kobe, however, did we learn of the terrible devastation: a great tidal wave at Kamakura, the near destruction of Yokohama and Tokyo, and the human suffering resulting from one of the world's worst earthquakes. It was estimated that 250,000 people lost their lives and 80 percent of the homes were destroyed. The great Imperial Hotel in Tokyo with its revolutionary floating cantilever construction was the only large building to withstand the quake and offer safety to the people. It had been designed by our American architect, Frank Lloyd Wright, and brought him instant acclaim. We were all shocked and saddened as we landed in Shanghai and said farewell to one another.

I was grateful that I could take the trip to Peking with Professor and Mrs. Osborn because on our arrival in Shanghai we learned that the train which we were supposed to take to Peking, the famous Blue Express, had been derailed on its way to Shanghai by bandits who had torn up the tracks. The passengers in the dead of night had been forced off the train in their nightclothes and made to walk barefoot over rough fields to a fort on top of a nearby mountain. The case was notorious because it was so bold and because so many foreigners were involved,—British, Americans, French, Italians, Danes, and Germans. When we arrived in Shanghai they were being held prisoners while negotiations went on between the bandits, the Chinese authorities, and the various consuls concerned. Because our train to Peking was heavily guarded by soldiers, we made the trip without incident although there was a little apprehension as we neared the spot where the holdup had occurred. Curiously enough this was one of the most beautiful spots along the way. We arrived there at sunset when the mountains were deep purple against the glow of the evening sky. The countryside all around was peaceful; only a solitary figure could be seen working in the fields.

After a long slow journey with leisurely stops at local stations along the way, the Shanghai Express finally arrived in Peking. We were deposited on a platform of the main station just below the thick medieval wall enclosing that part of Peking known as the Tartar City. There was great excitement as friends of the Osborns and representatives of Yenching greeted us and hurried us through the archway of a huge city gate to waiting rickshas. There the porters placed our baggage in separate rickshas while each of us mounted others that were to take us on a wide boulevard to the modern Legation Quarter. Here the Osborns waved good-bye; the rest of us went on to more native parts of the city. In a tiny *hutung* (a narrow street or alley) off Tung Shih K'ou we finally arrived in front of the impressive gateway of Yenching Women's College.

*   *   *

The letters and notes that follow, I found in a box which had not been opened for years. As I browsed through this material, reread my letters, and relived those wonderful years, I felt that they should be preserved. I thought of my grandchildren—and the great-grand-children whom I would never know. And like many an enthusiast for one thing and another I wanted the fun of explaining my enthusiasm for China and perhaps inculcating it.

As I began to weave this material into a story, I realized that many of the letters told of people and events which would be meaningless without some knowledge of Chinese history; this I have added. Of course, my letters give only a hint of the people and the country with such a wealth of paradoxes. But I offer them now just as they were written a half a century ago—mere fragments of those faraway days. I make no pretense for anything except my own reactions to a country and a people that I came to love.

I am no historian and I certainly have nothing to say to those who are familiar with China. But I believe the story of the Chinese people cannot often enough be told. Old as it is, new light is being shed on it every year. Meanwhile the Chinese are making history before our eyes. We need as never before to understand how they have come in our time to make such a sacrificial defense of a new way of life.

After I returned to this country I was often homesick for the streets of Peking with their colorful pageantry, for the Western Hills dotted here and there with tranquil old Buddhist monasteries, for the delicate fragrance of the *kui-hua* in the autumn, and a myriad of other things which remain indelibly in my mind. In a letter to a friend shortly after I left China I wrote: I have often tried to discover the secret of China's spell upon me. Sometimes I think it is the beauty of the country with its unique architecture, its art and philosophy; then again I am sure it is the quiet courteous gentleness of the people themselves, their delightful sense of humor, their strength of character, their loyalty, and their great capacity for friendship. Of course it is all of these things and much more.

China is where good fortune and an adventurous spirit took me when I was young. I have often wondered where an adventurous spirit will take those who will be young in the next century. Will it be into the depth of space—under the sea—back into the wilderness—or into cities still unborn? In this fast changing world of today it is impossible for me to imagine. But this I know, fulfillment will come to those who dare to follow the beckoning of opportunities that are bound to come to them, who dare to be true to themselves, and above all, who dare to trust that "something" which they feel deep within.

> What you can do, or
> dream you can, begin it.
> Boldness has genius,
> power, and magic in it.
> GOETHE

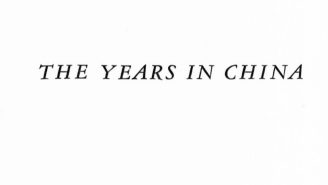

THE YEARS IN CHINA

Peking

Every highway leads to Peking.
CHINESE PROVERB

WHEN I ARRIVED in China in 1923, Peking was not only the official but the intellectual and cultural center of the country. Besides the foreign diplomats, the educators and missionaries, it attracted art collectors, scientists, writers, and world travelers. In those days the world came to Peking for it was one of the most majestic and fascinating cities in all the world—and whoever came was sure to fall under its spell.

Peking is in North China not far from the Great Wall built centuries ago to keep out the barbarian hordes from the north. It is surrounded by lovely fertile open country with the beautiful Western Hills only ten miles away. A massive wall with battlemented parapets like a medieval fortress surrounded the city when I was there. (It was taken down in the 1960s because bricks were needed, I have been told, to build an underground city as defense against a possible Russian nuclear attack.) The nine great city gates were solemnly closed each night to be opened at dawn the next day.

Within the gates were magnificence and splendor. There was the exotic beauty of architectural treasures dating back to the thirteenth century. There were handsome boulevards, open squares with stately colorful *p'ai lous* (archways of lofty columns), narrow twisting wall-lined residential streets called *hutungs,* all teeming with the life of a million people. Color was everywhere: in the red city walls, the gleaming yellow tiles of the curving roofs of the Forbidden City, in the saffron robes of the Buddhist priests as they stood near the red pillars of their Lama Temple, and in the uniform blue cotton garb of the coolies.

The Peking that I knew was a city of great contrasts. There were silken-gowned gentlemen riding comfortably in their rickshas; but there were also bent, straining coolies pulling heavily laden carts. Limousines passed the familiar two-wheeled covered Peking carts drawn by mules. There were telephones, electric lights, and telegraph wires bringing news from all over the world, but camels still brought coal in from the hills, young men and old carried heavy loads dangling from shoulder poles, and water carriers filled the earthenware cisterns in the houses without "self-carrying water." Behind the walls of the *hutungs* were lovely courtyards with the gardens and stately residences of the elite, the scholar-officials, and rich merchants. Outside, not far away, might be squalor and poverty or a beggar in rags.

What made Peking unique among the capitals of the world was its grand design, the majestic conception of the builder's plan. It was a triple-walled city. In the center was the Forbidden City where the Emperor lived amid palatial buildings that rise from beautiful white marble platforms; and from this "Great Within," as it was called, radiated the power of a whole empire. This central city was surrounded by a moat and two miles of massive walls. Surrounding this was the Imperial City with the fashionable residences of the Manchu and Chinese officials. It covered an area of two square miles and was once surrounded by walls of its own. Here are Central Park, Coal Hill, the Marble Bridge, and the artificial Imperial Lakes surrounded by old trees and buildings that were made for pleasure, worship, and repose. Outside these two was a third walled city taken over by the Manchus when they captured Peking in 1644 and called after them "The Tartar City." The defeated Chinese were at that time relegated to a large area outside the southern wall where they were permitted to live and work. This Chinese city, or Outer City, had walls of its own, only lower and with fewer gates than the fortified Tartar wall. So in Peking there were walls within walls, moats within moats, and massive arched gateways leading on to other gates.

Because Peking was considered the capital of the Celestial Empire, it was set in proper relation to the entire firmament. There was a Temple of the Sun outside the walls to the east and the Temple of the Moon opposite to the west. To the north was the Temple of Earth. This was extremely important to the Chinese because their whole world was based on agriculture, and it was here that the Emperor, each spring, would symbolically plow a furrow in behalf of all farmers. Opposite the Temple of Earth to the south was the beautiful Temple of Heaven with its triple-tiled roof of deep sapphire blue and its magnificent circular white marble altar which stands alone under the sky; it is one of the wonders of the world. Here at dawn after a night of purification the Emperor knelt at times of high ceremony to take upon himself the responsibility of the whole empire. This harmony between man and nature has always been important to the Chinese. If a flood, a drought, or any disaster occurred it was thought that the Emperor had in some way displeased Heaven from whom he received his mandate. To the Chinese all life is one and closely interlinked. "One cannot pluck a flower without troubling a star."

In the old Peking which I knew there was a low architectural profile, for buildings were seldom more than one story high. Only the palace roofs of the Forbidden City and the gate towers of the great city wall broke the skyline.

Yenching University

This institution will be based on the illimitable freedom of the human mind. For here we are not afraid to follow truth wherever it may lead nor to tolerate error so long as reason is left free to combat it.

THOMAS JEFFERSON

IN THIS FABULOUS CITY in 1919 during a time of infinite complexity and great promise, Yenching University came into being. Two small struggling mission colleges in Peking were merged under the leadership of Dr. John Leighton Stuart.

Dr. Stuart was born of missionary parents in Hangchow, a city which Marco Polo in the thirteenth century likened to paradise. He was educated in America and while at the Union Theological Seminary in Virginia made the decision about his future. He once said that it would be difficult to exaggerate the aversion he had against going to China as a missionary. He was not against the country but against what he conceived to be the nature of the life and work— "haranguering crowds of idle, curious people in street chapels or temple fairs, selling tracts for almost nothing, being regarded with amused or angry contempt by the native population, physical discomforts or hardships, etc., no chance for intuitive or studious interests, a sort of living death or modern equivalent for retirement from the world." But he did return to China and became head of the Greek department of the Union Theological Seminary in Nanking.

His scholarship and his knowledge of the Chinese language made him highly esteemed both in foreign circles and among the Chinese. Because his great interest was education, it is not surprising that when he was offered the opportunity to become president of this new struggling institution in Peking, he was willing to accept the responsibility, although he knew what problems were ahead.

Yenching means "Capital of the ancient state of Yen," a poetical allusion to Peking. In the beginning the university was practically penniless. There were only a few students, the buildings were obsolete, and their site undesirable. But Dr. Stuart's keen analysis of the requirements and opportunities of the times, his bold planning, and his untiring energy as well as his great capacity for friendship were to make possible for Yenching its phenomenal growth. By the time I arrived four years later, the university was a thriving institution. Student enrollment was at a peak, a beautiful new site for the university had been chosen outside Peking near the Summer Palace, and money was being raised in the United States for the magnificent new buildings already planned. When completed in 1927, Dr. Hu Shih called this one of the most beautiful university campuses in the world. Dr. Stuart had also attracted a distinguished faculty. I found there professors from the best-known colleges in Europe and America as well as Chinese scholars, many of whom had been educated abroad.

Although Yenching was a Christian college, there was no required chapel and no compulsory religious services. Christian and non-Christian students were admitted and treated alike. One's belief or its outward expression was regarded as a personal matter. As a Unitarian I never felt any discrimination nor was I for one moment made to feel uncomfortable. Dr. Stuart's purpose was to create a first-rate university. Together with his faculty he decided that its motto should be "Freedom through Truth for Service."

*   *   *

The North China Women's College, which had become a part of Yenching University in 1920, had a spectacular history. It began with three little beggar girls rescued from the streets of Peking by a Scottish missionary. Because he was a bachelor, they were put in the care of Mrs. Elijah Bridgman, widow of one of the first American Protestant missionaries to China. With these three girls and two others, she started a school which later developed into Bridgman Academy.

Gradually with the help of various missionary groups, the academic level of the school advanced, until in 1904 the first class was graduated with one year of college work. In 1905 it developed into a regular four-year college and became the first institution in China to offer higher education to women. Ten years later the college left the buildings it had shared with Bridgman Academy and moved to the old palace nearby called the T'ung Fu.

Here in the 1660s had lived the mother of the great Manchu Emperor K'ang Hsi, one of the greatest monarchs China ever had. The room where he had held audiences when visiting his mother had become the assembly hall of the college. Other buildings had been adapted for classrooms, laboratories, a library, faculty houses, and dormitories. Here I was to live in a little two-room, one-story house during my three years in Peking—three of the happiest and most exciting years of my life.

The T'ung Fu was typical of the old palaces in Peking. It consisted of many courtyards connected by gateways cut in the courtyard walls in the shape of a full moon. A high thick wall surrounded the great compound making the palace a kind of world by itself.

In this enchanting place I was taken on a path past many courtyards and ushered through a little gateway into what seemed to me a veritable paradise. The graceful branches of an elm drooped over the roofs of three houses built around three sides of a paved court. In the middle, facing the gateway was a handsome building with its curved roof extending over the pillared veranda, and pictures painted in gay colors showing under the eaves. This I was told was the reception room where I would receive my guests. On either side of the court were small identical houses.

The little house facing south was to be mine. Originally it had consisted of one room, but a partition had been put up making possible both a study and a bedroom. Both rooms were furnished sparsely. The stone floor was covered with a piece of old matting. A door with a paper window on either side opened on the court. There was no running water, no plumbing, no modern convenience of any kind. Yet there was an inexplicable charm about the place. And it was to be mine—all mine—the first house I ever had all to myself.

My first letter home was written the following afternoon when the sun had dropped behind the compound wall and nature had begun to quiet down for the evening.

September 10, 1923

Dear Family,

As I look into the courtyard of this fascinating old residence I can hardly believe it is to be my home for the next three years. You would understand my feeling if you could pass through the huge Chinese gateway, turn by the carved "spirit wall" and walk with me through the many courtyards and buildings of this seventeenth century ducal palace. A high stone wall shuts out the life of Teng Shih K'ou and softens the harsh cries of the street vendors to a romantic faraway call. There are many buildings—fifteen in all I should say—which were originally used for residences, a temple, a gambling house, and imperial reception rooms. The temple is by far the most beautiful. It is smaller than the other buildings and is now used for a reception hall and dining room. The original paintings of red and gold underneath the roof have been preserved, and the little animal ornaments on the roof still tell of its princely day.

I am glad to have arrived at this time of year for the flowers are still blooming in the gardens and the foliage of the trees and shrubs is green and full. The wisteria arbor by the gateway is heavy with foliage and I can imagine how exquisite it must be when it flowers in the spring.

It is difficult to convey to you the charm of the place. It is a beauty hidden in old curving roofs, in exquisite carvings, in ancient stone steps that have worn away gradually for centuries; in nature running wild in courtyards where an emperor once roamed; in moon gates and ivy-covered walls; and in the mingled sounds of the street that find their way to this secluded spot.

Peking is not yet a reality to me for I have not ventured outside our walls. But my glimpse of it from the train window and from the ricksha was quite thrilling: massive stone walls, huge arched gateways, yellow and green roofed palaces and temples; busy streets filled with vendors, rickshas, and other curious conveyances—and behind it all the purple Western Hills.

I am trying to make it seem real that I am actually in China, in Peking, in the T'ung Fu; but it is difficult. I feel that I am moving in a dream both fascinating and strange.

My dearest love to you all

I had arrived in Peking more than a month before the opening of the university so very few of my colleagues were at the T'ung Fu. But there to greet me and give me a warm welcome was the dean, Mrs. Alice Frame, a friendly outgoing person whom every one loved. Her young daughter Rosamond lived with her at the T'ung Fu—a lovely child who added much to our college life. Mrs. Frame was to become a dear and valuable friend for as long as I remained in Peking; I look back even now with gratitude for her understanding. It was she together with Wha T'ing, a servant who could speak a little English, who initiated me into the ways of Chinese life.

First of all I was introduced to my amah, Fu chin, who was to care for my room, wash and iron my clothes, sew, bring me hot water in the morning, and do whatever household thing I needed to have done. I was to share her with Dora Demiere, an attractive young teacher of French from Switzerland, who lived in the little house opposite mine.

Then arrangements were made for my Chinese lessons at the Language School; they were to begin the very next day. Because it was important for me to learn to speak the language as quickly as possible, Mrs. Frame had already engaged a private tutor who would come to the T'ung Fu three times a week for conversation. She assured me I would like him—a Chinese scholar who was an excellent teacher, demanding but patient and encouraging.

I was finally turned over to Wha T'ing who was to be available to do my errands, assist me in unpacking, and instruct me in the ways of our T'ung Fu household: the time and place of meals and how and where to get a bath. Wha T'ing was tall for a Chinese and very erect. I found him good natured and intelligent with a keen sense of humor. I liked him from the first. He said that he had selected a ricksha boy for me—one who knew enough English to help when I went shopping, and who would be waiting at the T'ung Fu gate every day to take me wherever I wanted to go. I could trust him completely, he said. As Wha T'ing helped me to unpack, he could see that I needed a little table for my typewriter. This he purchased for me at a fair not far from Teng Shih Kou—a fair held three times a month in the courtyards of an old temple called Lung Fo Ssu. "All foreigners love this fair," he said, "you go soon."

Mrs. Frame agreed that there was nothing quite like the fun and excitement of this great fair. "Go by all means," she said. But she urged me to resist as long as possible buying anything of value; she was certain that my taste would change as I lived in Peking. Then she initiated me into the great Chinese game of bargaining. "Never pay more than one half the merchant's asking price and it is well to begin your bargaining by offering one third." This sounded exciting, so when I thought I knew enough Chinese words to make myself

Entrance gate at the T'ung Fu with waiting rickshas. Note spirit wall
showing through gate.

Inside gate showing the carved spirit wall placed opposite the gate because it was believed that evil spirits could not turn a corner.

Inside my compound with reception hall and my house on left.

Gateway into my compound.

A touch of Chinese humor—little animals sitting on the curving roof of one of the T'ung Fu buildings. Note the moon gate.

My room, showing on the wall the piece of embroidery which was my first purchase in Peking.

My Chinese teacher.

Yenching students in a production at the T'ung Fu of an old Chinese festival play.

An ivy-covered wall and moon gate showing a paper window in the distance.

Two little beggar children outside the T"ung Fu like those taken from
the streets of Peking in 1891, when it all began.

understood, I asked my ricksha boy to take me to the Lung Fo Ssu fair.

I found the place thronging with people laughing and talking; there were young and old, rich and poor, Chinese and foreigners from all over the world. There was an air of excitement, a liveliness that one could not miss. At the many stalls crowded together in the various courtyards of the old temple, people were buying jades, ceramics, rare art objects, and antiques. Others were amusing themselves just looking on. Some crowded around the candy maker who, to the delight of the children, molded his fondant into camels, birds, boats, even pagodas. Artists sitting on the ground drew rapt crowds as they sketched with rapid strokes bamboos, chrysanthemums, birds, and fish.

Almost at once I fell in love with a beautiful makeup chest of teakwood with little Chinese figures of brass on the front and sides. The miniature drawers had delicate brass pulls and the top opened to display a lovely mirror. The shopkeeper, sensing my interest, stated his price; I offered him a third. He laughed but dropped his price a little; then I offered a little more—as much as I wanted to pay for it. He still laughed and shook his head so I sauntered away. At a nearby stall I bought a piece of embroidery for my wall, at the flower market, a little pot of freesia with its exquisite fragrance for my desk. I had fun at the bird and insect market watching an elderly gentleman buy his little granddaughter a pair of crickets in a bamboo cage. The Chinese love all insects. They put them in their paintings and on their choice porcelains. There is even a temple in the hills called the Temple of the High-Spirited Insects.

When I was ready to leave the fair, I could hardly believe my eyes— there was the shopkeeper with my chest. "It is yours," he said with a smile. He had met my price and I was honor-bound to buy it. How I loved that chest! I still treasure it today. So, flushed with the pleasure of my first purchases, I got into my ricksha and rode to Teng Shih Kou. Mrs. Frame was delighted with what I had bought and assured me I had bought them at a good price. Then with pride she showed me her most recent purchase at the fair—a bronze mirror of the T'ang dynasty, about one thousand years old, for which she paid ten dollars!

I soon learned that it was a great game among the foreigners to find out who had made the best bargains. Quite contrary to good taste in the West, in Peking it was not only proper to ask the price of any purchase, one was almost expected to do so.

When Fu Chin saw the piece of embroidery on my wall, she immediately told Wha T'ing who told his friend "the embroidery man" who promptly called at the T'ung Fu. On the day of his call, Wha T'ing appeared smiling at my door to say that there was a man in the reception room who had lovely things for me to see. He quickly added, "You do not have to buy. Today just look-see."

What I saw was ravishing. I was first shown a beautiful mandarin coat of warm beige satin with a wide band of deep blue waves embroidered on the bottom; six delicate round pictures of a gentleman in his garden were embroidered in soft shades of blue and ivory—in one he was alone in meditation, in another with his servant, still another with his lady; here and there were blue and pale yellow butterflies and peonies; the handsome wide cuffs showed little pots of flowers, miniature peacocks, birds, and cavorting frogs—the whole thing as carefully designed and as beautifully executed as a painting. There was a princess wedding coat of bright red satin, embroidered with bits of clouds, bats, and other symbols of good luck. There were pieces of embroidery with golden dragons and delicate phoenix birds; scroll paintings, and yards of exquisite tribute silk. I made no purchases that day but my delight in all these beautiful things was enough to assure the "embroidery man" he had found a new customer.

It was a Chinese custom, I learned, to buy things in this leisurely way. In the old days women did not leave their homes to make purchases. The merchants, with their wares wrapped in large blue cotton bundles, came to the homes and displayed their silks and satins to the ladies of the household. Antiques, silver, jewelry, and other precious things were also sold in this way.

But there were other ways in Peking to buy lovely things. I soon discovered the fascinating streets lined with excellent shops—Lantern Street, Jade Street, Silk Street, Brass Street, Furniture Street, and other streets where competitors were clustered together. There was a district famous for its Peking glass, where the glass blowers could make glass of many colors: imperial yellow, a heavenly shade of light blue, dark blue, green, and the lovely popular amethyst. A beautifully shaped bowl of carved imperial yellow glass is one of my treasures. (I saw one exactly like it at the museum in Vienna.) They made beads, glass flowers, glass fruit—anything that came to their minds.

Jade Street was one of my favorites for I came to love this pure smooth stone which the Chinese value above all jewels. There were necklaces, rings, brooches, bracelets; and it was here one bought the graceful jade trees. Jewelry shops also displayed beads and rings of amber, coral, lapis lazuli, and rose quartz. Ground lapis lazuli was often used in paintings; it is the background of a little picture of Buddha that I bought.

Two Different Worlds

Is it not possible that the ultimate end
is gaiety, music, and a dance of joy?
JAMES STEPHENS

AT THE T'UNG FU I was living near the old Imperial City with its strange and fascinating reminders of the past—a past when no railroads nor automobiles disturbed "the dreamy peace of Asia!" The Osborns and another friend from the *President Madison* were staying at the American Legation in what was called the Legation Quarter, an area of about three-quarters of a mile square near the south wall of the Tartar City. Here were housed all the ministers and their staffs representing about ten different countries; the chief envoys were not called ambassadors until late in the 1930s. Besides the legations there were a few other foreign houses and all the clubs with their swimming pools and tennis courts. Nearby were the hotels and banks.

Almost at once I was caught up in the social whirl of this foreign world. I was young and loved the sumptuous dinner parties, the elegant teas, the receptions and balls that were constantly going on. The dinner parties were great fun because we always went to the Peking Hotel afterwards for dancing. At the hotel the many dinner parties kept in separate groups so we always knew who was being entertained by whom. There were very few secrets in Peking!

What especially delighted me were the weekend parties at the Buddhist monasteries in the Western Hills. Houseparties and temples seemed incongruous to me at first, but the friends who invited me were always respectful of the monks and their ceremonies; the monks in turn were not disturbed for we stayed in the special courtyards and buildings reserved for guests. These weekends were a leisurely time. During the day we took lovely walks in the hills; at night after dinner we sat under the stars talking and enjoying the beauty and peace of our surroundings. The bonds of friendship were very strong in China because we took the time to know and enjoy one another.

I was invited to my first houseparty by Mrs. William Calhoun, widow of a former minister to China and one of the great hostesses of Peking. She had thoughtfully arranged to have one of the bachelors at the legation, Leon Ellis, call for me and see that I arrived safely at the monastery. We made the long trip in our rickshas and because the road to the hills had little traffic we were able to ride most of the way side by side. He told me about the monastery we were to visit—a very old one, built on the slope of a hill overlooking a valley. It was famous for a magnificent white pine—a tree native to North China, whose immense size and white bark made it an ornament for temples and tombs. So that I would not feel like a complete stranger, he told me something about the people whom I would meet there—all good friends of his. He told me, too, about the interesting events in Peking which he thought I would enjoy. When he learned that I loved music, he invited me to a concert at the Peking Hotel the following Sunday afternoon given by the White Russian orchestra, a weekly event. Later there were to be many other invitations—for diplomatic events at the Legations and for important Chinese affairs as well.

Mrs. Calhoun and most of the guests were at the monastery when we arrived. We joined the group in a courtyard with old cedar trees, lovely flowers, and singing birds. We were a congenial group; it was here that I met many of the people who were to be my dearest friends during my years in Peking.

As was usual with these houseparties, Mrs. Calhoun had sent servants ahead with carts carrying our beds, bedding, and all the food. Everything possible was done to make us comfortable. We were all amazed the first night when servants in white coats served a four course dinner with ice cream for dessert! Nothing was ever impossible in Peking.

Because I was young and unattached I was sometimes invited to her formal dinners in Peking when she entertained an important foreign visitor. For me unaccustomed to such impressive affairs these were unforgettable occasions. The "at homes" in her fascinating Chinese house on Wednesday afternoons were famous and attracted most of the foreign colony. At first I was surprised to find so many men attending these. The men in the States whom I knew did not go to afternoon affairs; as for my father—well, it would have been unthinkable, unmanly.

Invitations came by "chit" delivered by a servant. One's acceptance or regrets were usually written in the chit book: "Delighted" or

"Sorry." If a note were required, the messenger would wait quietly in our kitchen gossiping and sipping tea with Wha T'ing, Chu Pu, or other members of our household staff. When chits arrived everyone enjoyed them, especially the messenger to whom they gave much "face." He could recount the news of his household and learn much of ours in return. A messenger with four or five chits to deliver would know before he returned home who had dined with whom the night before—and how it had all gone. I soon discovered how it was that Wha T'ing could tell me in advance who would be at some party I was to attend. As time went on it was from him I learned about much that was going on in Peking—the quarrels, the love affairs, in fact the most intimate details of what went on inside the high walls which were supposed to assure privacy. I never encouraged this gossip, but one could not be in Peking long without learning that anything of interest spread rapidly in some mysterious way all over the city.

After the opening of the University when my classes began, I had to make engagements with myself in order to have time to do my work properly. It was not long before I realized that I had become involved with two very different worlds. This is hinted at in the following letter.

T'ung Fu
September 29, 1923

Dear Family,

I have just learned that I have half an hour to write a letter and get it in the mail that will catch the S.S. *Canada* at Shanghai. This is about the speed of Peking; it is positively dazzling! Already my calendar is filled with engagements until the 12th of October. In these first free days I have loved all the gaiety, but in less than a week classes begin and I must—in fact I want very much to get involved with the university life. I met all the members of our faculty at a weekend conference at the new site of the university. I never hope to see a more dedicated and colorful group of people—there were English, Scotch, French, Swiss, Americans, and both traditional and modern Chinese.

President Stuart is an amazing man. He opened the meeting with a stirring plea for loyalty and cooperation, a working together in such harmony as to bring to the university the greatest possible service. There were lively discussions at all the meetings carried on mostly by the men. Their keen penetrating minds and their amazing knowledge of China made a great impression upon me. There is no question that it is their deep faith in the work and purpose of the university which has kept their morale high. The equipment here is woefully inadequate and resources are terribly limited. A social hour each evening before dinner gave us all an opportunity to get acquainted. Those of us who had recently arrived could not help catching from the others the spirit of the new Yenching with its forward-looking thoughts. I think we all came away from the conference stirred by the unique opportunity Yenching has to blend the knowledge of the East and the West and to help instill a spirit of brotherhood between our peoples.

I have begun classes at an excellent language school. Because I am to be here only three years, I am learning only the spoken language—mandarin, the official language used here in Peking. I understand that there are many different dialects spoken throughout the country. Although the written language fascinates me, it is far too difficult for me to attempt in so short a time. Each character is a picture or symbol or a derivation or combination of these. There are some one hundred and thirty thousand characters in use today—a university student is expected to know at least six thousand! A private Chinese teacher—a scholar of the old school—comes to the T'ung Fu three times a week just to help me with conversation. So far he has been patient and very encouraging. Already he assures me that in a month or two I shall be able to speak enough words so that I can be understood. But I wonder! My greatest problem is with the tones—there are four of them. Each word has a different meaning according to the intonation of one's voice. It makes a difference whether you say it straight out, upward as in a question, downward, or with a diving inflection.

Imagine my delight to find that Mary Ferguson, a college classmate, lives in Peking. I have already been to her fascinating home and met her father and mother who have spent most of their lives in China. Dr. Ferguson, a distinguished scholar and sinologist, is an adviser to the Chinese government. He came to China under a Mission Board to found the University of Nanking. Within a few years he was asked by the Chinese government to found a modern college in Shanghai which has become China's M.I.T. Since the Republic, Dr. Ferguson has been adviser to each one of the presidents. Because of his great interest in Chinese art he was the only non-Chinese member of the committee on the Palace Museum when it was opened to the public. He has written several books and has been kind enough to give me a copy of his *Outline of Chinese Art*. Their home is filled with treasures: carved black teak furniture, exquisite scroll paintings, bronzes, and choice porcelains.

But more of all this later. This can only let you know that I am well, happy, and having the time of my life.

The opening exercises of the University took place in the large courtyard of the men's college. We assembled in the great hall and marched according to academic rank and years of service. The procession was dignified and impressive. Academic gowns represented almost every great university in the world. I was thrilled.

I shall never forget as long as I live what I saw as I reached the platform where I was to sit and turned to face the student body. There high against the clear blue sky was the American flag flying gently in the breeze. A lump came in my throat, for although I had looked at that flag all my life, never until that moment had I ever really seen it nor sensed its meaning. It was of my beloved country that I thought as the opening of Yenching in 1923 got underway.

It would be difficult to exaggerate the excitement I felt as I went to meet my classes the following day. But it was weeks it seemed before I could get them to come alive. For a while I thought I would never get through to these girls. They all looked alike and dressed alike in their straight blue cotton dresses with high necks and three quarter sleeves. I wondered if I would ever be able to attach the impossible sounding names to the proper girls. From the beginning they were kind and very polite but fearfully shy. In class they were silent. I had to work hard at this; but little by little their shyness vanished and their personalities emerged. When we began to have lively class discussions I discovered that some of them had a delightful sense of humor, all of them were earnest and hard working, one or two were so brilliant that they kept me on my toes every minute. A few of them I found to be exquisitely lovely with oval faces, delicate features, and bright dark eyes.

Just as I was beginning to see the Chinese as individuals, I learned to my great surprise that to the Chinese all foreigners look alike. It made me self-conscious to read in one of their themes: "All foreigners have a high nose, a loud voice, big feet, and a wide stride." For a while I made a desperate effort to speak softly and walk slowly.

However when I learned what the Orientals consider beauty in their women, I knew that we would always seem loud and gauche to them. The charming description that follows was in one of my first set of papers. I knew at once that I had a poet in my class.

A beautiful woman is neither taller nor shorter than the common people. Her face is the shape of a duck's eggs, pink in colour. Her eyes are like the phoenix's eyes, their brightness like autumn water down the deep river or like the twinkling stars above the heaven. She can send a message by her attractive eyes. Her teeth are as white as pearls. White jade is always used to represent the colour and smoothness of her hands. An attractive smiling must show her teeth.

A graceful motion is easy to make people notice her hands. Her hair is usually described as black silk, as bright and smooth as the feather of a crow. Beauty of walking is shown by her narrow and thin waist. As the willow leaves shaken by the winds can be held only by two hands, so the beautiful waist.

Walking also means the help of pretty feet. Her feet are as small as Chinese three inches, as thin as the shape of a water chestnut. She can dance by standing on a man's hand.

I gave my students great freedom in their choice of themes although I encouraged them to write about Chinese life and customs. The best of their papers I kept and still have after all those years. What did they write about? They wrote about their childhood and about their families, some rich and some poor; about the customs and festivals in the various provinces from which they came. A few wrote about their great poets, Li Po and Tu Fu who lived in the glorious age of T'ang —about Confucius, Mencius, Chuang Tze, and other sages of the classical age kept alive through the Confucian Classics. They wrote about the history of their great art of calligraphy and tried to explain to me the formation and meaning of the beautiful Chinese characters. They told about Wang Hsi-chih (321–375), China's greatest calligrapher whose script has been described as "light as floating clouds, vigorous as a startled dragon." Chinese writing combines ingenuity and artistry, they explained, "the brush never touches the paper but with a purpose."

Some wrote about the plight of women in the old Chinese society; others about the new woman emancipated since the republic, and of

the generation gap caused by the changing marriage and other customs. They wrote about the infamous "Twenty-one demands" made
by Japan when the Western world was too involved in the war in
Europe to protest; and about the violent protest against the terms of
the Versailles Treaty concerning China.

It was soon obvious that some of my students were traditionalists
and devoted to their old civilization; others were rebels who denounced the old. All of them were concerned with the welfare of their
country and deplored the domination of China by the Western Powers. Their themes were a revelation of human life in a changing society, a society full of the turbulence caused by the impact of Western
civilization on the ancient culture of their country.

I came to know personally something about this turbulence for I
lived in Peking during the Warlord era when first one Warlord then
another dominated the city. There were many Chinas when I was
there. But the old China was still in evidence wherever I went. It mattered little what Warlord was in control of the city, or how much
ideas were changing, for the life of the people remained very much
as it had been for a thousand years.

It surprised me to find that *David Copperfield* was a novel which I
was to teach early in the college year. Apparently the Chinese, who
had studied abroad in the late nineteenth century, had read Dickens'
novels widely and avidly. I was told that when many Chinese began to
adopt foreign names, it was quite common for them to choose the
name of a Dickens character. There might be a David Copperfield
Wu, or Oliver Twist Hung, or a Samuel Pickwick Wang. Although I
had enjoyed Dickens' novels—I had read most of them as a young
girl in the crotch of an old apple tree at my grandfather's house—I
agonized over my students who struggled with the original text. It
was my belief that they got little from the study of this work which
was so full of detailed colloquial description. I certainly did not enjoy
teaching it. Fortunately for the Chinese who enjoyed these novels
there were excellent translations. The literate Chinese read many
works in translation: histories, biographies, as well as philosophical
works.

If my students agonized over *David Copperfield,* they thoroughly enjoyed Shakespeare's *The Taming of the Shrew*. This play had been chosen because of the traditional Chinese mother-in-law who was herself a shrew. In fact the students showed such keen appreciation of it that we decided to give a few scenes from the play as a class project—something I learned to do at the Bennett School.

No one at the T'ung Fu could have failed to know what was going on, for the enthusiasm and excitement of the students involved were almost unbelievable. Of course everyone in the compound came to see the girls perform—including our busy dean. She was so surprised and delighted with the performance that she urged us to give a production of the whole play as a money-making project for the college. The students immediately nodded approval; so this we did, spurred on by her enthusiasm. In a letter home I wrote:

For nearly a month rehearsals of *The Taming of the Shrew* have kept me busy from morning until night although it was a joy to work with these girls. They are bursting with dramatic feeling. At first they were shy and awkward, but it took only a suggestion to get them into the spirit of their parts. Rehearsals were not always encouraging, for the Chinese hate to be coached—a matter of "face," I understand. But the performance went off beautifully. The girls kept the house in laughter every minute. The audience was mostly Chinese although a few foreign patronesses brought guests with them. We were delighted to have The Little Empress as one of our patronesses. I think the proceeds will amount to about $800.

Thus began my dramatic work at the college, not only at the Women's College but at the Men's College as well. A few of our performances were to bring distinction to the University and almost launched me on a career as a producer.

Chang Nge with the little white rabbit on the way to the Moon Palace.
Courtesy of Marz Minor, Kansas City, Missouri.

The Mid-Autumn Festival

O lovely lady Moon, now round and full and brilliant
Now like the pale crescent on the finger nail of my beloved,
From time longer than man's memory thou hast graced
The blue night sky with thy beauty,
Entering our halls by painted door and latticed window
To enchant the sleepless with thy silver loveliness.

LI PO

IT WAS FROM MY STUDENTS I learned that China once based its calendar, not like ours on how long it takes the earth to make its orbit around the sun, but on the rhythm of the moon. With the lunar calendar, the year begins around the end of February when nature itself begins a renewal with the coming of spring. The months differ in length as ours do but each represents a complete lunar cycle. There are the dark nights of the new moon, its waxing on to a perfect roundness, and then back again to darkness. With the lunar calendar the Chinese knew in advance the evenings when the moon would be the brightest; these came inevitably around the fifteenth of each month.

At the T'ung Fu as we approached the fifteenth day of the eighth moon, I found in a set of student papers the following theme.

Dear Goddess of the Moon;

Since the cold winds have sent forth the fragrance of the yellow chrysanthemums, we know that our Mid-Autumn Festival Day will come soon. May you spread your silvery light over the whole world, as you are tonight, without the trouble of the winds and the rain.

You will shine upon rich and happy people. They will have feasts and music awaiting you. They will have merrymaking in the great garden or large hall to enjoy your beautiful light. You will also shine upon the poor. They earn little and have many to keep. It is difficult for them to get ready an everyday dinner. Surely they will not be able to have a feast and no time to enjoy this bright moon. They can offer you nothing except a few drops of bitter tears by telling you of the hardships of life.

You will shine upon those who are apart from their beloved companions.

You will shine upon young people who are school boys and girls. They may have tea parties and plays to amuse your brightness. But, please do

47

not let these young people look at you with deep thought. In the silent and cold moonlight, it is easy to think about sad and far things. They may even think of their future with fear and doubt. The hardships and misery of human life—that is what destroys their tender and pure minds and makes people grow old and sad.

This letter was my introduction to the Mid–Autumn Festival held every year on the birthday of the Goddess of the Moon. It was written by Ling Jui T'ang, a very gifted and sensitive student who was to become a well-known writer and painter and a life-long friend. She and her father, a distinguished Confucian scholar and a former mayor of Peking, were to make possible for me some of my most delightful China experiences.

From Jui T'ang I learned about many of the Chinese festivals which were held throughout the year. Most of the festivals, she explained, were based on ancient legends. The legend of the Moon Goddess tells about Chang Nge who lived about 2,000 B.C. in a mountain cave with her Taoist husband. She discovered that a little white rabbit was mixing a potion which her husband intended to take in order to go to heaven. Because she was lonely she decided to take the potion herself and soon found herself transported to the Moon Palace where the "Western Mother" made her a goddess.

"Watching the Mid-Autumn Moon," the scroll painted b

On the eve of the festival Jui T'ang gave me a present, a little play which was her dramatization of that ancient legend. I saw how exquisite it would be to present this some moonlight night in one of the courtyards of our beautiful old T'ung Fu. Jui T'ang, too, was delighted with the thought and suggested it be given in the spring, at the time of her graduation from Yenching. Dr. John Ferguson, to whom I showed the play, was intrigued by the dramatization and had it published in *The China Journal of Science and Art* of which he was the editor. The play was given on a beautiful moonlight night in June, one of the outstanding events of the Commencement Week.

Peking was unbelievably beautiful on the day of the festival. Everything was bathed in warm sunshine and sparkled in the clear air of North China. As Jui T'ang had said, the streets were alive with children buying from the toy vendors paper Moon Palaces and all the accessories with which to act out the moon legend. The clay statuettes of the goddess and her rabbit were all made by the vendors and their families so no two figures were ever alike. Fathers and mothers were attracted by the steaming kettles of the itinerant restaurants and by the cooks calling out their special wares: "Come buy my moon cakes, Try my golden persimmons, my round melons, Feast on my chestnut soup."

I celebrated and bought a pot of lovely yellow chrysanthemums

n Chou. Courtesy of the Boston Museum of Fine Arts.

which I put on the steps of my little Chinese house. This delighted my amah who told me that their clear scent would prolong my life, for "the chrysanthemum" she said, "is the flower of immortality." Wha T'ing loved it also and promised to keep it watered for me every day. He said that all Chinese admired chrysanthemums because at the end they knew how to die with grace and dignity.

That night when the old T'ung Fu was radiant with the light of the full moon, Chou Ting Pi, another one of my students, brought me some delicious moon cakes and a picture of a lovely scroll painted by Shen Chou (1427–1500) called "Watching the Mid-Autumn Moon." It showed the painter and three of his friends gathered to feast and drink wine in a simple pavilion open in front allowing them to gaze at the moon. On one side of the painting Shen Chou had written his thoughts that night:

> When young we heedlessly watch the mid-autumn moon
> Seeing this time as all other times.
>
> With the coming of age respect has grown.
> And we do not look lightly
> Every time we raise the deep cup to celebrate a feast.
>
> How many mid-autumns can an old man have?
> He knows this passing light cannot be held.

Notes Written on the Great Wall
October 30, 1923

> A thousand years in thy sight are but
> as yesterday when it is past and as a
> watch in the night.   PSALM 90

A FRIEND FROM THE *Madison* visiting the Schurmans at the Legation and Miss Hotchkiss, a Scotch artist who is in Peking for the winter, invited me to join them on a trip to the Ming Tombs and the Great Wall, the first trip that every foreigner is urged to take. It was a glorious morning when they called for me in the Schurman car and we drove to the station in time to catch the eight o'clock train for Nankou about forty miles north of Peking. We went third class because that was the way we were told to go if we wanted to have a glimpse of Chinese life. We had expected that a third-class car would be like the others only harder, perhaps dirtier and more crowded. Not at all! When the train arrived we were shoved into a box car with a mob of Chinese who were laden with bundles, trunks, all kind of vegetables, crates of chickens, and wicker baskets full of pigeons. We were pushed over to the opposite door, where we stood for the greater part of the journey.

All around us on the floor were seated blue-garbed coolies with their queues wound around their heads, soldiers (probably many of them former bandits) in disreputable looking uniforms, one or two Chinese ladies dressed in light blue silk smoking cigarettes and drinking tea, and a few Chinese gentlemen dressed in black silk and wearing little black satin caps. We were the only foreigners on board. It is curious that we did not have a moment's fear—that is, after the pushing was over and we found ourselves settled in the midst of cabbages and mattresses. Our fellow travelers tried to converse with us but my Chinese was too limited for that. However the few words that I could speak pleased them; they smiled, shook their heads approvingly and said *ting hao*—"very good." After a while one of the ladies pointed to the adjoining kitchen-car and motioned us to go in. There we found a place to rest and were offered tea and crackers by a little Chinese boy who was delighted when I thanked him in Chinese.

The road to Nankou runs through innumerable villages which are always in sight of the Western Hills. At this time of year the whole country is golden. In the sunlight, the hills look dusted with old gold. The tiny stone and mud villages blend in with the harvest of golden corn which is thrown on the roofs to dry or hung in bunches over the door. On the immaculate mud floor of the yards some of the corn has been ground into soft yellow meal; in the corner the stalks have been piled to dry for fuel. The only touch of color is in the blue coats of the men who are grinding the corn or digging in the fields.

Nankou is a walled town at the foot of the hills built as the first link of defenses against the northern invaders. It was once an important stage on the caravan route to Mongolia, and still is to some extent. Above the town is the entrance to the wild and rugged Nankou Pass through which Genghis Khan and his hordes found their way into the fertile plains of North China in the twelfth century.

Today the town assumes importance only because of its railroad station and hotel. We arrived at the hotel about eleven and after leaving our bags started off immediately for the Ming Tombs seven miles away. In great excitement we picked out our donkeys and set off across the plains with our donkey boys. We rode for two hours through rugged country before coming to the peaceful valley where the thirteen emperors of the last Chinese dynasty (1368–1644) lie buried. Through the magnificent five-arched marble *p'ai lou* at the entrance to the tombs one gets a view of the whole amphitheater with the background of the hills protecting "this vale of the dead."

When we entered the "Triumphal Way," two-thirds of a mile long, we rode through a grand array of eighteen pairs of huge stone animals and ancestors until we finally approached the imposing sepulcher of Yung Lo, the greatest of all the Ming emperors. Three porticoes stand at the entrance of his tomb, opening onto an outer courtyard with twisted old cedar trees. In the inner court stands the great sacrificial hall where the rites of ancestor worship were performed in his memory. Three flights of marble steps lead to the terrace on which it stands and three massive portals with folding doors open into one vast room empty except for the table for offerings and a stand for the spirit tablet.

It is longer, I understand, than the transept of Westminster Abbey. Forty huge pillars, vermillion and gold, support the roof; in the ceiling are sunken panels worked in relief and lacquered with dragons. Above this temple and across another court is the actual tomb, the mound beneath which lies Yung Lo's coffin in its huge grave chamber. This is the sepulcher of the builder of all that is grand and impressive in Peking; the massive walls, the palaces of The Forbidden City, and the marvelous Temple of Heaven.

For a while we sat on the terrace under a cedar tree listening to the birds and the crickets. At that time I did not know about Golden Bell. It was Alan Priest, a young American art historian, who told me it was a special kind of cricket that sings in the countryside about the tombs of the Ming emperors. It is the subject of a legend which tells that one of the lesser consorts of the Ming court, who could not hope to be buried with her lord, found herself failing in health. One does not speak of death to an emperor, so the consort sketched a tiny cricket —a picture of herself, she said. She died and was entombed alone. When the emperor visited her tomb he was aware of a clear and delicate trill as of a tiny golden bell. He searched and found a little cricket—the cricket of his consort's sketch. From then on the cricket was called Golden Bell—the consort who could not be buried with her lord, but preferred to become a cricket and sing in the fields about his tomb.

In the late afternoon we started back to Nankou across orchards of persimmon trees; the fruit glistened like pure gold. The shadows and colors of the hills fascinated me. From a soft red-gold, they turned to a deep wine color and finally to a soft blue-gray when the sun had sunk behind them. We arrived in Nankou at dusk. It was good to get back to the inn, to sit before the fire and chat, and then to satisfy a ravishing appetite with a delicious dinner. Immediately after dinner we went to bed on straw mattresses which seemed as soft as down after eight hours of donkey riding.

We were up and off by eight o'clock this morning in the funniest train you can imagine. It was presumably a freight train but a small open boxcar was added to the front for the few passengers who were traveling, as we were, up the difficult pass to Ch'un Lung Chaiou. The engine pushing from behind puffed slowly up the narrow valley but had a fearful time getting up the steep bare hills. We had to back down every hill three times before we could finally get on again, but it was through such magnificent scenery that we did not begrudge one moment of delay. We sat on the platform of the car with our feet dangling over the front, gazing up into huge jagged mountains with fantastic shadows playing about them, peeping over the wall of a tiny village, or watching a stream of water plunging down into the gorge, tumbling as it went over white rocks past tall slender trees with only a tuft of foliage at the top. As we neared Ch'un Lung Chaiou we had glimpses of the Great Wall standing out clearly against the blue sky. From the station we walked about a mile and then climbed the steep ascent where we finally reached the Wall (2,000 feet above sea level). Here we were met by the inevitable beggars and by the men selling curios to foreigners: donkey bells, camel bells, carved flint, and old coins.

As I write I am sitting on one of the ramparts looking out onto the jagged hills which surround me. In every direction I can see bits of the huge wall crawling over the innumerable peaks. At times it is lost, as it dips into the valleys and between hills, but it is always sure to crawl up again and go rambling on as far as the eye can see. Far, far below me is the road that leads to Mongolia with its trains of camels, brown like the hills, and a few heavily laden donkeys. There is no vegetation anywhere except a few green trees sheltering a tiny village far away. Everything is brown: the hills, the wall, and the road. As the sun moves lower, the hills in the far distance are veiled in a purple mist. The song of the crickets, the faraway tinkle of the camel bells, and the cries of the goatherds and donkey boys are the only sounds. Here on the rampart where I am sitting is a bit of the ruin one sees all along the way—rocks tumbling from their places and others lying in scattered heaps where they have fallen down in the valley. On one of the ramparts below, two soldiers are stationed; I wonder how they could be needed in this isolated and peaceful spot.

Although this massive wall stands as a mockery to stone defenses, yet in its ruin we are made to feel the continuity of time. It was more than 2,000 years ago (220 B.C.) that the wall was built—a wall that stretches across half a continent from the shores of the Yellow Sea not far from Peking, to the mountains of Tibet, some 1,500 miles away

Top: The five-arched marble *p'ai lou* at entrance to tombs.

Center: The "Triumphant Way" showing pairs of stone animals and ancestors.

Right: One of the stone animals.

The Great Wall crawls over the hills.

A Chinese boy sits with me on one of the ramparts of the Great Wall.

(approximately the distance from Portland, Maine, to Denver, Colorado). It is one of the engineering wonders of the world made possible, I have been told, by the labor of half a million slaves and prisoners of war. A Chinese boy who followed me to this rampart has said that in ancient times watchers were stationed on every turret and tower, day and night. They used a code of smoke signals to summon help when the savage horsemen of Mongolia massed against the wall. It is not difficult to imagine armed horsemen dashing across the hills and hordes of invaders creeping over the brow of the peaks. Yet all around me now are only the lonely hills, the massive creeping wall, and rugged isolation.

I have a sense of history here that I have never felt before. The thought has come to me that men were working on this wall before my country was discovered or ever dreamed of; before Jesus was born, before Caesar and Pompey. In a place like this the years melt away and one is reminded of the Psalmist's words "A thousand years in thy sight are but as yesterday when it is past and as a watch in the night."

Winter in Peking

> Why should God speak in words?
> The four seasons follow in their
> course and all things come to life.
> CONFUCIUS

MY FIRST WINTER in Peking was mild and open. There was much to do and much to see so the weather was no obstacle. The following excerpts from letters to my family only hint at all that life in this fabulous city had to offer.

T'ung Fu
December 10, 1923

We have had our first fall of snow. It was only a flurry, but it came late one afternoon just as the lights were coming on. It was a fascinating sight to see the flakes falling against the paper windows and to watch the people hurry along brushing off every flake as it fell on them. The vendors on the streets covered their fruits and candies with huge canvases held by poles and spread out to four corners. Truly, it is the streets of Peking that intrigue me more than anything else. Here the people live; and here one gets the feeling of the Orient with the funeral and wedding processions, the slow steady stream of camels and donkeys, the squeaking water carts, and the squealing pigs being taken to market. The donkeys are now bringing mistletoe into the city for the Christmas season.

In the daytime it is thrilling to walk along the streets and the *hutungs* listening to the vendors each with his different call, ringing bells or twanging cymbals; smelling the delicious odors which rise from the great steaming bowls of the street restaurants; watching the tiny children playing shuttlecock or flying kites; observing ladies sitting by their doors smoking cigarettes or pipes; and best of all watching the silken-gowned gentlemen taking their caged birds to the tea houses. I shall never forget how amazed I was to learn that the Chinese have birds for pets as we have dogs or kittens. Nearly every little boy on the street is carrying some kind of bird tied to a small stick. Why the bird doesn't flutter about or try to get away is a mystery. I have never seen one that is not sitting peacefully on his little perch enjoying his airing. Some of the wealthy Chinese keep flocks of doves and pigeons for amusement. They tie bamboo whistles around their feet and let them fly about to make a whirring sound—like singing wires.

They never fly far away; generally they circle only over the houses from which they have flown. There are untamed birds that nest in the temple courtyards and the palace gardens in the Imperial City. Swallows fly down from the eaves; magpies, warblers, finches, and crows fly freely from court-yard to courtyard. Birds are everywhere. In fact the phoenix is held in so much honor here that one almost believes in it, accepting as fact that "it dances on moonlight nights on high terraces."

It is common to see fortune-tellers sitting on the street corners. Most of them have a bamboo tube of sticks and a book spread open before them showing a pair of hands. It is interesting to pause by one of them and study the crowd that gathers around. If anyone wants his fortune told the tube is shaken until a stick falls out. If it is long that means good luck, if short he is urged to pass on and try his luck another day. Storytellers, too, draw a rapt crowd, mostly coolies who squat in silence as they listen to tales of ancient heroism. This is the way the uneducated learn about their history. The narrator claps bamboo sticks, sings, or beats a drum according to the tale he is telling. There are jugglers, itinerant barbers shaving their clients, and itinerant dentists. Near the entrance to Lung Fo Ssu there is a sign in English reading "Insertion false teeth and eyes, latest Methodists."

I enjoy dropping into shops and talking with the shop owners who wear the traditional long gown and jacket. Chinese gentlemen are as cordial and as polished as any gentlemen I have ever seen. When I enter they are usually seated, leisurely drinking tea or smoking a long pipe. They rise immediately and bow most respectfully. When I speak in my limited Chinese they are always delighted. Even though I look around in the shop for an hour with-out buying a thing (as I often do, alas), they open the door for me or lift the curtain and beg me to come again. This human warmth is one of the outstanding characteristics of the Chinese people.

One of the tea shops is getting to be a favorite haunt of mine. I go there to buy tea or to get change for my ricksha boy. It has a handsome elaborately carved facade painted red with a touch of gilt and a fine old-fashioned interior where great canisters line the shelves filled with varieties of dried tea leaves. Fresh jasmine or dried chrysanthemum flowers are added later. The long-gowned proprietors always welcome me graciously and seat me at a large lacquer table. After a proper time—one must be unhurried not to seem uncouth—a sample of some recommended tea is brewed so that I may taste it before making a choice. This is served in little handleless white cups. My visits always mean a lesson in English for them and one in Chinese for me. There are seldom any other foreigners around so all the men

gather about me and ask questions as long as I will stay. Often they ask me
to translate a letter from America or to write an address on a package of
tea that is ready to be sent away. They tell me that tea is the supreme gift
of China and that there are two important points with tea, the leaf and the
cup. The best description of the leaf, they say, was written in 780 in the
Tea Classic: "The best quality of leaves must have creases like the leathern
boot of Tartar horsemen, curl like the dewlap of a mighty bullock, unfold
like a mist rising out of a ravine, and be wet and soft like fine earth newly
swept by rain." The porcelain industry, they say, owes a great debt to the
Chinese delight in tea and wine. This industry and the cultivation of tea
began at about the same time and in much the same locations (Kiangsi and
Chekiang)—areas where a chosen few could afford the finest tea and the
loveliest cups and covers. It has been said that the almost universal use of
tea instead of unboiled water has saved the people from countless intestinal
diseases—and it has soothed the nerves of mankind in every possible cir-
cumstance!

As interesting as the streets are by day, they can never quite compare
with the wonder of them by night. Paper lanterns hang above the shops,
silhouetted against the sky; paper windows throw out their soft yellow
glow with the fantastic framework standing out in black relief; ricksha
coolies run in perfect rhythm, gray against the blackness of the streets. The
figures of vendors are lighted by the glow of the fires in the street restaurants; steam rises from huge iron kettles and coolie faces bend over bowls
of food eaten rapidly with flying chopsticks. Here for me is the lure of the
Orient. Here is Peking.

You will be pleased to know that Dr. and Mrs. Ingram have invited me
to have Christmas dinner with them and their family. They are dear people who have spent most of their lives in China as missionaries. The whole
Ingram family is respected here in Peking by both the Chinese and the
foreigners. Their daughter, Isabel, a very good friend of mine, has just
been chosen as tutor to the little Empress. Isabel says she is very beautiful.
Apparently all the eligible Chinese households were searched in order to
find just the right mate for this last member of the Ch'in dynasty. Yet had
they searched the world over, Isabel thinks they would not have found her
equal. Their marriage last year was probably the last Manchu pageant.
Everything was done to fulfill the rites which have been elaborated through
the centuries to make the Son of Heaven's wedding the most marvelous of
spectaculars. Guests were dressed in their jeweled robes encrusted with

gold according to rank. There was music and all the courts were filled with flowers.

I do hope the box with my gifts for the family arrived in time for Christmas. You can't imagine what pleasure it gave me to send them to you. By the time this letter reaches Portland Christmas will be over, so let me end by wishing you all the Happiest of New Years!

*   *   *

January 12, 1924

Yesterday I saw my first big funeral—the largest in Peking for two years. The long procession began about eleven o'clock in the morning. It was an hour in gathering and it took about an hour for it to pass! All the time that I was watching I felt as if I were living in 1000 B.C.

First there were four camels with red silk thrown over their backs. Following them was an array of paper animals and men, a paper automobile, a ricksha, a tall paper pagoda and two huge dogs—symbols of good luck. All of these were to be burned at the grave. Then came a band followed by Confucionists, another band, more paper flowers and symbols. Lama priests and Taoist priests followed, still another band and so on until finally the male mourners appeared dressed in coarse white cloth, for white is always used for mourning. Behind them came the catafalque covered with gorgeous red embroideries. The huge catafalque that was to carry the body to the tomb was too large to go into the *hutung* where the deceased lived so a smaller one brought the body to Hatamen Street, one of the main boulevards. Here the casket covered with heavy red satin was moved from one to the other while priests threw paper money into the air to frighten away any evil spirits that might be lingering about. The children and the poor scrambled for this. Sixty-four bearers working in relays carried the massive catafalque. Following the body came the women mourners in white sedan chairs. Since the wife was dead, the first chair was empty; the next two contained his concubines. Along Hatamen Street straw houses had been erected especially for the occasion where the mourners stopped to drink tea and offer sacrifice for the departed one!

*   *   *

January 20, 1924

Last night Jui T'ang and her father took me to the theater to see Mei Lan-fang, the great Chinese actor. If I am to attempt to describe the performance to you, you must put away all the notions you have of a theater, for a stage and an auditorium are the only things we have in common. The audience gathers about eight-thirty when the first play begins; in the evening there may be as many as nine or ten. During the first plays, which are the least interesting, the audience drinks tea, eats fruit and candies, and smokes cigarettes. All this time the ushers go about throwing hot towels to their customers. Most of the ladies sit in boxes in the balcony; the gentlemen visit from box to box. To look at the audience one would never guess that a play was going on, and to look at the stage one is hardly more certain.

There is no curtain, and the orchestra sits on one side of the stage. It isn't until you have heard a Chinese orchestra, consisting of the three-string guitars, flutes, clappers, gongs, drums, and pipes, that you can conceive the meaning of the word noise; it is ungodly! The stage hands walk on and off the stage at will. Sometimes they come on stage to drink tea from a table placed at the back. If anything particularly interesting is going on, they crowd around the entrances and watch. The scenery is simple. Usually gates or walls are painted on cloth and held up by stage hands. If an emperor is passing under a gate with his soldiers, a piece of cloth is held up until they have all passed beneath, then the men walk off with the gate and stand in the back to watch the rest of the performance.

Everything is symbolic: the gestures, the costumes, and the makeup. When an actor stoops, the audience knows he is entering a door. Certain other gestures indicate he is mounting his horse. An actor carrying a wand tipped with white horsetail hair is representing a supernatural being. A red mask indicates a good character, a black mask an evil or cruel one. Waving ribbons can represent clouds, the wind, or the sea. Banners always indicate the number of troops of a general. In contrast to the scenery, the costumes are often elaborate; they are made mostly of silk with beautiful embroidery. An emperor, for instance, always wears a yellow gown embroidered with a dragon, for yellow is the imperial color and the dragon the imperial symbol. There is very little action in Chinese plays, or "operas" as they are rightfully called because of the falsetto singing. Much of the acting consists of traditional postures and gestures which require great skill if they are to be performed correctly and gracefully. However the performances usually end with a battle or a remarkable acrobatic stunt, and sometimes with lovely Chinese dancing.

The best play or opera is always reserved until the end. Last night Mei Lan-fang did not appear until twelve o'clock. He is a remarkable actor taking only women's parts, for as yet no women are allowed to appear on the stage with men. He is slight of build and extremely graceful, acting generally in the delightful old legends of China. At the end of this particular opera there was an extraordinary dance in which he went down to the bottom of the sea to get a pearl from an oyster. It was done with great artistry. The Chinese seldom clap or show much enthusiasm although they love the theater. Once, when a famous child actor gave a performance, the audience rose with a shout of applause and clapped spontaneously. During a performance of Mei Lan-fang they will applaud but with great restraint.

I want to know more about Chinese drama so I shall go to the theater as often as my tiny salary will allow. Jui T'ang tells me that the theater in China, which has always been immensely popular, is centuries old. The pantomine, plays, and operas are based on ideas, stories, or historic episodes that go back thousands of years. In the past, raised platforms over a street or in a field often served as a stage. At the fairs in market towns and on other special occasions a performance by a dramatic troupe was usually part of the program. Curiously enough, the flowering of the Chinese dramatic genius came under the Mongols in the thirteenth century. Ever since 1215 Peking has been the center of Chinese drama.

*   *   *

Peking
February 3, 1924

There have been two fascinating Chinese parties which I must tell you about for one at Jui T'ang's house reflects the old China which so intrigues me, the other reflects the new.

Here in Peking there are several young American men representing their colleges as I am representing Wellesley. Because we are all involved with Chinese education in one way or another, we are drawn more than most foreigners into the life of the Chinese people. Alan Swede, one of the Princeton men and a genial soul, has made many Chinese friends. One, a wealthy young man educated abroad, has recently returned to Peking with many Western ideas. Because Alan was eager to have me meet him and see his house filled with Chinese treasures, he took me, as his date, to a large and impressive party there. Besides Alan and me, there were only four other foreigners.

The Chinese family who gave the party had all lived in America or Europe, so the home and the clothes were not entirely Chinese. Most of the men wore foreign evening clothes although the women for the most part were in their native dress. The house was very beautiful—a large Chinese house with modern comforts. The Chinese curios were magnificent: a room of blue and white porcelain, another of green and white jade, and for me the most beautiful, a room of exquisite carved ivory.

It was interesting to see how these Chinese of the elite society entertain themselves. In one room mah-jongg was being played with extremely high stakes, in another bridge was being played, again with high stakes. One huge room was cleared for dancing where an orchestra of White Russians played Western music. Here Alan and I spent most of our time. It surprised me to find that the Chinese are good dancers. In fact these cultured Chinese are no different from our finest Western men. Some of those I met had studied at Oxford, Edinburgh, and Heidleberg—others at Harvard and Columbia. Many diplomats were there. I found myself talking to W. W. Yen, China's foreign minister, who had been ambassador to Germany and Denmark. I was also introduced to a man who had been a representative to the Washington Conference. He and I had a long conversation for, of course, he knows Charles Evans Hughes (our Secretary of State) and had met his daughter, Catherine, a college friend of mine.

All of the guests spoke English even among themselves; only once in a while did I hear a word of Chinese. To speak English is considered very smart among this group. However, some of the guests had come from different provinces and spoke English because there is no common Chinese dialect. Toward the end of the evening I was introduced to a fine looking young Chinese named Arthur Tsu-kuang Lin. As we talked I noticed that he was wearing an Alpha Delta Phi pin. I told him that I had a brother who belonged to the same fraternity in a small college in Maine called Bowdoin. He smiled and exclaimed "Bowdoin is my college, too," When I asked him if he knew my brother Proctor he said "Proctor! We were classmates and good friends; we met in Boston just before I sailed for China this fall." You can imagine what fun it was to talk with him. Such an experience makes one feel very much at home anywhere in the world.

Going to Jui T'ang's house was like going to a different world. Her party was in honor of Rabindranath Tagore, the Indian poet who was given the Nobel Prize for Literature a few years ago. He has been in Peking lecturing at the Chinese universities on the subject "Asia for the Asiatics," a popular subject among the students as you can imagine. Because I had met him last year when he gave a reading at the Bennett School, I invited him to have tiffin at the T'ung Fu and to speak afterwards to my students about his life and his school in Bengal. He was happy to accept and the students were enthralled, especially Jui T'ang.

A Peking street with one of the city gates and gate towers in the distance.

A heavy load being carried on a shoulder pole.

One of the impressive *p'ai lous* in Peking.

A load of melons on the familiar wheelbarrow.

Steaming bowls in a
street restaurant. Note
paper windows in
background.

Street restaurant in winter. Note padded clothes of the men and
the man in the distance with a queue.

A typical Peking cart.

Part of the official's funeral showing mourners in their white robes.

Outside the city wall showing, on the extreme right, Ch'ien Men,
one of the principal gates of the city.

Camels bringing in coal from the hills.

Pagoda, Summer Palace, showing Western Hills in the distance.

Tien An-Men, Imperial City.

Some of the magnificence within the Forbidden City.

Peking street scene from scroll celebrating Emperor K'ang-hsi's birthday (1712).
Note Peking cart, shoulder poles, wheelbarrow, and store lanterns.
Courtesy Harvard-Yenching Institute.

It was because of her enthusiasm, that Jui T'ang's father invited him to their home to meet some noted Chinese artists and musicians who come once each month to paint, write, or listen to music. He kindly included me. Unlike the other party, here was the traditional China, a typical home of an official and Confucian scholar. Within the walled compound were several courtyards and separate houses similar to the T'ung Fu. We were received in a large reception room furnished simply with handsome carved teakwood furniture and pieces of bronze. Lovely scroll paintings hung on the walls; by the door stood a beautiful tall porcelain vase filled with plum blossoms. There was not a trace of Western influence.

The guests were mostly Chinese gentlemen in their long, dark blue silk gowns and short black jackets. Several wore the traditional little black satin cap tipped with a red button. They were all charming and gracious. The only Chinese women were Jui T'ang and her mother. Besides Tagore and his Indian friends there were two other foreigners besides myself, the former Mrs. Willard Straight and her new English husband Leonard Elmhurst. They are connected with Tagore's school in some way and have suggested that I spend a year there on my way back to America. Tagore was enthusiastic about the idea—what do you think about it?

During the evening the artists made several sketches for us; you would be amazed to see how they work. In painting a flower, for instance, they begin with the blossom and then paint the leaves and the stock. It is all done in a minute with the most casual strokes of the brush. Each one of us was given a sketch to take home so I chose a graceful spray of bamboo. Jui T'ang's father, an excellent calligrapher, was asked to show us how Chinese characters are made. He sat at a table with his brush holder, his ink stone and slab, and placed his left hand firmly on the top. With his right hand held high, he took a brush and made his strokes with precision and power. His characters were striking and bold. I thought they were handsome although it was obvious that only the Chinese who were there could fully appreciate their artistry. Jui T'ang explained that calligraphy is often regarded by the Chinese as the highest art. She quoted Arthur Waley who once remarked, "In the West writing is a convenience, in the East it is almost a religion." Every literate Chinese, she said, has spent years in training his hand and eye in handling the brush and acquiring a feeling for design and composition. Chinese writing must always show strength, grace, and above all, individuality. Jui T'ang is very proud of her father's writing.

After the ink stone and slab were put away, a musician played on three different instruments. One was a *peh-pah,* a harp of four strings over a

thousand years old, handed down by a famous musician who had carved his
favorite poem on the back—a poem written by Wang Ch'ang-Ling in the
T'ang dynasty. Jui T'ang read a translation for us. It began:

As I lie forgetful of wordly cares in the Southern Pavilion
I draw back the curtain to see the rising moon;
Tranquil waters and woodland lie bathed in the glorious moonlight.
The shadows dance on the paper windows.
The moon waxes and wanes without end
As the present gives way to the past!

Before the evening was over Tagore, a gentle quiet man with a soft high
voice was persuaded to read some of his poems. In his long flowing Indian
gown he was very impressive; his dark deep-set eyes lighted up as he read.
For his last poem he chose one which he thought was in harmony with the
Confucian tradition.

Where the mind is without fear and
the head is held high;
 Where knowledge is free;
 Where the world has not been broken
up into fragments by narrow domestic
walls;
 Where words come out from the
depth of truth;
 Where tireless striving stretches its
arms towards perfection;
 Where the clear stream of reason has
not lost its way into the dreary desert
sand of dead habit;
 Into that heaven of freedom, my
Father, let my country awake.

This was a fitting end to an evening of the "Old China" which was
so soon to fade into the mist of history.

* * *

If the winter in Peking had been mild and open, the winter in
Maine had been unusually severe. Every time the temperature plunged

to zero or below or when a blizzard was raging outside, my mother would think of me in a house with paper windows. Could they really keep out the cold, she asked. Did they not get torn or blown out in a winter storm? I finally wrote:

February 25, 1924

And now for the paper windows which mother has been asking about in every letter. No, they are not covered nor replaced in the winter. And they never get torn because they are protected by a frame made of small pieces of wood fitted together to make an interesting design. At night it is lovely to see these designs silhouetted against the soft yellow light.

I must confess that at first I was a bit dubious about these windows myself. But they do keep out the cold quite as much as glass. At least with a little cast-iron stove in my living room I have been comfortable at all times. I haven't felt the cold here any more than I did at home. There were several bitter days when I hugged the fire, but I remember days in Portland when we hugged the fire, too. My bedroom is unheated, so many mornings I have waked to find the water in my pitcher with a film of ice. On these days I stay snug in my bed until my *amah* comes with hot water and calls "Six piecy-panty day." I have bought a camel's hair puff which is wonderful; it keeps me warm whatever the weather. I am told they last forever for when they get matted, as they often do at the end of winter, they are opened and the camel's hair washed, puffed, and dried in the sun.

One does have to dress much warmer out here than at home for it is necessary to be out of doors so much. All of our meals are served in a separate building, and we must cross a courtyard and crunch through the snow even to take a bath. But one of the joys of living in a Chinese compound is that one is always conscious of the beauty of the heavens. None of the classrooms are heated so I teach in a fur-lined coat which I bought for a song; the students all wear padded clothes, as do most of the Chinese people. Fortunately, our lively class discussions help to keep us warm. And of course, remember we go about in open unheated rickshas instead of warm electric cars!

In the Legation Quarter, the homes as well as the banks and hotels are well heated as at home. But most of the foreigners whom I know prefer to live in Chinese houses which have so much more charm. At formal parties it is not easy to keep warm in our evening clothes, so I always take something extra to throw over my shoulders. However, I find that when people are having a good time together they can always manage somehow. Of course it is good to have the comforts of home—the central heat, the running water, and all the other things that we take so much for granted in America—but they are not really essential. Here one learns to adjust to the inevitable and to make the best of it. One can be happy without all of our creature comforts. I think what makes my Chinese friends happy in spite of their primitive living conditions are their many interests; they love art, poetry, philosophy, music, good food, and good fellowship.

Temple of the Great Awakening

> When you ask why I dwell here docile among the Far Green Hills, I laugh in my heart. My heart is happy. The peach-blossom watches the river running—but remains content. There is a better Heaven and Earth than the busy world of men. LI PO

I HAD PLANNED with Ruth Chen, a Chinese friend and colleague at the T'ung Fu, to spend part of our spring vacation in the Western Hills at a beautiful old Buddhist Monastery called Ta Chieh Ssu, "Temple of the Great Awakening." We were to be gone long enough to make the trip to the famous monastery built on top of Miao Feng Shan, the sacred mountain far beyond Ta Chieh Ssu.

On the morning of our departure, Chu Pu, the servant who was to accompany us, knocked at my door at five o'clock to say that the cart had arrived, the beds, bedding, and the provisions already packed, and he was off. There was an hour before dawn would break, so I dreamed awhile of hills, temple bells, and stars until the first gray light shone through my paper windows. Ruth was waiting when I arrived in the dining room so I hastened through my breakfast in order that we could be on our way.

Our ricksha men were waiting for us outside the T'ung Fu gate and sped us out beyond the city wall across the plain to the summer palace. The wind had begun to blow as we left the city, but it had died down so quickly that I did not give it a thought. By the time we reached the palace there was no wind, the sun was shining, and the crisp air seemed as clear as crystal.

Here we left our rickshas, and after much bargaining mounted the donkeys that were to take us to Ta Chieh Ssu. Only the merry tinkling of the donkey-bells could match our spirits. We rode for an hour through many tiny villages before we reached the road leading directly to the mountains. It was here that the wind, which had already begun to blow again, suddenly grew fierce; dust was whirled everywhere. A dull, ominous yellow light came into the sky as we drew near the mountains. The wind increased and the dust became unbearable. We knew then that we were caught in a severe dust storm. In the spring great winds come from the remote Mongolian desert carrying large quantities of sand mixed with yellow loess. They blow past the northern mountains and the Great Wall through the Imperial hunting forests into Peking.

At a steep pass through the mountains we had to dismount, for the path was rocky and uneven. The fierce wind and blinding dust prevented us from making much of any headway. It was cold, so cold that my fingers were numb as I tried to feel my way along the rocks. When we were finally through the pass and on the road again back upon our donkeys, it was colder than ever. Fortunately we had brought our rugs so we wrapped them around us and bent forward to cut the wind. Because the dust was blowing directly against us, the poor beasts could hardly move. It grew colder and colder. I had to dismount again to get warm. It was difficult to fight the wind and I could guide my steps only by the tiniest squint. Once in a while the wind would die down so that we could see about us. Only desolate hills, rugged paths, and a solitary figure walking by a cart or a loaded donkey. On our donkeys again we went miles through mountain passes and across plains with only a tiny hamlet here and there. As I hugged my donkey to keep the dust out of my face, I could occasionally hear the donkey bells of a fellow traveller who was passing very near.

The storm continued to rage as the sun sank lower and lower. I wondered if we would ever reach the monastery that night. When I questioned the donkey boy about the distance still to cover, he answered with oriental calm: "Two hours more!" My back ached from leaning forward; my head ached from its cramped position. I was cold, bitterly cold; my eyes and mouth were full of dust. Two hours more! But what was to be done? It would take us as long to turn back. It was impossible to try for another temple for neither of us knew where we were, and it would probably be difficult, if not dangerous, to stop at a farmhouse along the way. We must go on. We wrapped our rugs around us a little tighter and hugged our donkeys a little closer. Then gradually the wind began to die away and the dust to settle. The quieting of the wind lifted our spirits. If only the cart which we had sent ahead with Chu Fu in the morning had arrived, we might even have a hot supper waiting for us. Spurred on by these thoughts we seemed to give new life to our donkeys, for they began to run again.

By the time the sun had gone behind the mountains, the wind had died down. Ahead of us, on the slope of a mountain not more than half a mile away was a line of cedar trees and a glimpse of a red wall through the green. "Ta Chieh Ssu," cried the donkey boy.

Inside the monastery gate a coolie was waiting to tell us that our servant had arrived and that everything had been prepared for us. He guided us to a higher courtyard through another gate and into the temple court. Here we were to have one of the temple houses where we could look out onto the marble steps, onto some glorious old cedars, and listen to the temple wind-bells! Chu Pu heard our voices and came out to greet us. He could hardly wait to show what he had prepared. Our beds were set up, a fire glowed in the stove, a kettle of water was boiling, and tea was already on the table. Blessed Chu Pu, blessed fire, blessed food!

After we had washed, had our tea, and warmed ourselves a bit, we discovered that we were in a room with a shrine on which were three small Buddhas. As we stood near them, our door opened and an altar boy brought in pieces of burning incense which he placed upon the little altar. This was the beginning of the evening worship so he invited us to follow him. In every building and before every idol and tablet he placed the burning incense.

By the time we returned to our house, dinner was ready: fried chicken, green peas, toast and coffee, peaches and cake. No one ever had a more delectable meal by the light of a candle. Outside a breeze began to stir the little bells hanging from each corner of the temple roof. For a moment we sat in silence listening to their soft, delicate tones. We had travelled since early morning, we had braved a savage dust storm; now it was heavenly to rest in this peaceful old monastery —a place of tranquility so typical of the Western Hills.

Dogs were barking and bells ringing as I opened my eyes at six o'clock the next morning. There was an hour of blissful waking until Chu Pu knocked at the door with our warm water—then after break-fast out into the sparkling sunshine. The altar boy returned after his morning duties to ask if we would like to look about the monastery. He was a handsome youth with a warm friendly manner. Ta Chieh Ssu, he told us, was built toward the end of the 12th century, one of the "Eight Resting Places" of a Chin emperor as he was travelling in the Western Hills. Later under the Mings the monastery was so prosperous that it could serve 200 monks daily in the great refectory. In those days the guest rooms of the monastery accommodated thousands of pilgrims on their way to Miao Feng Shan; the huge ovens smoked continously to feed them. Today few fires are ever lighted because there are no longer Imperial patrons to use this as their travelling palace.

The priest's house was opposite ours, and here we met the honored *ho shang*. Most of the priests whom I had seen around Peking were dirty, coarse, and often repulsive. Perhaps that is why I was so amazed and delighted to find in this faraway monastery a priest whose beautiful face was lighted by a cordial smile, whose appearance was immaculate, and whose welcome could not have been more gracious. He wanted us to see the great K'ang Hsi's throne room in a garden court which was shaded by magnolia trees. He said, "Come often to this court to feel its soothing atmosphere." As we went from court to court he pointed with pride to a superb ginkgo tree hundreds of years old. And he showed us a spring of clear water spouting from a dragon's mouth into a stone basin fringed with wild iris, violets, and ferns. He asked the altar boy to show us the storerooms which we found filled with huge crocks of grain and salt vegetables. Dried golden corn hung from the ceiling and huge fat bags of yellow meal were piled in the corner. A white and yellow cat prowled through the crocks and jumped into a hole as we opened the creaking doors.

Inside the first courtyard where we dismounted from our donkeys, men were braiding *kao-liang* (a tall grain) into a large mat. In a little shed to the right, a donkey was pulling a grinding stone which crushed corn into soft yellow meal. Everything was orderly and alive. In the gardens outside of the monastery walls coolies were tending the first green shoots shielded from the north by tall *kao-liang* stalks. The orchards extended far up the mountain in back of the monastery; one huge orchard had been terraced for growing vegetables. I sat for a moment just outside the monastery gate. In front of me was

The entrance to the summer palace on the way to the Western Hills.

The camel back bridge and pagoda at the Summer Palace.

The Western Hills.

A court of Wo Fo Ssu, one of the first monasteries I visited, and its famous white pine.

Listening to the wind-bells hanging from the corners of the temple roofs.

The temple court at Ta Chieh Ssu.

The high-pillared temple hall with the three huge gilded Buddhas.

The bronze incense burner, Ta Chieh Ssu.

The honored *ho shang*.

Of what importance if the roof be low
When beneath it plum blossoms grow.

The monastery garden in the spring.

the lane through which I could see the distant purple hills. The sun poured down upon me; magpies chattered in a pine tree. It was good to be alive!

The temple service was going on when we returned at noon. All the altar candles were lighted, and the priest in his rose-colored robe was placing incense before each Buddha. In the beautiful open court-yard there was a huge bronze brazier where the priest lighted a paper tablet taken from the altar. While this was burning he knelt down, poured a libation upon the ground after which he kowtowed three times and then walked silently away.

After an early lunch we climbed part way up the mountain behind the monastery. Our path led by tiny mud huts belonging mostly to goatherds; otherwise we saw only the brown barren hills. In the valley were many fruit trees—peach, apricot, and pear—but at this time of year only the buds had begun to swell. We walked by a dried bed of a mountain stream. Huge rocks had been dashed together and sent tumbling down the hillside. Then the rains had ceased, so the rocks were to lie there until unborn springs should burst forth and dash them further. After an hour of climbing, we came to a hut where an old man was working in his little garden; a grandson played nearby. The old man smiled as he stepped forward to greet us and urged us to go inside to rest. The little place with its low ceiling and white walls was comfortable and cozy. It was pleasant to sit and chat for awhile with this kind old man; and we were both touched as Ruth translated some Chinese characters written on his wall:

> Of what importance if the roof be low,
>   when beneath it flower plum blossoms?
> What matter if one's destiny be humble,
>   when within it is fragrant friendship?

We wound our way slowly down the mountain. On a terrace under-neath a solitary pine tree, a father and son sat smoking their pipes as they looked off into the beauty of the distant hills. "From the foot of the mountain," says a Chinese poet, "many are the paths ascending in shadow, and many the feet, silk shod or shoeless, that follow them.

But from the terrace all who climb behold the self-same view, and travel to the same ultimate goal."

It was late when we finished our evening meal, but the gates were opened for us. We walked out into the brilliant night, to the sweep of a star-filled sky, and to the silence broken only by the sound of the wind-bells as they were caught now and then by the evening breeze.

In order to be in good shape for the difficult trip to Miao Feng Shan, we spent the next day hiking and climbing. By noon we had climbed more than a thousand feet. Ruth then returned to the monastery but I stayed to rest underneath a huge pine tree. On the edge of a nearby hill two goatherds were climbing with their herds. Their faint cries and the wind whispering through the pine were the only sounds. As they reached the top their figures were silhouetted against the blue sky. Leisurely they walked along the brow of the hill while the goats behind them nibbled on the burned stumps of grass. They sang a slow monotonous tune; across the distance it was very beautiful. It sounded of peace and leisure and contentment. I was reminded of other shepherds of long ago.

Another herd made its way up the hill where I was sitting. When the goatherd spied me he flung himself on the ground, took out his long pipe and began to smoke. He was a handsome youth with black hair down to his shoulders. As he sat looking out towards the hills he began to talk and pointed here and there, only once in awhile looking up to see if I were listening. He seemed carried away by what he was telling although I could understand only a word or two. It was only after he had noticed that the last goat had passed way beyond us that he took up his staff, waved good-bye, and went on his way again. As he was leaving he pointed to a hut halfway down the valley saying that was his home and I should stop there for a cup of tea. These huts are all more or less the same. They consist of one room with a *k'ang* (a large stone platform about two feet high which is used for a bed), a Chinese stove where there is always a kettle of tea, and a small ancestral shrine. I stopped at one on my way this morning; in the courtyard I saw seven goats, three pigs, a cat, and two dogs, beside a whole flock of hens. The old lady who greeted me was a garrulous soul with a loud shrill voice; her daughter-in-law, about twenty years old, was a thing of beauty. When I looked at her sad face I was reminded of a poem written by Fu Hsuan (A.D. 278):

> How sad it is to be a woman!
> Nothing on earth is held so cheap.
> Boys stand leaning at the door
> Like Gods fallen out of Heaven.
> Their hearts brave the Four Oceans,
> The wind and dust of a thousand miles.
> No one is glad when a girl is born;
> By her the family sets no store.

That evening I stayed up to attend the late service at the Temple. It was midnight before I was ready for bed. The last reverberation of the temple drum had ceased and a deathlike stillness had descended upon the place. Our room lighted by one guttering candle seemed possessed by moving shadows. I felt the stony glare of the three Buddhas behind me until I found myself looking around to make sure that everything was well.

I went to sleep thinking of the service I had just seen. In the yawning darkness of the high pillared temple hall only the outline of the three huge gilded Buddhas could be seen. A tiny wick burning in a bowl of oil on the altar gave the only light. Those still shining figures, the loud hollow echoes of the huge drum, the heavy scent of incense, the music of the chanted "sutras" and the small figure of the altar boy kowtowing incessantly before the images had held me spellbound. I felt as if I had looked into the soul of a stranger.

At six o'clock the next morning we started off across the plains to the village where we were to get the old caravan trail leading over Yang Shan, a mountain 3,000 feet high, which we had to climb before reaching Miao Feng Shan. It was a gray dawn and pieces of white paper flapping from the innumerable grave mounds gave a ghostly effect. Yesterday was a day sacred to the dead when every country person is supposed to visit the grave of his ancestors to burn incense and paper money celebrating what is known as the Tomb Festival. The pieces of white paper were left to show that the grave has been visited. Along the way we passed many men and women working in the fields preparing for the spring planting of peanuts and sweet potatoes; these farmers have a hard life but they never failed to greet us cheerfully. We also passed a little school house where we heard the children reciting their lessons in unison. Here we stopped and entered the building cautiously. When Ruth explained to the teacher that I was an American interested to know what the children were learning, she gave me a little paper textbook which she insisted that I keep. Then she asked the children if they would like to recite something for the American lady. They smiled, sat up straight, folded their hands, and fairly shouted a selection from one of the classics. I was sorry that we could not have stayed longer.

An hour's tramping brought us to the old mountain trail which was made of huge flat cobblestones taken from the beds of the mountain streams. They were white from the travel of a thousand years; as we ascended we could see them shining far above us. At times we skirted the edge of sheer cliffs as we climbed and climbed leaving goatherds, swineherds, and cowherds far behind us. Gradually a mist settled over the plain and the surrounding hills; we seemed cut off from all human life. The wind began to blow but there were no trees to shield us; there was no sign of life anywhere except for a few mountain birds which plunged into the crags. We had climbed only three hours before we reached the top, but the ascent had been so steep and rugged that we ached from weariness. We flung ourselves upon the ground and let the wind blow over our weary bodies.

With the thought of a descent ahead it did not take us long to rest. Shortly we were looking down into the valley and across to the mountain we had yet to climb. As we descended the south side of Yang Shan it was like another land. Instead of the bleak rugged terrain of the north side, here was intense cultivation: myriads of rose bushes grown for the petals and leaves to be used in tea and wine, fruit trees, and terraced gardens. Bright colored birds flitted from tree to tree singing their ecstasies. Below was the picturesque village of Chien K'ou gay with peddlers and food vendors. Then across the valley, we came to a tiny village at the foot of the sacred mountain. In the narrow paths there were pigs and goats and untidy bare-bottomed children running about. Boys were leading straggly donkeys. Old men and women slept or smoked their long pipes in the doorways. Beggars were lying in wait for pilgrims.

Here we found coolies with sedan chairs ready and eager to take us up the long steep trail to the monastery which we saw towering far above us. Half way up, the coolies stopped to rest and to wipe the perspiration from their bodies. As I watched them I wondered how it was possible a thousand years ago to build a monastery on the top of this remote mountain, and why such a site should have been chosen in the first place. When we reached the summit, it was easy to understand. None of the temple buildings had any artistic merit and the priests and acolytes were unimpressive. But the beauty and majesty of the place were beyond words to describe for the monastery is perched like an eagle's nest on the top of the steepest of the Western Hills. We could see for a hundred miles—not only distant Peking but even the Nankou Pass and the Great Wall as it crawled along the hills. No wonder it was here for the last thousand years that Buddhists from all over the north of China made their pilgrimage in the time of roses.

For hours it seemed, I was content just to sit and look out upon those endless mountains, up into the expanse of sky; to ponder the wonder, the majesty, and the mystery of this great universe. Here the boundaries of time and space seemed almost to disappear. Was it in a place like this that the psalmist wrote: "Before the mountains were brought forth, or ever thou hadst formed the earth and the world, even from everlasting to everlasting thou art God." On that mountain top I came to understand why in Chinese art there is so much contemplation, why man appears insignificant in relation to these high mountains and powerful streams. Man is only a part of life together with the birds and beasts—while the great laws of heaven and earth are constant and eternal.

One cannot live one's life on mountain tops; but like Herbert Spencer, one can take from them the awareness that "amid the mysteries, which become more mysterious the more they are thought about, there is one absolute certainty, that man is ever in the presence of an infinite and eternal energy from which all things proceed." We left the monastery in the early afternoon. As we made our long way back to Ta Chieh Ssu down mountains and across valleys we were tired as we had never been tired before; but we were both deeply moved.

We had our supper that night in a little pavilion nearby the spring. It was easy in the stillness of the early evening just to listen to the sounds of nature: the rippling water, the chorus of the peepers and the birds' songs. Toward dusk there was a subtle change in the singing. The day's end always adds a melancholy tone—the sound of nesting. Through the trees we could see the glory of the sunset spread across the sky, then slowly fade into the creeping darkness.

Once again the gates were opened for us and we walked out into the brilliant night. We spent our last evening sitting quietly under the star-filled sky; not even the temple bells broke the silence. We looked out across the moon and Venus out beyond the galaxy. Is there life out there we wondered? After a while Ruth asked quietly: Do you ever wonder about the purpose of this great universe and about the meaning of life?

As she spoke thoughts drifted into my mind which had been stirred by my own questioning, by my Quaker Bible teacher, by the philosophers whom I had studied. And we talked of these things: the nature of man, of human society, the world, the universe. I remembered what a great teacher had once said to me when I asked if his idea of God had changed as the vastness of the universe unfolded. "It is not in these dimensions that the confirmation of my faith rests," he said. "It is to be found in the meaning I experience at the point where the universe touches my life and I become in my awareness a part of reality—if not a part of its purpose."

Ruth was reminded of what Buddha had said two thousand years before.

> Be ye lamps unto yourselves.
> Be your own reliance
> Hold to the truth within yourselves
> As to the only lamps.

When at last we started back to the monastery, we stopped to look down into the valley which was beginning to glow with the light of the moon. And as we looked out once again across the stars, Ruth said: "Just think, the questions we have thought about tonight have teased men's minds since the beginning of time. Back in the days of Confusius, Chuang Tzu asked:

'Do the heavens revolve? Does the earth stand still? Do the sun and moon contend for their position?—Is there some mechanical device that keeps them going? Or do they merely continue to revolve inevitably of their own inertia?'"

And I remembered the great passage from Job which I had learned in college:

> Then Jehovah answered Job out of the whirlwind, and said,
> Who is this that darkeneth counsel
> By words without knowledge?
> Gird up now thy loins like a man;
> For I will demand of thee, and declare thou unto me.
> Where wast thou when I laid the foundations of the earth?
> Declare, if thou hast understanding
> Who determined the measures thereof, if thou knowest?
> Or who stretched the line upon it?
> Whereupon were the foundations thereof fastened?
> Or who laid the cornerstone thereof
> When the morning stars sang together,
> And all the sons of God shouted for joy?

A half a century has passed since that night at Ta Chieh Ssu—a half century during which there has been a gigantic leap forward in the knowledge of life. Man has smashed the atom, made a bomb which can destroy the world, made a computer, walked on the moon, and sent a satellite into the depth of space; oceanauts have now lived for weeks at the bottom of the living sea. But still there are no answers to those eternal questions. We inhabit a mystery and the best of scientific wisdom recognizes that this is so. We still do not know what produces life on earth. "Man can make a weedkiller, but he cannot yet make a weed." Will the horizon forever recede? Will there never be an end of the trail?

Jacquetta Priestly, a distinguished archeologist said recently: "Those scientists who live as whole, imaginative men do not believe that anyone has proved that their minds, their individual psyches are nothing but chance responses to chemical and molecular games played on the skin of the earth.—Let us have the courage to accept the inner experience that tells us that we are something more—and that we may be part of a process that is something much greater still."

Loren Eisley has put it more simply: "We are compounded of dust and the light of a star."

Peking Temples

IN CHINA TODAY there is little religion as we think of it; but when I was in Peking there were many religions. They existed peaceably side by side, for the Chinese were a tolerant people not given to strong religious convictions or antipathies. They were willing to let each man seek truth in his own way believing, as an old proverb says, "Each cult has a truth and each truth a cult." Indeed over the centuries, all kinds of religious thought had been introduced into China. Official sanction had been given to various forms of Buddhism, to Mohammedans, to Jesuits and other Catholic orders, to Protestant Missions, to Orthodox Missions from Russia, as well as to their own philosophical and ethical systems like Taoism and Confucianism. For thousands of years the Chinese were able to maintain a level of tolerance that the West might well envy for as Arthur Waley has said, "in China there was no Index, no Inquisition, and no Holy Wars." To the Chinese this would have been unthinkable. To them the wisest attitude was to accept the important truths of each religion on the basis of one's own experience.

The ease with which a Chinese could accept Taoism, Confucianism, and Buddhism was well known. Also well known was the Chinese practice of "hedging about eternity" by inviting priests of all religions to participate at funerals. Dr. Ferguson told of Fu Hsi (497–569), inventor of the revolving bookcase, who was always represented as wearing a Taoist cap, Confucian shoes, and a Buddhist scarf. In the T'ang dynasty during the reign of Ming–huang (712–756) which he considered one of the most brilliant eras in China's history, Ch'ang-an, then the capital, became not only the center of religious proselytism but also a great cosmopolitan city where Syrians, Arabs, Persians, Tibetans, Koreans, and other people of widely divergent races and faiths lived side by side. This presented a remarkable contrast to the violent religious and racial strife then prevailing in Europe—and still prevails even today, alas.

It is no wonder that I found temples everywhere in Peking. There were more than a thousand of them, although in the 1920's many were deserted, with weeds growing on the roofs and birds nesting in trees in the empty courtyards; very few Chinese ever entered them. Besides temples there were also Christian churches and mosques. It was believed that the last Manchu emperors ruled about as many Moslem subjects as the Sultan of Turkey and the Shah of Persia combined. The most famous mosque was built by Ch'ien Lung in 1746 for his Mohammadan concubine; this was no longer standing when I was in Peking. But at the other mosques on Fridays, the Mohammedan Sabbath, services were held regularly at two o'clock in the afternoon. It is interesting that like most imports these mosques had succumbed to Chinese influence for they all had Chinese roofs instead of the domes and square towers of minarets.

One of the famous sights in Peking was Yung Ho Kung, commonly known as "The Lama Temple" although it was not really a temple but a monastery. Originally it had been the palace of Emperor Yung Cheng transformed for religious uses after his accession in 1722, for in China the birthplace of a sovereign could never afterwards be used as a dwelling. Beyond the impressive entrance with its yellow-topped *p'ai lous* were the spacious grounds with fine buildings and handsome courtyards. Here in the shade of the spreading trees where magpies and blackbirds flittered about, the monks walked to and fro telling their beads.

I never attended a Lama service in Peking, but friends who had saw a resemblance to the Roman Catholic Mass. According to Chou-tzu, the Lamas have the crosier, the mitre, the cope, the service with responses, the censor, the rosary, and the Processional. Lamaism never had the nobility of the original Buddhist conception for it was full of demonology and superstition. Their annual festival was a grotesque Devil Dance. Although the Lama priests were a picturesque group with their orange and red vestments and yellow helmet-shaped hats, those that I saw in Peking were for the most part lazy, dirty, and often vulgar—far different from the monks at Ta Chieh Ssu who represented a different form of Buddhism. Yet those who knew this monastery well, mostly scholars who had access to the monastery library, spoke of many Lamas who had not only genuine religious feeling but vast learning as well.

Once this monastery had both religious and political significance.

It was the former residence of the Living Buddha and the home of 1,500 priests. It had enjoyed official patronage, for the Emperors bestowed upon it substantial grants hoping in return to strengthen their hold on their distant provinces of Mongolia and Tibet where the order had enormous influence. When I was in Peking these days of prosperity were over. The monastery was unkempt and beginning to show signs of ruin. Even so, the monastery continued to be a spiritual as well as a social center of the Mongolian life in Peking.

The temple which was of most interest to me was the Confucian Temple built by Kublai Khan in 1307; it had the distinction of sheltering the great Stone Drums which were national treasures. In size and beauty this temple was second only to the one in Chu-Fu, the birthplace of Confucius in Shantung province. Unlike so many of the monuments in Peking which were in partial ruins, this temple was kept in excellent condition. The roofs glistened with perfect tiles and the red and gold painting under the eaves was clear and bright. It was shaded by ancient cypress trees and surrounded by an aura of calm. Here on Confucius' birthday a colorful and impressive service took place. It was my good fortune to attend this ceremony in the spring of 1924 and to my family I wrote:

Yesterday I went to a ceremony at the Confucian Temple here in Peking, one of the two big sacrificial ceremonies held there during the year. Most of the ceremony, which lasted for more than two hours, was held in a huge courtyard where the century-old cypress trees were casting shadows on the marble walks. Those officiating wore their beautiful ceremonial gowns and the Chinese musical instruments were brought out of the temple for this special occasion. There were all kinds of drums and flutes; small bells and an enormous bronze bell, cymbals of brass, wood, and glass. Many of the instruments are centuries old. The musical stones hanging from carved frames, the lutes with thirteen reeds were all invented before Confucius was born. They had been collected originally to call the Heavenly Spirits, to instruct the Emperors in their duty, and to inspire men and women with love of virtue.

Besides the twenty officiates there were some thirty musicians in blue robes who came and sat by the instruments. Following these were boy dancers who did a sword dance which I thought might have been handed down from the old battle kings. There is nothing warlike about it now for it is done slowly to the accompaniment of beautiful Chinese music. The dances and the procession of the officiates constitute most of the service which the foreigners are allowed to see. The sacrifice takes place inside the temple. Before the tablet to Confucius were placed an ox, a sheep, and a pig to be offered as sacrifices. I have been told that when the ceremony is over the servants who have in any way helped with the service are given a share of the meat. On either side of the altar were trays with fruit and nuts—also offered as sacrifices. We could not see this, of course, but Chinese friends who were there told us about it. Nobody but the highest Confucian scholars are allowed into the temple during the service.

While the sacrifice was going on, the musicians played on lyres a hymn of praise to Confucius and the boy choir sang hymns called the "Odes to Peace." I was told that this music was played exactly as it was played twenty centuries ago. In Confucian temples, unlike the Buddhist temples, there is not an idol to be seen—only red tablets with gold inlaid characters in honor of Confucius and some of his most famous disciples.

The Stone Drums were in a long entrance gateway, five on a side; they are about three feet high, made from mountain boulders, and supposed to date from the Chou dynasty (1122–755 B.C.). The records on these monoliths have long fascinated archeologists for they are said to be the oldest relics of Chinese writing on stone in existence. The writing is a series of ten odes, a complete poem cut on each drum. The stanzas celebrate the hunting and fishing expeditions of a feudal prince who lived about 1,000 B.C., a time when David reigned in Israel and Homer sang in Greece. Many Chinese poets have praised these 3,000 year-old stones, blackened over the years by repeated rubbing. Han Yu, a distinguished T'ang official, scholar, and poet tells something of the vicissitudes of these drums. In a long poem that became a classic, he says they are lying in the country, abandoned and neglected, overgrown with moss and dirt. Cows rub their horns on them, herd boys strike flints on their surfaces. To him this is dreadful. He urges someone to help him arrange for these precious relics to be taken to a place of safety, like the Imperial Temple at the capital (then at Ch'ang-an). Before Han Yu died the drums were actually taken out of the fields and put in a Confucian temple, eventually to come, almost intact, to the beautiful temple in Peking.

Beyond these drums one enters a lovely courtyard with six yellow-tiled pavilions. Three flights of stairs with a magnificent spirit ramp in the center lead from the courtyard to the main building called "The Hall of the Great Perfection," one of the most beautiful buildings in Peking. It was here in this "Hall of Perfection" that the sacrificial ceremony took place.

When I told my students that I had attended this ceremony there was a quick reaction. Most of the students were opposed to Confucianism as a state religion and believed that Confucius himself, a very simple man, would have deplored not only the animal sacrifices but the elaborate ceremony which I had seen. Yet they all knew the *Analects of Confucius,* a collection of his sayings, because this had been used as a textbook when they were in primary school. The old method of teaching, which was still in effect in parts of China when I was there, was to make the student memorize and recite the whole book, word for word. The students all agreed that as children the meaning of these sayings was only half understood, but gradually as they got older the philosophy was digested, absorbed, and for most of them became a part of their being.

They were eager to share some of the sayings with me.

The noble type of man is modest in what he says and surpasses in what he does.

Better to do a kindness at home than walk a thousand miles to burn incense.

Learning undigested by thought is labor lost; thought unassisted by learning is perilous.

Liberty is the luxury of self-discipline.

Who is the great man? The great man is he who cannot be tempted by wealth and honor, who cannot be budged by poverty or lowliness, and who cannot be bent by authority and power. That is the great man.

He who governs by his moral excellence may be compared to the Pole Star which abides in its place while all the stars bow toward it.

Confucius was asked: "Is there a single saying that one can follow as the motto of life?" The master said, "Perhaps the principal of fair dealing and consideration: Never do to others what you would not like them to do to you."

These quotations and the lively discussion which they provoked gave me my first insight into what Confucius had meant to the Chinese people over the centuries. Before I went to China, I knew practically nothing of Confucius. Things are very different today. Our youth are exposed to all the cultures of the world. As Toynbee said a quarter of a century ago "Our own descendants are not going to be just Western like ourselves. They are going to be heirs of Confucius and Lao-Tse as well as Socrates and Plato; heirs of Gautama Buddha as well as Isaiah and Jesus Christ; heirs of Mohammed as well as Elijah and Peter and Paul—heirs (if still wallowing in the Serbonian Bog of politics) of Lenin and Gandhi and Sun Yat-sen as well as Cromwell and George Washington and Mazzini."

I Buy a Pony

In the spring dawn I awake unconsciously
Hearing the birds' song everywhere
The sound of the wind and the rain came last night
How many blossoms fell?

CHOU T'ING PI

ONE OF THE REASONS for my appointment at Yenching was to make possible a long delayed furlough for Grace Boynton, the head of the English Department at the Women's College. As she was leaving for America immediately after the Commencement Exercises, she began in the spring vacation to sell her possessions—including her beautiful bay pony. Because I had learned to ride at the Bennett School, Miss Boynton had trusted me to ride the pony when he needed exercise. I desperately wanted to buy him and so did Alice Boring; we decided to buy him together.

April 18, 1924

Dear Father;

This is the first morning since I have been in China that I have been up at daybreak. But it is really spring now, and this morning, I am riding out to the Western Hills on a pony which Alice Boring and I have just bought together. I wish you could know the joy I have had since I bought him! You may think me extravagant for doing this, but I am sure that what I have done is right. You see, in Peking it is utterly impossible to get any exercise without a pony. One can't walk on the streets because of the filth and dirt; even to go to the next hutung I usually get into my ricksha. Of course tennis is possible but no one plays here in the T'ung Fu, so I have to wait until some one offers to take me to the club.

When I was catching one cold after another, I realized how much I needed exercise. Just outside of Peking there is beautiful country. I knew that if I could only get out into it, I should feel like a different person. The pony we have bought is one of the best in Peking. When I found that we could buy him for sixty dollars it seemed too good to be true. It all happened just after your check arrived so I consider him your present. As for the expense of keeping the pony: for stable rent, food, and the use of a riding coolie we each pay six dollars and a half a month! This is all reckoned in mex, of course, which means in American currency about three dollars. Even with my meager salary of $65 a month this is something I can afford.

These glorious spring days must make you think about getting down to the island. My plans for the summer are beginning to take shape: I shall give a course at the Peking Summer School until the middle of July; then in August I am hoping to take a trip to Mongolia. Plans are indefinite, but this is what I want to do more than anything in the world.

On my pony at the Gobi Desert.

The Month of May

A gentle breeze is blowing, butterflies
are frolicking. Flowers are blazing,
honey bees are buzzing.   TU FU

THE MONTH OF MAY was as lovely as everyone told me it would be. I remember it well not only because of its exquisite beauty and the festive occasions described in the following letter to my mother, but because it was in this month that I first learned of an event which profoundly changed the course of history in China. It was also a month when I became closer to Jui T'ang and her father and sensed a little more what life was like as seen through their eyes.

T'ung Fu
May 1, 1924

Dear Mother,

I have just been out picking some red roses which are growing in profusion in our courtyards. I have never seen nor dreamed of such an abundance of flowers. To have lived through a spring in this old T'ung Fu is an experience of a life time. As I look out into the courtyard, I can see a willow with its dainty branches drooping over our moon-gate wall and a flowering almond, a mass of pink against the background of an old gray stone building. On either side of a tiny pathway, lavender and white lilacs have burst into flower and three tiny yellow butterflies are playing about them. The wisteria over the arbor has not yet blossomed, but the pods are getting very full and there is a touch of color at the tips.

Never shall I forget the night of the full moon when we had a reception in our front courtyard. The air was filled with the fragrance of lilacs. And the bright silver light shining on the curving roofs was sheer poetry. The nights here are sparkling; the stars look as if they would burst and the moon is pure silver. No wonder that all the Chinese poets sang of moonlight. Often when I am returning late from a party and everything is quiet and peaceful I love to linger in the moon-gate and gaze on all the beauty of these courts and old buildings. No matter what else I get out of my three years in China, I have already shared in the mellow beauty of an age that has passed.

Have I told you that Leon Ellis has been transferred to Guatamala? As you can imagine there were many farewell parties for him. For two weeks I hardly had a tiffin or a dinner at the college.

There was one party at the legation given by Jefferson Patterson which outdid every other party of the year. I arrived about eight-thirty, when most dinners begin out here, and was escorted to the house by a gateman who took me on a path lighted on both sides by handsome horn lanterns, each one hanging from a tripod. The drawing room was already filled with guests—the men in their tails and white ties, the women in their most elegant gowns. Various cocktails and hors d'oeuvres were being served by Chinese men-servants dressed in their long white gowns and short black silk sleeveless jackets. There was a festive hour before dinner was announced; then each woman was escorted to the dining room by her dinner partner.

The table was laid for twenty-four guests—a dream of silver, candles, and peonies. As is usual with these parties, at each place was a set of wine glasses: white wine was served with the fish course, red wine with the meat, and because this was a festive occasion there was champagne with the dessert. The men remained in the dining room when dinner was over to smoke their cigars and drink their port. We women went again into the drawing room where we sipped liqueurs.

By the time the men returned to the drawing room, a Chinese magician and an artist had arrived to entertain us—both fascinating. After they left, an orchestra began to play in the dining room which had been transformed into a dance floor. At midnight supper was served as elaborate as the dinner had been. Then came more dancing until the wee small hours.

I am going to miss Leon, for it was through him that I was invited to many diplomatic affairs. Just before he left, he took me to a reception given by the President. It took place in one of the palaces in the fabulous Forbidden City taken over after the republic for government residences and offices. When we arrived, we entered the palace court between lines of soldiers standing at attention; then we crossed a lake in a curious kind of covered boat. At the other side, a band played until all the guests had arrived. After we wandered for a bit through the lovely gardens we went into the reception hall where I saw the most interesting and glamourous group of people I shall probably ever see: the diplomats of every nation and the wealth and influence of all Peking. I was fascinated by the Japanese ladies who came in their gorgeous kimonas. They are certainly among the most beautiful women in all the world—such grace and delicacy! The Chinese, their black hair combed smoothly back with a white jade flower at the neck, were beautiful too; they came in their embroidered silks and satins, and their dazzling jewels. It all seemed like a dream to me for I can never get used to pomp and ceremony.

*   *   *

On the fourth day of the month, a brilliant young professor from Tsing-Hua University, who had recently been elected president of an association of English teachers of which I was secretary, came to have tea with me at the T'ung Fu to discuss what he had in mind for the next year's program. Long after we had finished the business at hand, he stayed on to discuss the differences between China and the West and how these differences were likely to affect China in the modern, industrial world. He saw the essential difference a cultural one—the Chinese tradition based on human consideration, the search for tranquility and order, for moderation and compromise, while the West was committed to the principle of law, competition, and individual self-interest.

For him this gap was a gigantic one which he believed would not easily—if ever—be wholly bridged. It was this basic difference which he felt had been the cause of friction ever since Westerners had come to China. He saw the West dynamic, restless, expansionist, individualistic—qualities which were the exact opposite of those engendered in the Chinese people for centuries.

He was one of the many Chinese who valued the good things which the West had brought to China—especially such institutions as Yenching and the Peking Union Medical College. And he appreciated the Christian missionaries, most of whom, he believed, had taken the pains to understand the Chinese people and had done much splendid work among them. What troubled him at the moment was to see growing among his students, a bitter antiforeign feeling as they came to understand the extent to which their country was being controlled by Western nations. He wanted to know if I saw any of this among my Yenching students. At that time I did not, but it was only a matter of months before I did.

Because we were meeting on the anniversary of the May Fourth Incident of 1919, a very important anniversary to the Chinese as I was to learn, he was eager to tell me about his part in it. The incident was sparked, he said, at the end of the war when the peacemakers at Ver-

sailles decided to leave in Japanese hands all the former German concessions in Shantung Province. The Chinese people had expected, as
one of the Allies, that the control of this province would naturally be
restored to China. They had entered the war believing in democracy
and the institutions of the West. They were elated over the proclamation of Woodrow Wilson's "Fourteen Points" and the declaration of
the "war aims" of the Allied Powers. But when this decision of the
Peace Conference became known there was a public uproar.

He was a student at the National Peking University at the time and
one of a group organizing a demonstration for "National Humiliation
Day" on May 7 to commemorate the signing of Japan's Twenty-One
Demands. However, when news broke of the Shantung decision the
students were so shocked and angered that 3,000 of them held a mass
demonstration and paraded through the streets of Peking shouting
"Down with the traitors"—"Boycott Japanese Goods." Students from
other universities joined them. He was one of several who presented
protests to the foreign legations; other students burned the residence
of the pro-Japanese foreign minister; some even attacked the Chinese
minister to Japan who happened to be in Peking at the time.

Police and troops moved in. They attacked the students; some were
killed, others wounded. The prisons were full of demonstrators, Yenching students among them. But order was not restored. Telegrams
were sent to students in all the major cities of the country and a
nationwide strike was called. From May 5 to June 4 patriotic teams
were organized to distribute leaflets and to make speeches of protest
among the people. He said that what had begun as a spontaneous
eruption developed into a political force that swept all over China.
Protest spread among the merchants who closed their shops; there
was a boycott of Japanese goods which lasted for more than a year.
Labor unions staged strikes and joined in the broadest demonstration
of national feeling that China had ever seen.

As a result of this nationwide outburst, the Chinese delegation at
Paris refused to sign the Versailles treaty—a treaty which his father
considered one of the most uncivilized papers ever written and one
that would surely lead to future wars.

The May Fourth Movement (as it came to be known) not only
brought the new ideas of democracy and science and this wave of

patriotism together in a strong anti-imperialist program, but it also made the students suddenly aware of their power. Many began to rebel against the past, against the ancient traditions and customs, blaming them for much of China's troubles. In fact he believed that this Movement might well prove to be a turning point in China's history—as indeed it proved to be.

In a letter to my family I wrote:

To talk to these young educated Chinese makes one certain that the Chinese are not a decadent race as so many Americans think, but rather that their tremendous powers have been lying dormant and will some day be awakened to surprise the world. The eagerness of my pupils to gain knowledge of all kinds, their infinite patience, and their willingness to work to the limit of their strength also make me believe that before this century has passed China will take an important place among the nations of the world.

*   *   *

On a warm sunny day toward the end of the month, Jui T'ang and her father invited me to join them on their annual visit to Chung Siao Hsi, a Buddhist temple famous for its peony terraces. At this time of year, peonies have burst into blossom in all their glory and at Chung Siao Hsi I saw every kind of peony that grows, every size and every color. Some of them were tremendous, four and five hundred years old. There were exquisite ones of gleaming white, others equally beautiful of delicate pink and deep rose. There were very rare ones of deep purple and pale fresh green.

For me the most magnificent was one of pale yellow so large it filled the entire center of a court. As we stopped to admire it and enjoy its fragrance, Mr. Ling bent over to cup a handsome blossom. Lifting it toward me he said, "Now perhaps you can understand why the peony is the favorite flower of my people, why we call it our national flower. As you can see this plant has had loving care for hundreds of years." There were four flowers, he said, that were traditionally held preeminent in China—the peony, the plum blossom, the lotus, and the chrysanthemum.

He told how the Chinese love of flowers had been rewarded by genius in their cultivation. Vast wisdom had been handed down orally from generation to generation. In fact one of the great gifts of

China to the West, along with tea and porcelain, had been the many shrubs and flowers brought back by our botanists during the past two hundred years—the azalea and rhododendron, two of my favorites, among them. We talked of the Summer Palace near Peking where there is a two-hundred-year-old wisteria and a three-hundred-year-old lilac. Where a whole hill called the flowery mountain is a mass of peonies of blended colors and where a lake is a carpet of pink lotus. He knew well "uncle Li" the old gardener of the Empress Dowager, Tz'u-hsi (the old Buddha), who had built the palace and who could not bear to see her favorite flowers die. She used to say that trees and flowers become more charming when they are old. If they are treated well, they will never die. One day "uncle Li" discovered that her favorite peony tree was rotting at the roots. An old gardener told him not to worry but to wash the roots in sesame oil. This he did. Eventually the plant was cured and did so well that from that time on he treated all the old flowers and trees with this treasured oil. For as long as the Empress lived and he was her gardener, the flowers and trees all flourished.

It was a rare experience for me to wander leisurely through the temple courts seeing through their eyes the beauty I had not been fully conscious of before—the curve of a petal, the shape of a leaf, the subtilty of a color. As Jui T'ang stopped to sketch a flower she quoted an old Chinese saying, "Whoever enjoys a thing possesses it." Her sketches and paintings are all typically Chinese—"the flowers talk to you, the birds fly, all nature is alive." In one of the courts we passed a superb ginkgo tree said to be 1,000 years old—a tree, Mr. Ling said, which originated in ancient China and is the sole surviving link between trees and ferns. The ginkgo is sometimes called the maidenhair tree because of its ornamental foliage. Peking residents flock to see it in the autumn when the leaves turn golden.

It was a delightful surprise when Mr. Ling took us into one of the temple buildings to be served a delicious Chinese feast. How well the Chinese know the secret of variety and flavor in foods! That day I was introduced to bird's nest soup, asparagus and bamboo sprouts, sharks fins, the tenderest duck, glacé nuts, almond paste, rose wine, and any number of other delicious dishes.

Jui T'ang's father was not only an important official and a great scholar—he was a charming gentleman. He was always very kind to me because of my interest in his daughter and my appreciation of her talents. He was extremely proud of her accomplishment at Yenching and especially delighted with her dramatization of the Festival Plays which I had encouraged. At the banquet which he gave at the time of her graduation from the college, I was flattered to be given the place of honor. I knew that the relationship between pupil and teacher was a unique one in China but I felt far too young to be so honored in the presence of many older and distinguished Chinese.

It was not until thirty years after Jui T'ang graduated from Yenching, when I read *Ancient Melodies,* the enchanting book in which she tells of her childhood, I learned that her distinguished father had had six wives or concubines—a measure of his great wealth.

Jui T'ang was the daughter of his fourth concubine, the next to the youngest of his twelve children and his tenth daughter. All of his wives and children lived together within the high wall of his impressive residence—usually in separate courtyards. The house in the first courtyard contained his drawing room, seldom used except when he entertained important guests. The second court was "Third Mother's" where she lived with her four children and her slave girl Peach Blossom. Jui T'ang's mother and her four daughters lived in the third court with "Fifth Mother" who had no children. Her father's study and sitting room were in the last court; "Sixth Mother" lived in one wing of this court. Behind these, was a beautiful garden cared for by their beloved gardener, Lao Chou.

When Jui T'ang was still a child, she learned that her birth had brought much sorrow. In her book she writes:

I was a good-natured child, perhaps because I was Mother's fourth child and the tenth daughter of the family and naturally neglected. So I got used to this neglect. From the daily chat of my mother's maid with my elder sisters, I knew that I had chosen a most unfavourable time for my arrival in the family. Although my mother was living in a large household of forty or fifty people, there were only two who knew she had given birth to another baby girl. One was Chang Ma, Mother's maid, the other was Wang Sen, the old gateman who was sent to fetch the midwife. Mother would have given anything to keep the news a secret as long as possible. With tears in her eyes she implored her maid several times. Chang Ma also repeated with tears: "Don't tell people about the baby coming; that will only make them say she's got one more...." One more what? She was choked by tears, she could not speak. As Chang Ma described this, she often concluded by saying: "It seems nowadays the heavenly gods have closed their eyes. How unfair they are; they would not give a good-hearted woman like your mother a son. They grant good luck to those wicked ones and allow them to enjoy the unhappiness of others." Mother was only twenty-three or twenty-four at that time. She always swore that she would not have any more children.

Whenever I thought of Jui T'angs's mother after reading this book, I thought of the poem Yuan Tu had written one thousand years ago.

> Entering the Hall, she meets the new wife;
> Leaving the Gate, she runs into her former husband.
> Words stick; she does not manage to say anything:
> She presses her hands together and hesitates.
> Agitates moon-like fan-shed pearl-like tears—
> Realizes she loves him just as much as ever;
> That her present pain will never come to an end.

In spite of the fact that Jui T'ang was a girl, she was undoubtedly her father's favorite and most gifted child. At the age of six she was observed by an artist friend of the family, Wang Chin-lin, drawing pictures on the white garden wall with a piece of charcoal—pictures of flowers, people, landscapes. Wang Chin-lin who was one of the court painters was amazed at what he saw. "Have you a teacher?" he asked. She told him she had no teacher. "Your drawings have good style" he said; "you have talent and some day you may become a great painter. We must see that you have a good teacher."

Thus it was that Jui T'ang became the pupil of Miao Sun-Yun, the famous artist who had been the favorite painter of the Empress Dowager. On the day that she was to be presented to the artist, she went to her father's sitting room with Wang Chin-lin. Mr. Ling said to his friend: "I hope you are right that Jui T'ang will some day be a great artist. I could not bear to see her become the kind of artist who knows

Rabinbranath Tagore with some of my students.

Jui T'ang at the T'ung Fu.

Some of Jui T'ang's sketches.

My Foster-Mother took me out to fly kites on a fine day

A page from Jui T'ang's book, reproduced with her permission.

In Chinese painting "flowers talk to you, the birds fly, all nature is alive."
Birds and Blossoms. Woodcut from the Ten Bamboo Studio (1644). Hu Cheng-yen,
the Master of the Ten Bamboo Studio, was considered the greatest of the Chinese
woodcut artists. Courtesy of the British Museum, London.

These peonies could have grown at Chung Siao Hsi.
Flowers, by Yun Shou-p'ing (1633-1690).
Hanging scroll.
Courtesy of the British Museum, London.

Lady and Attendants in a Garden.
Scroll on silk by Leng Mei, Ch'ing Dynasty, Reign of K'ang Hsi.
Courtesy of the Museum of Fine Arts, Boston.

The Goddess of the Moon—
Jui T'ang's dramatization
of the old festival play
produced at the T'ung Fu.

only how to waggle her brush to make pictures." To Jui T'ang he said: "If you want to be a great artist you must remember my words: never do any picture which you do not want to do. Paint everything for your own sake." Then he added laughing: "You should not try to please anyone, even though he be your father."

After Yenching Jui T'ang followed in the tradition of her family giving her time to calligraphy, painting, and writing. She made a place for herself in contemporary Chinese art and letters and became one of the Keepers of the division of painting and calligraphy at the National Gallery in Peking. In 1927 she married Chen Yuan, a professor at the National Peking University and editor of *Modern Times* a magazine published by the University. They had one daughter.

When the Japanese war began in 1937 she moved to Western China and did her share of war work in addition to her writing and painting. She lived through the terrible civil war and remembers with horror the galloping inflation and the terrible suffering that it caused. She was forced to sell practically everything she owned just to keep alive. A gold bracelet bought only enough food to last for a few days.

Since 1949, when the Chinese Civil war ended, Jui T'ang has been living and painting in England and Europe. Her paintings have been exhibited in London and Paris, as well as New York and Boston. Her work was first seen in America in 1943 when Dr. Hu Shih, our Chinese Ambassador, lent one of her landscapes to the Metropolitan Museum of Art in New York for their exhibition of contemporary Chinese painting. During her stay in Boston she was a guest in my home in Wellesley. At the time I was principal of the Dana Hall School, so I persuaded her to give a demonstration of Chinese painting in our art studio; the students and faculty members were enthralled. When the news came that the Boston Museum of Fine Arts had bought several of her paintings there was great rejoicing. Jui T'ang's style of painting is called *shih-hua,* poetic painting. The term goes back to the eighth century when it was said of the poet-painter Wang Wei (699–759), "there is a picture in his poetry, and poetry in his painting."

She was encouraged to write the story of her life in Peking which she called *Ancient Melodies.* Although she wrote in English her book has all the flavor, feeling, and poetry of the Chinese. When it was published in London in 1954, V. Sackvell-West wrote the introduction, J. B. Priestly nominated it as Best Book of the Year, and Andre Maurois in his introduction to her Paris exhibition called it *ravissant*.

I have visited Jui T'ang frequently in her apartment in London. We go to the theater together and to Chinese restaurants; but London is not Peking. The bond that keeps our friendship strong is our memories of the happy days together in that eternal city of Asia. The look in her eyes sometimes tells me how sad it is for her to be so far away. To me she will always be Jui T'ang, although after Yenching she took Su-Hua as her pen name—a name used today by her family and all of her Chinese friends.

During my last visit with her in London she gave me one of her paintings. It shows two swallows in the drooping branches of a willow tree. There is a poem on the painting which reads:

> Just two little swallows
> 　　in the shade of the willows
> Returning to the home they remember.
>
> Painted by Ling Su-Hua one spring day
> as she was thinking of the past.

The Goddess of the Moon

> Instead of going to heaven at last
> I am going all along.
> EMILY DICKINSON

June 9, 1924

Dear Family,

Last night my heart's dream came true. Jui T'ang's dramatization of the ancient legend of "The Goddess of the Moon" was produced in the temple courtyard of this lovely old T'ung Fu. It was a glorious night. Because of "Commencement" a large audience had gathered and everyone was in a happy and expectant mood.

There are only two scenes in the play—the first in a lonely mountain cave, the second in the Moon Palace. Jui T'ang not only wrote the play but painted all the scenery. The effects she created were remarkable. For the moon palace we had a huge round frame made to fit into the stage which she painted purple and yellow. As she was working on it I nearly had heart failure for it looked simply impossible. But when the lights were played on it from the back of the audience, it looked exactly like a full moon rising over the horizon. There was a storm of applause when that scene opened and it *was* beautiful. The costumes were exquisite. I did the whole thing at my expense and since it was my first attempt with a Chinese play I didn't spare a penny. A famous Chinese actor trained six of our most beautiful girls for the dancing, and the students of the men's college furnished the Chinese music.

I wish you could have heard the applause at the end. As far as anyone knows this is the first time a festival play has been given in English. In the audience were several professors from the Chinese universities who came up afterwards to congratulate Jui T'ang. Among them was P. C. Chang from Tsing-Hua, the college made possible by the indemnity money America returned to China after the Boxer Rebellion. His brother is Chang Poling, the distinguished head and founder of the famous Nankai University which so impressed Charles Eliot when he came to China after his retirement from Harvard. Both brothers are extremely interested in drama. P. C., as everyone calls him, studied drama at Columbia University and Chang Poling introduced a drama club in his Middle School as far back as 1909. P. C. wants to collaborate with us in producing other festival plays in English. We have agreed to discuss this in the fall—it sounds exciting.

Tomorrow I am off to "the hills" for a week. I am fearfully tired after this strenuous year and I shall welcome this week of rest and quiet. Dora Demiere, my Swiss friend here at the T'ung Fu, is going with me. We are to have a house (belonging to Yenching) and two servants all to ourselves. That sounds luxurious doesn't it, but our entire expenses for the week won't be over five dollars each. It is a joy to be in this land of servants, chiefly because it leaves one free to do so many of the interesting things which life offers. Goodness knows, I am willing to cook and wash dishes when I have to, but there are many other things I prefer to do. The nice thing here at the T'ung Fu is that all of our servants are just like friends.

How Mother would love to entertain out here. Tell the cook: "Tea for fifty," or "dinner for twelve" and that is all one has to do. The cook plans and orders the food and the number-one boy arranges the table. With two servants to serve, things generally go off very smoothly. I have given several parties here at the T'ung Fu. Most of my friends have never been here before and are ecstatic about the place. The fact that some of the guests come from the legation or are well known in Peking gives the servants "face." They always know in advance who is coming for Wha Ting delivers my chits. Both Chu Pu and Wha Ting are determined that I shall repay my social obligations handsomely.

If I ever invite more guests than can be taken care of properly, dishes or silver are borrowed from the household of one of the guests. It is a common experience to go to a dinner party and see one's belongings on the table—this has happened more than once here at the T'ung Fu. Occasionally a servant appears whom I have never seen before. It turns out that he is a friend or relative of Chu Pu who has arrived to *pang mang* (to "help our haste"). Everything is planned so far in advance that I am always confident that things will go well. All of us are cheerful as we await the moment when it will be announced: "the guests' rickshas are at the gate."

After a party I always go to the kitchen to thank Chu Pu, Wha Ting and any others who have helped. Once when my guests exclaimed over some delicious cakes with frosting that resembled little pink roses, I asked the cook how he got such a lovely color. He picked up a glass of pink water and beamed as he took out a piece of red flannel. Holding it up he said gleefully, "piecy amah petticoat."

I have to smile when I think of how ignorant I was last year about living conditions here. I shall probably never live more comfortably nor more luxuriously in all my life. And as for food! For the past month or more, we have been having delicious fresh asparagus, green peas, string beans, and what father would revel in—oodles of the most delectable tiny cucumbers. Strawberries and apricots are in abundance now. Nearly every night for dinner we have strawberry or some other kind of fruit ice cream. We have Chinese food only three times a week; I wish it were more often.

Now I must dash to get this letter in the mail so that it can catch the steamer sailing from Shanghai on Friday. The roof garden is open at the Peking Hotel; we dance there nearly every night. Peking is as festive as ever.

Summer in Mongolia

—light-hearted, I take to the open road
Healthy, free, the world before me.
I inhale great draughts of space;
The east and west are mine and
The north and south are mine.
Whoever you are, come travel with me.
WALT WHITMAN

MONGOLIA HAD INTRIGUED ME ever since Professor Osborn had told me on the *Madison* about the expedition of the American Museum of Natural History. I had met Roy Chapman Andrews, the leader of the expedition, for he had made the trip from the Gobi desert in order to be at the station in Peking to meet the Osborns and to take the professor back with him to the site of the explorations. Mongolia, the expedition, and the scientists connected with it were topics of conversation wherever one went. There were other famous scientists, well known in Peking, working in Mongolia at this time; among them were Sven Hedin, the famous Tibetan explorer, and Father Teilhard de Chardin, the distinguished palaeontologist and author of *The Phenomenon of Man*.

So when the time came to make plans for my first summer vacation, it was natural that I should think about Mongolia. How exciting it would be, I thought, to see this fascinating land, the land of Genghis and Kublai Khan who in the thirteenth century had created one of the greatest empires the world has ever seen, one that comprised all of Asia—and Europe as far as the Dneiper River.

Two colleagues at the T'ung Fu, Alice Boring and Dora Demiere, always ready for an adventure, became intrigued with the idea also. Dr. and Mrs. Ingram, who were planning a trip to Mongolia themselves, asked us to join their group. Plans were beginning to take shape when friends at the legation tried to discourage us.

"The United States government can give you no protection," they warned, "nor guarantee your safety because of the swarms of bandits operating there." They explained that hundreds of soldiers, remnants of a defeated army, were scattered all over the Mongolian plateau north of Kalgan. Since they could exist only by robbery they had become a menace. "If in spite of this danger you persist in going," they added "by all means go unarmed but take along a supply of calling cards which you should make as impressive as possible." Dr. Ingram, who knew the country well, believed the bandits were interested only in the rich caravans going back and forth between Kalgan and Urga, the capital of Mongolia. Because he was convinced they would give us no trouble, we proceeded with our plans.

It was decided that Dora and I would leave early with Shin Ling, our Chinese servant, and meet Alice and the Ingram party at the Swedish mission at Gulchaggan. On July 15, with our supplies and our pony, Shin Ling departed by train to Kalgan where the railroad ended. There he was to bargain for the Peking Cart in which we would travel and acquire the necessary coolies to help us on the way. A day later Dora and I followed. We arrived safely at the mission at Kalgan where we expected to stay only a night or two, or until Shin Ling had completed his arrangements. It was two weeks before we finally left. Torrential rains day after day made it impossible to depart sooner.

Finally, on August 1 a tiny streak of blue appeared in the sky. It was on that day that Dora and I climbed into our Peking cart and began our journey—leaving Kalgan and the twentieth century far behind us.

Our road to the Waushan Pass that leads to the Mongolian plateau was a dry river bed winding through a long valley. At the base of the hills on either side nestled mud-roofed huts and Chinese inns. Along the way we were to stop at these inns which are enclosed in a compound with several small houses and a large courtyard for the carts and the animals of shepherds and travellers. The inn itself is a fairly large one-room building with a Chinese stove opposite the door. On either side of the stove are raised platforms, called *k'angs,* on which people eat and sleep. My notes taken on the trip began later that day.

Just out of Kalgan
August 1, 1924

Try to imagine us sitting on a *k'ang* of a tiny Chinese inn together with an old lady, her son, the innkeeper, and his two children. Outside there is a steady dripping of rain, and the many carts in the yard

are drenched. Our road, the river bed which an hour ago was absolutely dry, is now a torrent rushing by only about two hundred
yards away. It is two o'clock; we are only a few miles out of Kalgan,
yet here we must stay—literally covered with flies—until tomorrow
morning anyway. We are thankful that we reached this place of
safety, for if we had been travelling in the river bed when the storm
broke it is dreadful to think what might have happened.

We had not gone far when almost without warning there loomed
ahead of us the darkest cloud I had ever seen! At first I thought it
must be a mountain; but as it gradually grew darker and darker I
knew that it was a cloud portending a terrific storm. We had just
arrived at this tiny inn yard when the first drops came. The coolies
quickly threw our bags into the inn and covered the rest of our things
with oil cloth. It poured all the time we were eating our lunch, but
we rather enjoyed the coziness of the inn and this first native experience.

Suddenly there was a terrible crash; the small children began to
cry, the men rushed out to the gateway shouting fiercely. We looked
out; rushing past the entrance gate was a terrific force of water. I
ventured out and saw the river thundering by with huge masses of
mud rising higher and higher. By this time there was real danger of
the water rushing into the inn yard. Men were leading their horses
and donkeys up the hillside; children were rushing about madly. All
the time the rain was pouring, the river pounding, and thunder
rumbling.

I went back into the inn for Dora and together we rushed up the
hill with the others. There had been no time to think of saving any
of our things; we stopped only to get our money. Streams were pouring down the mountainside, and by the time we reached a safe height
we were both drenched. On the opposite bank we could see a village
which had been utterly destroyed by a flood the week before. Was
all that misery going to be repeated? Gradually, however, the clouds
began to break and the rain became a drizzle. We rushed back to the
inn to pack up what things we really needed. Food, a change of clothing, and money were packed into one small bag which we could keep
with us in case of trouble.

When the rain finally ended and the pounding of the river became less intense, we decided to follow the others back into the inn. So here we sit under a black sky ready to run if there is another downpour.

At five o'clock that afternoon the weather cleared and left us with blue sky, thick mud, and hopes for the morrow. We took advantage of our delay to get acquainted with the dear old lady who offered to share her house with us. There she sat cross-legged, happy as could be, smoking her long thin pipe, and swishing a fly stick to keep away some of the thousands of flies that swarmed everywhere. She wore the usual coat and pants of coarse blue cloth. Silver ornaments decorated her hair, ears, and arms. Her feet were bound within tiny high heeled shoes—a custom centuries old. Curiously enough those "lily feet" which must have caused untold suffering, had an aesthetic and even an erotic value. Bound feet as well as queues for men were given up after the revolution and are seldom seen now except in the country-side. We tried to converse with the old lady but it was difficult to make her understand. The children were afraid of us and clung to their father who was standing on the floor leaning over the foot of the *k'ang.* He was a handsome man as he stood smoking his pipe. His head was bound with a white coarse cloth and his coat was open at the throat showing his bronze skin. Every once in a while he went outside to join the crowd of shepherds who were to spend the night at the inn.

There was no room for us in the inn so the coolies prepared our bed in the cart. The *jui taos* (bed rolls) were spread out with one large camel's hair puff to cover us and a large net put up to keep out the flies and mosquitoes. We had our supper at six in the innkeeper's house. We made tea and cooked rice which we ate with bread and prunes. At seven we were in bed in our cart surrounded by pigs, cows, donkeys, horses, dogs, and hens. At the inn besides ourselves there were only two Chinese women with twenty-five men—mostly shep-herds in charge of the carts and the animals. Because there was never a moment of fear, we went to sleep almost as soon as our heads touched the pillows.

How it was possible to sleep at such a time I cannot understand but the next thing I heard was the crowing of roosters; in the courtyard the pigs were grunting and squealing, the donkeys braying. I looked out in the gray dawn through rain. I could see the old lady standing in the doorway still smoking her pipe. I looked at my watch; it was five o'clock, the hour we had set to start once again on our way. I listened for the river, but the pounding had ceased. That was the only comforting fact, for the rain was dripping constantly and the yard was full of mud and water. Again I went to sleep; when I awoke at eight o'clock carts were moving and the rain had nearly stopped. Three yellow-robed lama priests, who had spent the night at the inn, rode away just as I looked out. Two of the carts were ready to start, and the cows and pigs already gone—a good sign in spite of the gray sky and the mud.

August 3, 1924

It was noon when we left the inn and were back again on the river bed, thick with mud. In America it would have been unthinkable to travel on such a road with a heavily loaded cart. It was continually getting stuck. But the coolies good-naturedly pulled and pushed, until finally at three-thirty we left the river bed and began on foot the long climb up the rocky pass that would lead us to the great plateau. There were about twenty carts making the ascent. The air was filled with the crashing of carts over the rocks, the cracking of whips, and the yelling of the drivers urging on the frightened mules and ponies. As we climbed higher and higher, a wonderful panorama stretched out around us. It was beautiful looking back onto the distant hills with the afternoon sun shedding a soft purple light upon them. In the far distance loomed the mountains of the Shensi border. Above us crawling along the rim of the plateau was the Great Wall, the original part now mostly in ruins.

When we finally reached the top, the clouds set in again and we had to make our way through a thick drizzle. It was here that we understood the reason for the quick rising of the river. There must have been a deluge, for the dirt road had been washed out and the plain filled with small ponds. If the torrent had started at the top of this steep pass nothing could have stopped its terrific force as it roared down to the river bed below.

Through thick mud, we made our way to the inn where we were to spend the night. As the sun went down, the wind began to blow and it was cold. It was eight o'clock, dark and windy, when we saw the lights of the village. They looked cheery and inviting. But when the cart stopped in front of the inn door and we caught a glimpse of the dark, dirty room inside filled with coarse looking men, we realized that our cart, once again, would have to serve for our only shelter. When the innkeeper saw that we were women, he had one of his men sweep a part of the *k'ang* far in the corner insisting that we sit there to drink a cup of tea. If I had been dying of fatigue and thirst, I doubt that I could have crawled into the filthy corner. Our coolies cleared the cart quickly, spread out our *jui taos,* and put up the net. By the light of one candle and with our invaluable sterno, we managed to toast some bread and make coffee inside the cart.

We attempted to sleep, but all night long men went in and out of the inn to urinate, talking in loud voices, splashing in the mud, and lighting candles. At four o'clock in the morning the first exodus began; from that time on the men were departing with their animals and carts.

The innkeeper's wife and family lived in a house at the farther end of the compound. We had to make a visit there this morning, but the place was so dirty and the children so diseased that we left just as soon as we possibly could. In the house were the old mother, the daughter-in-law, and three children. The youngest child, about two years old, was being nursed by its mother who looked up wearily and asked, "Do you do it this way, too?" The other two children clung to their grandmother's trousers. Their clothes were patched and half on, their heads and faces so dirty I could not stand to look at them. Surprisingly the old woman was clean and offered the usual hospitality. She poured tea for us, dished out food as well, and seemed hurt when we told her that we were not hungry.

Because we were cold, we decided to have our breakfast in the inn. No sooner had we found a place on the *k'ang* when seven soldiers on horseback came galloping into the yard. Dora and I looked at each other and held our breath. Were these the inevitable bandits? For a moment the air was tense because they came in shouting and pushing each other. They quickly spied us and immediately quieted down— after all young foreign women were a rarity in these Chinese inns. They stared at us in amazement. Then they nodded and smiled. When the cook had served them some thick noodle soup from the huge iron kettle on the stove, they crouched over their bowls drawing the food into their mouths with the aid of chopsticks and suction. In no time they had finished; then they all settled on the *k'ang* as close to us as possible.

The soldier nearest me was fascinated by my riding boots. As he felt of them he exclaimed so gleefully that I feared he would take them away from me. But he didn't. In fact they all proved to be friendly, good-natured, and eager to talk with us. Fortunately I thought of our calling cards. They roared with laughter when they saw them and grabbed for them eagerly. When they read my card they shouted "mei-kuo jen," (American) and up went their thumbs —always a sign of hearty approval. Americans, I was happy to discover, were held in high esteem wherever we went.

In exchange for our cards, one of them offered us a cigarette. When we politely refused he asked in surprise "Didn't Jesus smoke?" They all lighted cigarettes and after taking a puff or two they left, jumped on their ponies, and waved good-bye. I had a strong feeling that this *was* a group of bandits. If so, Dr. Ingram was right when he said that they would give us no trouble.

We left the inn in bright sunshine. Before noon we had reached Chang Pei-hsien, the only postal station for miles around and home of the famous bandit who controlled all the region north of Kalgan. We had ridden for miles across barren plains so it was a relief to see the tiny village ahead of us. The road ran through the middle of the town. On either side were mud huts, houses, and shops. Three foreign influences were in evidence: a cigarette shop, a motor supply shop, and a Christian church. The keeper of the church saw us as we drove into town and insisted upon taking us to his home to meet his family. In contrast to the other Chinese houses which we had visited this one was immaculate; and his wife and baby were as neat and clean as could be. He made tea for us, brought eggs to take on our journey, and refused to accept a cent.

Never shall I forget the beauty of that afternoon. Huge white clouds and blue sky stretched out before us and the Mongolian grassland sparkled in the sunshine. The meadows, lush with green silky grass, were filled with all kinds of wildflowers: forget-me-nots, honeysuckle, larkspur, Queen Anne's lace, iris, and dandelions; here and there fields were yellow with mustard. Occasionally there was a pond as blue as the sky. Mud villages were scattered about, most of them flooded by the recent rains. Sheep and horses grazed in the pastures; shepherds with their long poles dashed across the plain on their ponies; occasionally a caravan of ox carts passed us going from Urga to Kalgan. This was wilderness with freedom, expanse, and beauty. There was a strange loveliness about the late afternoon light; long deep purple shadows stretched everywhere. A fresh cool breeze blew against my face. I felt a wonderful new surge of life.

Our Peking cart which had literally been our home for days was to take us only as far as the mission station at Hallong Usu. Since the driver was to take a pouch of mail from the mission to be posted in Kalgan, I began the following letter to my mother:

This is our fourth day out of Kalgan and we are having an afternoon rest at a tiny Chinese inn. You would smile, I think, if you could see us travelling in this Peking Cart, much more primitive than the old caravan carts which were used to cross America a hundred years ago. It is surprisingly comfortable when we get it packed with our bedding.

For the first day and a half, our road was a rocky river bed winding in among the hills; then came the very difficult ascent to the top of the pass where we went through the narrow gateway in the Great Wall onto the plateau. The last two days have been on the Mongolian plains. This is beautiful rolling country with cultivated fields, green pastures filled with wild flowers, and hundreds and hundreds of sheep, cattle, and horses. It is interesting to watch the Mongolian shepherds in their bright red coats dash over the plains on horseback; they are magnificent riders. One, attracted by our cart, wheeled around to greet us this morning and shouted "hello." We were amazed to find that he had been in France during the war. He was very proud of the little English and French he had learned and was eager to tell us that he had been part of the labor force which China had sent to Europe to help the allies behind the lines. We find everyone here very friendly—especially when they learn that I am an American.

For four days we haven't seen a foreigner, haven't slept in a bed, nor taken off our clothes. The Chinese inns are too dirty to sleep in, but we always stop in the inn yard to be near a water supply. Most of our cooking is done on two sterno lamps inside the cart. This noon we helped the innkeeper to catch a hen for our dinner. It was the first meal in four days that we have had much of anything but bread, cheese, coffee, or tea. We had been told that we could buy eggs and vegetables all along the way but on account of the flood everyone has been loath to sell. Yet it is surprising how good bread and cheese can taste when one is really hungry!

Mongolia is much more beautiful than I expected. The air is exhilarating and from now on there should be plenty of good food: milk, eggs, chicken and vegetables. I have brought my pony with me and expect to ride a great deal. What a joy it is to be out in the country once again!

I wish you could see the crowd that gathers around us wherever we stop. At the moment on one side of me is a group of men—on the other, women and children. The women are rather attractive with their elaborate head-dresses; but they walk with great difficulty because their bound feet are no more than three or four inches. To them we are very, very strange. They laugh and giggle at us like children. They ask to feel of my clothes; my stockings, shoes, and especially my middy-blouse. The collar hanging at the back mystifies them. The men watch fascinated as I write. They look with wonder when we brush our teeth. We have come from a world across the sea, a world totally unknown to them. "America" and "Europe" are mere names. A few have heard from soldiers returned from the war that men in that far land had fought among themselves and that their own country had in some vague way been involved. "Are you for us or against us?" they ask. They grin when we tell them we love their country.

The Chinese servant whom we brought with us from the T'ung Fu boils water for us, keeps crowds away when we eat, covers our cart at night, and loves to take our pictures. The carter, too, looks after us. The other day when we could not buy eggs or chicken, he brought us delicious fresh peas which I am sorry to say he had stolen somewhere.

That night we were the solitary occupants of an inn yard. We took as a sign of good fortune the tip of a rainbow in the east. We ate our supper by starlight; the air was so clear it seemed as if I could reach up and touch the sky. By nine o'clock we were in bed.

August 5

We were up and off this morning by 6:30. We watched a blood red sun climb above the horizon and hide behind a dark screen of clouds, but they broke by nine and gave the sun a chance to counteract the bitter west wind blowing. The villages are getting farther and farther apart and soon we shall leave our last Chinese settlement behind us.

Although we have been in Mongolia ever since we reached the plateau, everything so far has been Chinese: the inns where we have stayed, the mud-walled huts, the tiny villages, and the people. For nearly a hundred miles from Kalgan it has been all the same, the blue-clad Chinese everywhere. It is they who have cultivated the fields of wheat, oats, barley, and potatoes. The Mongols, who are most at home on the back of a horse, herd their sheep, goats, and cattle, leaving to the Chinese farmer the cultivation of the vast plains.

As we move on to Hallong Usu we shall pass near our first Mongol village, so Shin Ling has brought us big sticks to fight off any dogs that may attack us. The Mongolian dogs are ferocious creatures because they feed on human flesh. The Mongols do not bury their dead; they put the body on a cart which is driven fast over rough ground. Somewhere the body falls off and is left to be eaten by dogs, eagles, and wolves. It is believed that the sooner the body disappears, the sooner the spirit will pass into heaven. This gruesome practice is very difficult for us to understand; even some Mongols cannot bring themselves to leave their beloved dead to be devoured by animals. They burn their corpses and send the ashes to repose in some holy place. It is because the dogs feed on the dead that they attack the living. It is never safe to approach a Mongol settlement except on horse back armed with a club, for every family and every caravan has one or more of these dogs.

Hallong Usu
August 6

Yesterday I rode my pony over rolling hills and through meadows of wild flowers. Cattle were grazing everywhere. There was warm sunshine and clear fresh air—a wonderful afternoon. I arrived at the mission before the others and announced our arrival at 5:30. No sooner had I dismounted than one of the Mongol servants cried "Wolves." He jumped on my pony and dashed across the fields chasing four wolves that had killed one of the big sheep. Wolves are everywhere in Mongolia; the Mongols fight a continuous war against them.

The cordial welcome of the Emersons, the Swedish couple in charge of the mission, has been very touching. Although we are complete strangers everything has been done to make us feel comfortable. Last night was the first night since leaving Kalgan that we had a meal seated at a table. The savory odor of cooked mutton that greeted us on arrival had whetted our appetites for the delicious dinner we were served. And we had our first bath and our first night's sleep in a bed. When I was asked to say grace at breakfast this morning, it was not difficult to find words to express my thankfulness.

This mission is extremely simple. It consists of a small foreign type house and several Mongolian tents called yurts. Ten orphan children have their homes here; for thirty others it is a school. There is also a dispensary to which Mongols come from all around, mostly for the treatment of venereal diseases which are prevalent. Because of their lack of cleanliness almost every kind of skin disease appears; and eye trouble is common because of the sandstorms and the constant smoke inside the yurts. The Emerson's beautiful children play with the Mongol orphans as if they were kin. What will they grow to be like in this tiny mission miles and miles away from civilization?

We have had our first peep into a Mongolian yurt. This is a circular latticed framework covered with white felt and dome-shaped on top like a beehive. In the center is a round fireplace. A flap at the top can be opened to let out the smoke. Since wood is scarce, dried dung is used for fuel. Women and children with baskets on their backs are often seen gathering it. This does not blaze like wood but it glows; and, as they say, it can boil a pot. The vivid coloring of these Mongolian women, the first we have seen, is striking; they have black eyes, red cheeks, and brown skin. They are tall and straight. Since they do not bind their feet they are strong like the men. Their elaborate headdresses of coral and silver are handsome and are worn by all women who are married.

The only other guest at the mission is a Mr. Birkland, a genial Swede who has recently arrived from Urga after travelling sixty-six days with a caravan of ox carts. Last night he told of the hardships he had encountered on the way. When he had finished, he said seriously, "I know now it's not so easy to die." Since our carter left early this morning to return our Peking cart to Kalgan, Mr. Birkland will accompany us to Gulchaggan. It had been arranged by Dr. Ingram that someone at this mission would be available to guide us safely through the most difficult part of our journey. Mr. Birkland very kindly volunteered. The Emersons not only refused to take any money for food and lodging but when it came time to say good-bye gave us a generous supply of food for the road.

At a Mongol Settlement
August 7

As we left Hallong Usu, Dora rode in a high two-wheeled Russian cart with a Mongol guide, while Shin Ling took our baggage in an ox cart. Mr. Birkland and I rode our ponies. It was dusk with the golden sunset turning to saffron as we reached the first Mongol settlement, obviously a poor one; here we would have to spend the night. Mongols expect to offer hospitality to any traveller asking for a night's rest, for hospitality is the law of this land. There is never any thought of recompense. Vicious dogs jumped at us as we approached the yurts but they were tied up securely after we were properly received.

We had our supper in the open and watched red Venus rise above the hills. Gradually as darkness set in, the black night was filled with the magic of a million stars. As we sat quietly enjoying the evening, Mr. Birkland said "Tell me about your American Indians. They have always seemed to me akin to the Mongolians." Both he and Dora had an idea that Indians roamed all over our country and were amazed when I told them I had never seen one. But I could tell them a little about Indian folklore because the islands of Casco Bay where I have spent most of my summers were the summer "hunting ground" of the Abnakis, the name of the five great tribes of Maine. I told them, too, about the Canadian Indian Chief who was asked by a friend of mine: "Are you an Indian first and then a Canadian or are you a Canadian and then an Indian?" He replied calmly, "I come from some miles near the Arctic Circle in the north country. I live with the snow, the ice, and the sharp wind in the winter; with the streams, the flowing waters, the sun and the blossoms in summer. These flow into me and I flow into them. They help me and I help them. I am a part of them and they are a part of me. I am not sure what you mean when you say Indian or Canadian."

When we went into the yurt which had been offered to us, the red glow of the fire in the middle of the room gave the only light. On the floor we could distinguish an old woman sitting cross-legged smoking her pipe. As we entered she smiled, blew at the fire, and lighted a wick in a bowl of oil. We could guess at the filth of the place so we spread oil cloth on the floor where we were to sleep to prevent the insects from crawling on us. The old woman was to sleep there too. After taking down her hair, she wrapped herself in an old cloak and lay down by the door. This was latched for fear of the dogs which are always let loose to roam the compound at night. She tried to close the flap at the top. But we refused to allow this for the odor of the tent was vile and the smoke nearly blinded us.

Mr. Birkland insisted upon sleeping in the ox cart although I much preferred sleeping there myself. He would not permit this so I crawled into the dirty, dark yurt, wrapped a blanket around me and tried to go to sleep. Not long after the dogs were set free, there was a terrifying noise as if they had all rushed to attack someone. It was a savage sound; I was glad for the protection of the yurt. Above this noise I heard the voice of the Mongol holding back the dogs and Mr. Birkland shouting, "May I come in?" The dogs had surrounded the cart and were about to jump on him when he stood up and cried for help.

He finally lay down in the yurt at our feet—but none of us could sleep. We dozed off and on, but at the first light of dawn we were up. The old woman was up with us and to our surprise she washed her face and hands and combed her hair. When she stepped out into the light we saw her for the first time, dirty, barefooted, and ragged; yet on her head was the elaborate Mongolian headdress of coral and silver.

We were on our way again as the sun rose behind a soft film of cloud which covered the sky and cast a rose light over the land. The hills were enveloped in a thin lavender mist. It would have taken a poet to catch the delicacy of the morning. We reached a large lama temple about nine o'clock and stopped there for breakfast.

Since the Mongol with the cart was no where to be seen, Mr. B. jumped on his pony to see if he could find him. No sooner was he out of sight than the horse harnessed to the Russian buggy where I was sitting began to stand on his hind legs and back down a hill. The two-wheeled cart would tip over at the slightest provocation, so I got ready to jump. I started to free my feet just as the buggy overturned catching my left foot as it went. It was the first accident of the kind I had ever had, so when I heard my foot snap I thought I had broken it. When I found I could walk with only a little pain, I said nothing about this to Mr. B. when he returned. We ate a huge breakfast and walked through the temple before harnessing the horse again.

This was a typical lamasery with the various buildings on the side of a hill. There were hundreds of priests about, ranging from very young boys to old men. Some had calm, good faces, but most of them were coarse and sensuous. Although their wine-colored robes were soiled, their color was picturesque against the gray stone of the walls and porticos. Two-thirds of the male population of Mongolia are priests, each family being obliged to send at least the first son to the temple. They are not allowed to marry, but they are seldom refused a woman when they visit in a tent. This is the cause of the great amount of syphilis and gonorrhea in the country. It is said that nearly 90 percent of all the men and the women have been afflicted by this disease.

The Emersons told us that the Living Buddha who died last June in Urga was so diseased near the end of his life that he became blind; drunken orgies were very frequent in his house and licentiousness of all kinds indulged in. If another Living Buddha is chosen, astrologers will help to determine the direction in which the soul has fled. After the place has been discovered all the children born at the moment of his death will be brought together at the age of two when the clothes of the Buddha will be put before them. Which ever child reaches for the clothes will be the next Living Buddha.

It is strange to think that the Mongols who once controlled half the known world lost their importance chiefly through religion. Kublai Khan, grandson of Genghis, wishing to civilize the Mongols, sent a message to the Pope for a hundred Christian missionaries. Denied this request he encouraged the introduction and spread of Lamaism, the degenerate Tibetan form of Buddhism to which his first wife had been converted. It gained a profound hold on the people and led directly to their decline morally and physically. The Lamas preached indifference to the affairs of this world and held up the life of a monk as the highest ideal. The people were brought up to put their faith in rewards bestowed in a future life—a faith which destroyed the terrible energy of their forefathers before whom the whole world had trembled. Lama temples now dot the land. The support of these, together with the monasteries in which throngs of idle priests live, has impoverished the country.

As we continued our journey, the road began to ascend and became a stony path winding in and out between high rock-tipped hills. Several eagles were perched on the rocks and others swarmed noisily into the air. Cultivation had ceased. The fields were wild with blue grass and brilliant flowers; the hills looked as if huge rocks had been tumbled over them; there was not a tree in sight anywhere. Villages were very far apart, so that it was possible to ride for hours without meeting a soul.

The first large Mongol settlement we passed was the home of a rich official and here we stopped for a cup of tea. Within the compound wall were four huge yurts and a few Chinese mud houses. We were received by the official in the first yurt which was comfortably and beautifully furnished with Chinese chests, rugs, and tables. The place of honor was opposite the door, on either side of which were three rugs or cushions; in front of these were small tables. As always a fireplace was in the center. Mongol tea and sesame cakes were set before us, but the tea, different from anything I have ever tasted, was salty and made me very thirsty. It was made with brick tea, rancid butter, and fine ground meal. The official was a charming man and a gracious host accustomed to entertaining foreigners. Although he owns considerable property which he rents to the Chinese for vegetable gardens, his wealth is in his horses.

When we started on the last lap of the road to Gulchaggan, the horse harnessed to the buggy began to fuss again. Our Mongol guide mounted my pony and, taking the leading rein, led the horse at breakneck speed for the rest of the way, the buggy careening wildly. At the top of the last hill, the Mongol stopped and pointed out Gulchaggan at the farther end of the valley. Here he put on a long gray coat tied at the waist with a blue cloth. Across the plain he fairly flew until we reached the gates of the mission. We were received with great dignity by the entire Mongol household; each one bowed low to greet us. Our Mongol jumped from the pony the moment he saw his mother and bowed his knee before her as she came with out-stretched arms to embrace him. It was a touching introduction to our Mongol household.

Miss Wickland, in charge of the mission, had not expected us so soon. But in keeping with the extraordinary hospitality everywhere things were made ready for us in an instant. Within half an hour I found myself in bed, for the ankle which had continued to pain ever since we left the temple, utterly failed me when I once extricated my-self from the Russian buggy.

Gulchaggan
August 14

Gulchaggan, which is between 5,000 and 6,000 feet above sea level, is delightfully cool. Dora tells me there is no village higher in all Switzerland. The air is clear and invigorating. Sunsets here rival any that I have ever seen—the nights are even more brilliant than those of Peking. Alice and the Ingrams have arrived making a full and jolly household. As soon as I can ride my pony we are taking two exciting trips: one to a sacred mountain to see all kinds of wild life, the other to the edge of the desert.

I have been here now just one week and this is the first day that I have walked comfortably. Mr. Birkland has been frightfully upset over my accident and has hardly left me for a moment. But I haven't minded being laid up. It has kept me quiet for a week and because of it I am completely rested. It has also given me plenty of time to read and to learn more about this amazing country. What I have learned has astonished me.

It seems incredible that this land over which we have been travel-ling could possibly have any great political significance. Although it is half the size of the United States, it has only 2,000,000 inhabitants widely scattered and loosely organized. There is not in this vast area a single mile of railroad. The scientific expeditions and the Russian Bolshevist officials use motor cars here and there, but transport is mostly by camels, ponies, or ox carts. There is no telephone, no tele-graph, no postal system. I have not seen even a paved road.

Mongolia consists of Inner and Outer Mongolia with the Gobi desert in between. Most of the country is still unknown. On the map are only a few names and some of these do not even represent a town

or a trading post; they are names of mountains, springs or wells
which, when the traveller finds them, are not in sight of a single
habitation. There are fertile plains and good grazing land. Some
mountain ranges covered with forests are known to contain great re-
serves of gold, copper, iron, and coal; but by far the greater part of the
country is waste and desolation to be crossed only by camel caravans.
The people are nomads; they roam the wide plains, break tracks
across the deserts, or migrate over the mountains. The temperature in
summer often goes above 100° with no available shade; in winter it
plunges to 50° below zero.

But Mongolia is the pawn of three countries. China needs more
fertile land for its cramped and hungry millions. Only one-ninth of
China's land is arable yet 80 percent of its people are peasants. Mongolia offers them that land and Chinese settlers have already taken
over much of the farm land in the south. Russia has long been the
dominant influence in the north. Mr. Birkland who lives in Urga says
that Soviet advisers now supervise educational matters, provide for
military training, and supply funds for the economic development of
the country. Mongolia borders on the western side of Manchuria,
China's wide frontier north of the Great Wall—larger than France
and Germany combined. Here Russian influence confronts Japanese
interests. The Russian-controlled Chinese Eastern Railway crosses
Manchuria from west to east and the Japanese-controlled South Manchurian Railway from south to north. Japan is in desperate need of
the bare necessities of survival which she sees available in Manchuria:
fertile grasslands, coal and iron, grain and waterpower. Russia and
Japan have already confronted each other here in a war that ended by
the treaty of Portsmouth, New Hampshire, in August 1905. President
Theodore Roosevelt was awarded the Nobel Peace Prize for his wisdom and tact in bringing an end to these hostilities.

Those who know this country well prophesy that some day another
clash will come, for the Russians are a people who have an old tradition of a destiny to be fulfilled in Asia. How ironic it would be if this
land, which was the cradle of life on this earth, should ever be a
battleground of the races of man or the final meeting place of East
and West! Here in quiet, peaceful, and beautiful Gulchaggan it is
too incredible even to think about. (Yet, seven years later in 1931,

Japan invaded Manchuria, an act which led eventually to World War II. And now as I write in 1976, Soviet divisions totalling nearly a million men with up-to-date weapons are deployed along the Mongolian border, the most sensitive of the Chinese-Soviet frontiers.)

Hongor Obo
August 19

We left Gulchaggan in the early evening when the sky was aflame with the setting sun and travelled most of the night by the light of the full moon. After three hours rest under the stars, we were off again at sunrise with our caravan: five carts, eight horses, two oxen, two cows, two calves, three dogs, and three servants. We often travel at night because the days are hot.

This sacred mountain is unlike the grassy plains; it is covered with huge rocks and tiny fir trees. On the top of the highest peak is an obo, a round sacrificial pile of stones built as an offering to Buddha. In the center are poles on which are tied prayer-flags, pieces of cloth and scarves, all faded and whipped to ribbons by the winds. These are offerings of pilgrims and travellers. This kind of religious monument is common in Mongolia. Almost every high point of land near a trail or a road has its own obo. Travellers climbing to the top of these usually add a stone or two. From this peak we look out upon a sea of rolling hills. At the foot of the mountain is the old caravan road that leads on to Urga. In the distance can be seen the white line of the Gobi desert.

We have pitched our tents in the valley. Every day we have been riding our ponies across the plains following all the interesting valleys and canyons along the way. There are many cool deep ravines with tangles of low spreading trees and massive rocks over which tiny streams are trickling down from the mountain tops. Often we have seen flocks of white cranes daintily catching grasshoppers. Marmots are everywhere on the plains bobbing in and out of their burrows. Mongolian sky larks jump out of the grass almost under our ponies feet; then they soar high in the sky flooding the air with their song. The Chinese come to catch the nestlings because in Peking they bring a good price. Climbing to the ridge of a low mountain range the other day, we saw antelopes grazing. These graceful creatures, if frightened, have been known to reach a speed of sixty miles an hour. Gazelles and wild asses are seen everywhere.

One still night Dora and I slept in the open near the obo. We watched a golden sunset as the long blue shadows filled the crevices of the hills. Shepherds were driving their flocks across the plains and a solitary horseman was riding slowly along the road toward Urga. The restful hills bathed in the soft evening light stretched out as far as the eye could see. Just as the evening star appeared, we heard the sound of distant bells and saw silhouetted against the sky a long line of camels in an enormous caravan. They came quietly out of the shadows and slowly disappeared in the glow of the Western sky. As they made their way toward Urga and beyond, they were following one of the great trade routes made long before the travels of Marco Polo. Two thousand years ago the caravans passing this way might have been carrying the precious Chinese silk on its way to Sogdiana in Central Asia. (Sogdiana today is called Uzbekistan, a thriving Soviet Central Asian Republic, not far from where the Russian cosmonauts landed after the Soviet-American space flight.) This was an important crossroads for the trades of all the world when this meant China, Rome, Parthia, and Afghanistan. All of these traded with each other by caravan either directly or indirectly. From here went the Chinese silk on its way to Rome via Syria, for Rome had already acquired a taste for the products and luxuries of the Orient. Chinese silk came to play an important part in the problem of Rome's balance of payments for Chinese silk had to be paid for in gold. As the taste for silk spread, Tiberius (437) prohibited the wearing of silk because it was undermining the Empire's economy—a complaint one has heard quite recently and a reminder of how very old some of our recent problems are.

Here too, gathered Indians, Chinese, Persians, Jews, Greeks, and Syrians. Their exchanges went far beyond material goods for the world was then in a state of religious ferment. Monks and missionaries journeyed with the caravans spreading the doctrines of Buddhism, Zooastrianism, Manichaeism, and eventually Nestorian Christianity. It was at this time that Buddhism spread eastward to China. Although the Chinese have never shown much ardor for religion,

The dry riverbed, our road to the Waushan Pass.

After the deluge.

Our Peking cart on the road again.

The steep, rocky Waushan Pass.

On the plateau at last.

Mongolian shepherds with their flocks. Note camels in distance.

Morning coffee in an inn yard.

A crowd that gathers around as I write.

Shin Ling on a *k'ang* of a Chinese inn.

A cook working the bellows of a Chinese stove.

Riding toward the land of the Mongols.

The quiet beauty of Mongolia.

A typical yurt with a water cart and one of the ferocious Mongolian dogs. *Below:* Mongolian women with their elaborate headdress.

The home of an important official. Note the tops of yurts behind the wall.

The official in his elaborately
furnished yurt.

A lama monastery. *Below:* Looking toward an obo built as an offering to Buddha.

Our campsite and the two Mongols
who followed us everywhere.

Thirsty camels at the desert.

Watching a desert sunrise.

A camel caravan that came out of the shadows and disappeared
in the glow of the western sky.

A Mongolian prayer ready to be taken to the gods.

Buddhism at one time was a popular faith. Its gentle, compassionate teaching had a strong appeal for many Chinese at times of stress and difficulty. Millions of converts were made. (Although Buddha was a contemporary of Confucius, Buddhism was only a minor sect until the great King Asoka of India became a convert around 260 B.C. The missionary zeal of this philosopher sovereign transformed it into one of the great religions of the world. It has been said that Asoka's vast empire enjoyed perhaps the most enlightened rule known in the history of mankind.)

These slow camel caravans used to make their way over thousands of miles. From China they had to cross the mighty mountain chains of the Pamirs, which had isolated China from the west for thousands of years, and then across the fertile plains of Sogdiana. Today just to make the seven hundred mile journey from Kalgan to Urga will take a camel caravan at least seventy days.

The exhilarating air and the brilliance of the night made it difficult for me to go to sleep. As I lay in the stillness I could not help thinking of Mongolia as it was 700 years ago when Genghis Khan welded the fierce Mongol tribes together to form one of the greatest military forces and to create the greatest empire the world has ever seen. His imperial highways spread out into China, India, Persia, Russia, and beyond. Along the way were military and post stations, the necessary grain stores and pasture lands. It is said that more than 10,000 posting stations with 300,000 horses made possible unhindered traffic throughout this mighty land. The Khan's messengers could spring from horse to horse at the subsidiary posts and continue their journey travelling from 250 to 300 miles a day. Tu Fu's famous poem describes these marvellous horses!

> See his wiry build, almost angular and rugged.
> See his two ears, erect and sharp like bamboo shoots
> See his four hoofs, fleeing with the wind.
> This is a horse for the conquest of space
> To him one may entrust one's life.
> When one has a flying steed like this, a thousand
> miles are nothing.

This was a time when Mongolian roads were thronged with couriers, caravans, and envoys going to and from the Mongol court at Karakorum. Booty came from every land, princes from Russia, skilled craftsmen from Paris, Damascus, and Peking. I marvelled at the thought of this fabulous, but cruel, world.

Then suddenly piercing the silence, there came from a distant hill the long howls of wolves, mournful and savage. As I listened, they seemed to me a portent of the evil that is always lurking in the shadows—corruption, decadence, greed, inertia—waiting for the first sign of weakness in order to creep in stealthily to destroy—to destroy even the greatest empire of the world.

At the Edge of the Desert
August 24

The Gobi desert is a part of Mongolia but only in the western section is it the desolate waste which is usually associated with it. In the eastern part where we are it gradually changes into a rolling plain covered with sage brush. It is difficult to tell where the desert begins because in the sand, here and there, are bunches of tall grass with long slender silver-tipped blades that sway in the breeze; soft bushy pink grass grows close to the ground. As one would expect, there is a very little water here except surface ponds.

Mongol villages lie at the edge of the sand with herds of camels, horses, sheep, goats, and cows. The two-humped camels fascinate me; sometimes if they are in need of water one hump lies limp. Strangely enough, this is good grazing land for camels. They grow thin in the grasslands, but they thrive on sage brush and thorny vegetation. On the way to our camping site last night we passed a herd of nearly a hundred camels drinking from a small pond. They are stately creatures utterly unconcerned about anything or anybody.

All along the way from Gulchaggan we have been invited to stay at Mongol settlements. The Mongols' food consists almost entirely of mutton, cheese, and tea so whenever or wherever we have stopped we were sure to have mutton served in some form. At the Mission we have it morning, noon, and night. It is a monotonous diet, yet on a trip like this we cannot afford to be fussy; we are grateful for the warm hospitality of these people. Nearly every night Mongols have come to our camp to visit. They sit by our camp fire examining everything about us. In turn we see their pipes, snuff bottles, rings, and the silver ornaments on their tobacco pouches. On one of these visits a Mongol suddenly jumped on his pony and rode off, returning shortly with a pair of fieldglasses which he showed to us with a wide grin. These are a never-ending source of wonder to all the natives. The Chinese call them *chen lo yen,* "thousand miles eyes."

We visited a silver smith the other day and bought some interesting jewelry. An official arrived while we were there and invited us to take a pinch of his snuff as it was passed among the men. Then we all sat down for a cup of tea together. The official drank from his own silver dish; we were served our tea in Chinese cups.

On our return to camp that night we crossed huge dunes of rippled sand. As the sun dropped below the horizon, the world was suddenly on fire. The whole sky was ablaze. The sand was burnished gold, even the distant mountains were aglow. It surpassed anything I had ever seen. It was long after that final blaze of light that the sky slowly faded into the night and over this land sea lay the quiet calm of a desert evening.

The next morning I woke before dawn and slipped quietly out of my tent. In the awesome stillness there was not a sign of life. Then gradually as the eastern sky heralded the dawn, light and color came back into the world. As I looked out onto the barren earth stretched endless before me, I was reminded of the time eons ago when the waters receded and the steppes of Asia became the mother of the continents. And I thought of the scientists working patiently somewhere in Mongolia to unlock the secrets of the dim past. I did not wonder that one of them, Father Teilhard de Chardin camping near the edge of the desert, was moved to pray on Easter Sunday:

Since once again, O Lord, in the steppes of Asia, I have no bread, no wine, no altar I will raise myself above those symbols to the pure majesty of Reality, and I will offer to You, I, Your priest, upon the altar of the entire earth, the labor and the suffering of the world

Teilhard was a Jesuit priest from an old aristocratic French family. He had a brilliant scientific mind and a great heart, both of them big enough, a Peking friend once said, to encompass the whole world. They had given him the insight to discern the rising tide of destructive forces which were threatening our planet and had led him to call on all mankind to unite in building the earth—in making the world a home for all people.

"The Age of Nations is past," he said, "The task before us now, if we would not perish, is to shake off our ancient prejudices and to build the earth. . . . The natural units of humanity must achieve harmony through the very variety of their racial characteristics—characteristics which can enrich one another. Remain true to yourselves," he urged, "but move ever upward toward greater understanding and love. At the summit you will find yourselves united with all those who from every direction have made the same ascent. For everything that rises must converge." The constant goal of both nations and individuals, he believed, must be to achieve this unity if we are to have any fullness of life on the earth.

Teilhard's theory of evolution and his attempt to reconcile science and religion had kindled a fierce controversy within the Catholic Church. By some he was acclaimed as "the saint Thomas Aquinas of our age,—a new Galileo." Others denounced him as "the old Trojan horse of Catholicism," a man of dangerous theories. Of Galileo whose discoveries about the solar system the Catholic Church did not accept for two hundred years, he said, "I keep his bust in my room because the Church owes him at least this much." Nothing could shake his belief in the infallibility of evolution—the progress of the universe from elemental matter through the advent of life, animal consciousness, and human thought toward God. Man did not descend from an ape, he used to say. He ascended.

While teaching at the Catholic Institute in Paris, he wrote an article suggesting that original sin was not an historic fact but largely a theory to explain the existence of evil. The Jesuits were so shocked at this that they ordered him, for his own sake before Rome acted, to stop teaching and stick to scientific research, preferably as far from France as possible. So under the auspices of the Paris Museum of National History, Teilhard obediently sailed to China. (The Jesuits might have had second thoughts had they foreseen how his scientific work with the Peking Man confirmed his objectionable theory. Actually he believed Peking Man to be a woman and always called her "Nellie.")

Teilhard had many devoted friends in Peking. He was witty and gay and he loved people. What an increase there is in man's power, he used to say, when he catches the breath of affection or comradeship; what fulfillment when he finds that he has glimpsed the wonders of a kindred spirit. The world is round, he was fond of saying, so that friendship may encircle it.

Lost on the Plains

August 29

Our return trip to Gulchaggan was under cloudy skies. Then for two days we had steady rain. On the third day the rain stopped; by afternoon the clouds broke with enough blue sky appearing to make us believe the weather had changed. About five o'clock Alice and I decided to go for a short ride before supper to exercise our ponies and to get some fresh air for ourselves.

Before we left, Miss Wickland warned us never to get out of sight of the mission. She explained that it was easy to get lost on the plain. Although the land looks flat, it is really a rolling surface full of slopes and hollows—each one looking exactly like all the others. "Just remember," she shouted as we mounted the ponies, "there are no landmarks here in Gulchaggan except the mission."

We started across the plain galloping at full speed glad to be out in the open again, but always looking back at the mission. Soon there loomed ahead a hill which tempted us. Climbing to the top of it we looked out on endless hills. Upon one that looked fairly close was a row of poles resembling the top of a Turkish temple. "Let's go that far," I said, "and then turn back." We looked toward the mission, then took careful note of our position. From this particular hill the plain and the mission were both clearly visible and directly south. We rode and rode soon discovering that our hill was much farther away than we had imagined.

Eventually we reached the hill, discovering that what had intrigued us from the distance was an enormous obo. Evidently there had just been a sacrifice, for the obo was covered with prayers printed on pieces of paper with a picture of a horse stamped on each. We had learned at Hongor obo that during a service when these are thrown into the air it is believed the horse will take the prayer to the Gods. We picked up several for souvenirs then looked about us. Toward the north was a beautiful rainbow. Here and there the sun shone through the clouds making the rolling hills look more than ever like the waves of an angry ocean.

As the sun began to set we started back. We headed for the hill which we thought would give us our direction. But from the top, neither the mission nor the plain was anywhere to be seen. I thought the plain was in one direction, Alice thought it was in another. We compromised. Before we had gone very far, we saw in the west a black storm sweeping in our direction. If we were to avoid the storm we had to find the road across the plain. We galloped at full speed to the top of the highest hill which we could see. But still the plain was nowhere to be seen; it was swallowed up by the hills. The clouds scudded across the sky putting now this hill in shadow, now that. We were completely lost and bewildered. We both had a feeling for the direction yet a wrong turn—ever so slight—meant winding endlessly among the hills. Thunder rumbled ominously. Now and then a flash of lightning pierced the sky.

As we scanned the horizon we saw in the distance someone riding a white horse. We galloped toward him praying that he would know the way to the mission. He was a Mongol who could neither speak Chinese nor understand what little Mongolian we knew. But he was on a road and a road leads somewhere, so we followed him at a gallop. It began to pour just as we saw in the distance the walls of a lama monastery.

To our great relief we entered the courtyard. But what a dismal sight, not a person anywhere to be seen, only a horse dripping wet tied to a pole. The temple building was empty, but we saw a yellow-robed priest disappearing in a house beyond. We followed him and asked if he knew the Swedish mission at Gulchaggan. It was difficult to know whether he understood what we were saying; nothing could move him into the rain. But at least he opened the door to let us in.

Our talking roused other priests who crowded around and stared at us in unbelief. Among them was one who spoke Chinese; from him we learned that Gulchaggan was thirty li (ten miles) away. He insisted that we spend the night at the monastery when we first suggested his riding back with us. He would see that we were comfortable and would get us safely back in the morning. We explained that our only reason for not accepting his hospitality was the thought of our friends at Gulchaggan. Again we urged his riding back with us.

"I have no horse" he said, "and there is none to be had."

"What about the horse outside?" I asked.

"He does not belong to the monastery."

Finally, I suggested that he ride on one of our horses—at least one of us could go to relieve the people at the mission. The rain poured torrents at that moment; again he refused. But I knew that we *must* get back; once more I pleaded. He looked at me, smiled, and finally gave in. Alice and I flipped a coin to see who would go and who would stay. I was to go!

The lama put on his hood, took a crop, and outside mounted the pony. Never as long as I live shall I forget the sound of the horses hoofs splashing in the mud as we rode off into the black night! Alice was left behind in the care of the head lama. The rain made her good-bye sound far away and faint.

On the road it was almost impossible to see ahead. This lama priest and I crossed plains, followed roads, crossed other plains, and other hills. Never a sign of even a Mongol yurt—nothing but the rain and the sound of the horses hoofs on the wet ground. We rode on and on; still there was no light anywhere to be seen. Did this man *really* know where I wanted to go? If he did, could I trust him to take me there? Could he possibly know where he was going in the blackness of the night? Fear overcame me and I felt weak and faint. How foolish I had been to insist upon returning to the mission at night with a complete stranger! I thought of all the terrible things that could happen to me—and no one would ever know. I began to be sick. Then as a kind of miracle, the twenty-third psalm came into my mind, a psalm which had always had a special meaning for me ever since my grandmother had taught it to me as a child. "The Lord is my shepherd, I shall not want. I shall fear no evil."

Gradually I gained control of myself. And I saw this man as he really was, a lama priest very reluctantly doing a great favor for me. I kicked my pony and rode up side of him. In Chinese I said, "You are very kind to do this for me." He replied, "It is nothing." As we rode for a while in silence the thought came to me how very important it is what we put into our minds. It was not long before a tiny yellow light gleamed ahead. He spoke something to me and pointed. I knew we had reached Gulchaggan.

As soon as we were near enough for the dogs to hear us, they barked and told of our arrival. Lanterns appeared in all the yurt doors. The courtyard became full of people waving and shouting, "What happened? Where is Miss Boring?" When it was learned that she was safe, I was sent to change my wet clothes. Thankfully, we all sat down together and had a cup of tea. To reward the lama for his kindness he was given a choice of articles and was delighted to accept a bolt of cloth; money was of no interest to him. When it was decided what Mongol would return with him, the rain had ceased. Jupiter appeared briefly between the clouds as the two Mongols started back across the dark plain for Miss Boring.

It was nearly midnight when she arrived. Because we were far too excited to go to bed we talked about our frightening experience as we ate a light supper. We learned of the great concern everyone had felt at the mission, of the bonfire that had been lighted as a beacon for us, of the Mongol who had been sent in search of us. When he had returned alone, all hope had been given up of finding us until daybreak.

We were chagrined because of the trouble and worry we had caused. But Miss Wickland assured us that we were not the first foreigners to be lost on the plains. Only the Mongols who have a "feel of the land" never get lost. Then she smiled and said "If only you had given your reins to the ponies, undoubtedly they would have brought you back safely to the mission."

That was our last adventure, for in two days we said good-bye to Miss Wickland, to the kind Mongols who had served us, and were on our way back to Hallong Usu, to Chiang Pei-shien, and the Wasushan Pass. As we went through the narrow gateway of the Great Wall we took a last lingering look at Mongolia with its great open spaces and its natural beauty—this place which had given us such warm hospitality and such a sense of peace and freedom.

Ahead was the magnificent vista of distant hills and below the dry river bed which was to take us back to Kalgan, a city where two worlds meet—the world of railroads and automobiles, and the world of ox carts and camels. Each is unconcerned about the other. Camels stepped haughtily over the railroad tracks to kneel for the unloading of their packs brought from across the desert, while automobile horns blew and trains puffed. Mongolia was to fade into a beautiful dream as our train pulled into the station at Peking and brought us back from the Middle Ages into the twentieth century.

Back in Peking

Look thy last on all things lovely
Every hour. Let not night
Seal thy sense in deathly slumber
Till to delight
Thou have paid thy utmost blessing.
WALTER DE LA MARE

September 9, 1924

DEAR FAMILY,

You can't imagine how good it is to get back to this lovely old T'ung Fu again. It was just a year ago today that my ricksha deposited me outside our gates and I stepped into this old palace walking through the various courtyards to my little compound. It is all as enchanting today as it was then.

But the best part of getting back is to find so many letters from home. For your beautiful birthday letter and the generous check many, many thanks—I was on the ragged edge of my checkbook. Our board has gone up to 60 mex a month—practically half of my tiny salary. Thank you for remembering to send the soap and toothpaste. These are luxuries out here.

Invitations have begun to fly in for all sorts of things; however I can't go at the pace I went last year. It was great fun for a year, but after a while that kind of life begins to pall. With Miss Boynton on furlough I must assume the headship of the department and devote more time to college work. My courses, which are all elective this year, promise to be very challenging. I have been given a course in drama open to both men and women students—also the responsibility for all the dramatic work of the college. All of this thrills me; I just hope I shall be equal to the job. And speaking of drama, imagine my surprise last week when the president of The Peking Players, an international theatre group, asked if I would be willing to put on their big winter production. This would be lots of work; but they have promised plenty of assistance so I am tempted. I have been toying with the idea of Gilbert and Sullivan's *Iolanthe* which I saw produced at Bennett just before I left.

There has been fighting between some warlords in the plains not far from Peking. At night some of the streets are full of soldiers, for battles never take place after dark nor when the weather is cold and rainy. They wear gray cotton uniforms with tea pots and paper umbrellas tied around their waists. Around their sleeves they wear colored bands indicating what army they belong to; these are pinned on with safety pins because they frequently change from one army to another. Here in Peking the fighting is not taken very seriously; it seems almost as if they were playing at war. There is very little bloodshed and little interference with the ordinary activities of life.

I am thrilled to be back in Peking. What a glorious city this is! After the dirt roads and open spaces of Mongolia, I am more impressed than ever with the handsome boulevards, the pageantry of the streets, the splendid vistas through the great city gates, and the massive Tartar wall crowned with its high gate towers. These towers are said to be ninety-nine feet high, a proper height for beneficent spirits, according to geomancers. There are great archways under the towers. These are made of granite while the imposing gates are of thick wood studded with huge nails.

Yesterday I went for a walk on top of this wall. In the clear autumn air I could see far and wide, for the city is low and spacious. It was easy to pick out the splendid monuments which rise above the maze of *hutungs*—everything oriented to the axis of the Forbidden City.

I have never made the complete circuit of the wall for it is a distance of some twenty-five miles. Originally several horsemen could ride abreast there, but today there is only an uneven pathway that meanders through a luxuriant growth of weeds, grasses, and wild shrubs. This neglect is typical of much of Peking today. However, above the Legation Quarter between Ch'ien Men and Hata Men, the two principal city gates, there is a paved walk kept in good condition. This section was demanded by the Western Powers after the Boxer defeat because it was from this vantage point that the Chinese bombarded the "foreign devils" in 1900. This is still controlled and patrolled by the various legations so that never again might they run the risk of being fired upon from it.

For me the most interesting part of the wall is the Observatory, called by the Chinese the "Star-gazing platform." Here are the great bronze azimuth and globe given by Louis XIV to the Ch'ing Emperor K'ang Hsi. And here Kublai Khan put his terrestial globe and models of six astronomical instruments given to him in 1267 by a Persian astronomer. Here also were the instruments of Kuo Shou-ching, the famous Chinese hydraulic engineer whose instruments made in 1276 were considered the finest in the world. It excites me to think of Peking in those days when Arabs, Venetians, Persians, Russians and many others were drawn to this fabulous city of wealth and culture. Even papal envoys resided at the great Khan's court. Travellers came mostly by land routes over Central Asia—a few by sea routes in the south. Stories are told of a Mongol envoy born in Peking about 1225 who visited Byzantium and Rome in 1287 and saw the King of England in Gascony and Phillip the Fair in Paris! It was a great and magnificent age, but it lasted only a century from 1260 to 1368.

I always leave the wall by the ramp near Ch'ien Men, because it is through this Front Gate that I get one of my favorite views of the city —the vast sweeping lines of the palace roofs with their yellow tiles shining against the background of the Western Hills. For everyone these are a symbol of the colorful past and will always dominate the city regardless of what changes take place around them. Roofs and walls are among the most distinctive features of Peking. The colors of the imperial roofs are spectacular, not only imperial yellow, but also green and deep blue. Besides this splendor, the roofs of princely houses have a touch of Chinese humor—little animals sit side by side on the curving edge.

Now as always the huge city gates are solemnly closed at night to be opened at dawn the next day. Yet these gates and the fortified walls, forty feet high and forty feet thick, have not been able to keep the invaders from this inscrutable city. The Mongols and Manchus broke through by treachery, the Western Powers by their weapons, and finally in 1911 by "the force of ideas against which no wall can stand."

Dr. Ferguson has given me a fascinating book about the history of Peking; it begins with a little town named Chi built on this site as far back as 1100 B.C. (about the time of the siege of Troy). There is a yellow-tiled pavilion about two miles north of the Tartar City which covers a tablet on which the Manchu Emperor Ch'ien Lung wrote: "Here stood one of the gates of the ancient city of Chi." However, it was not until two thousand years later (A.D. 915) that there was a metropolis where Peking now stands. This city was called "Yen-ching" or "Swallow Capital," a name commemorated by our Yenching University. It had a circumference of twelve miles, it contained a palace, and was surrounded by a wall thirty feet high with eight gates.

But it was when Kublai Khan left his great Mongolian encampment at Karakorum and came to Peking in 1264 that Peking for the first time became the Capital, not only of all China but of a great world empire as well. Many have told of the Mongol splendor of "The City of the Great Khan"—palace grounds with halls for residence and audiences, courts for parades and entertainment, artificial hills and lakes, parks with many fruit trees, and on the grassy plains, animals of the chase so dearly loved by every Mongol. Roads and waterways were improved and post stations with relays of hundreds of thousands of fast horses established for official use. The Grand Canal, begun in the sixth century was completely restored under the direction of the famous Kuo Shou-ching and extended to Peking, making a waterway from Hangchow of 1,000 miles. Marco Polo said of the great Khan "the most powerful lord in respect to forces, to land, to treasure that existeth in the world or ever was in the world from the time of Adam until now."

Kublai's fame spread over the whole empire. Vassaf, a Persian, wrote: "Although the distance of our country from the center of the Mongolian realm, the focus of the universe, is more than a year's journey, the glory of the great Khan's deeds has reached our ears. His laws, his justice, the profundity and fineness of his spirit, the wisdom of his decisions, his amazingly good government are, according to famous merchants and learned travellers, so enormously superior to anything which has been known in the world, that one ray of his glory would suffice to throw into the shade all that history has to relate of the Roman Caesars, the Arabian Caliphes, the Indian Rajahs, and the Seljuk Sultans."

According to tradition, Kublai Khan's wife wept when she saw in the newly acquired city of Hangchow the luxurious palaces of the defeated Sung Emperor. "It came to me," she said, "that the Empire of the Mongols will end this way some day."

Two hundred years after Kublai Khan, in 1429, it was Yung Lo, the great emperor buried in the impressive sepulchre which I saw at the Ming Tombs, who built the magnificent Forbidden City, when Versailles was an insignificant shooting lodge, the Kremlin surrounded by a wooden palisade, and Hampton Court not yet begun. Some of Peking's finest monuments were built at this time: the stateliest bridges, the lovely lakes and gardens of the Sea palaces, the Altar of Heaven and the Altar of Earth. In fact, the city today remains very much as it was in the time of Yung Lo, one of the oldest "living" cities in the world.

*   *   *

During the summer, Jui T'ang had written another festival play which she called *The Seventh Day of the Seventh Moon*. It was based on a legend which had been made into a popular opera called *The Marriage of the Heavenly River*. China's most famous actor, Mei Lan-fang, appeared in it often. The legend tells of a goddess who comes to earth and falls in love with a handsome cowherd. The "Western Mother" discovers their romance and punishes the goddess by taking her back to Heaven and making her a star. The grief-stricken cowherd searches for her in vain. Finally his love softens the heart of the "Western Mother" and he, too, is brought to Heaven. He becomes a star and is placed across the silver stream (our Milky Way) from his loved one. Once a year on the seventh day of the seventh moon, they are allowed to meet by walking across a bridge made by the wings of magpies.

Jui T'ang had already shown the play to P. C. Chang and to a well-known cousin of hers, Feng Kan Kwang, a patron of the great actor. They were both delighted with it. I was, too. So one afternoon we all had tea together and discussed how and where the play should be produced. It was agreed that I would direct the play, Feng Kan Kwang would borrow the costumes from his friend Mei Lan-fang, and P. C. would be responsible for the dances, the posturing, and the music.

A cast was chosen and rehearsals begun immediately after the opening of the University. The invaluable help of P. C., as well as the magnificent costumes of Mei Lan-fang gave the performance so much promise that the Peking Players, of which I was a member, begged to let them present it as their opening event. This we did. The performance exceeded our fondest hopes. It took place early in October in their little theatre and charmed a foreign audience, many of whom had never seen a Chinese play. Jui T'ang was overwhelmed with its enthusiastic reception.

This association with P. C. was the beginning of a wonderful friendship. It was through him and his friends that I came to have some understanding of the great forces that for more than a century had been changing the shape of their world.

He called at the T'ung Fu one day and brought with him Hu Shih, at the time a professor of Chinese philosophy at the National Peking University. Both were charming and brilliant young men deeply involved in China's Cultural Revolution. Hu Shih was one of the "greats" of contemporary China, the one responsible for the movement to replace the classical Chinese with the living spoken language. It was an unforgettable experience to talk with him. "New and living thoughts," he said, "can never be expressed in a dead language, however beautiful—something Europe discovered in the Middle Ages when Latin was dropped for the vernacular." The many books and magazine articles which he had written were all in *pai-hua*. His latest book published in Shanghai just the year before was about ancient Chinese philosophy. When I told him of the lively discussion I had had with my students about Confucius, he promised to bring me a copy of it.

Both P. C. and Hu Shih had studied in America. What had impressed them most about our country was its optimism, its energy and alertness in contrast to what they called the resignation of the East; it was this spirit of optimism they had both brought back to China. Although they valued the magnificent products of China's past—the bronzes, porcelains, jades, the calligrapher's art, and the delicately painted pictures, they agreed that China must be more than a museum; it must align itself with the democratic, scientific West and become a modern nation.

We had a fascinating hour together, all too short, before joining a group of their friends at one of the famous restaurants in the old Chinese city outside Ch'ien Men. P. C. wanted to give me a typical Chinese feast to celebrate the success of *The Seventh Day of the Seventh Moon*. I described it in a letter to my mother:

There must have been at least fifteen courses. Some were exotic dishes which I didn't care for; but there was bird's nest soup which I do like— made not from sticks and straws but from a gelatinous substance secreted from the glands of a little swallow when making its nest; and delicious meat balls, moo shi pork, a variety of vegetables, fish, and Peking duck. I had my first hundred-year old eggs, which of course are not "hundred-years" but preserved in lime for a year or two. The yolks turn a dark gray and the whites a greenish yellow—not very appetizing but dipped in soya bean sauce they are quite good. My favorite dish is Peking duck which is always served toward the end. The skin is roasted to a delicious crispness then cut with a thin slice of meat and wrapped inside a thin flour pancake with a delicate sauce, a dish fit for a king! The feast ended with a delicate almond soup.

Wine is served throughout a Chinese meal—to "aid digestion" but in thimble cups. It is always hot and only sipped. Since it is an important part of any feast, old fashioned invitations often read "the wine cups have been polished to await your pleasure." Besides wine and good food there was sparkling conversation and good fellowship. How well the Chinese know how to enjoy life! Every one of us did justice to the feast and after that meal I could understand why P. C. said "In America you eat in order to live but here in China we live in order to eat." With a smile Hu Shih put it this way: "Food is one of the things that has meant most to the Chinese through the ages along with drink, clothing, poetry, and music." To prove it, he recited a poem written in the first century, b.c.

> We go to the Golden Palace;
> We set out the jade cups.
> We summon the honoured guests
> To enter at the Golden Gate.

> In the eastern kitchen the meat is sliced and ready—
> Roast beef and boiled pork and mutton.
> The Master of the Feast hands round the wine.
> The harp-players sound their clear chords.

The cups are pushed aside and we face each other at chess:
The rival pawns are marshalled rank against rank.
The fire glows and the smoke puffs and curls;
From the incense-burner rises a delicate fragrance.
The clear wine has made our cheeks red;
Round the table joy and peace prevail.
May those who shared in this day's delight
Through countless springs enjoy like felicity.

As I came to know these intellectual Chinese and listened as they talked, I became aware of the seething restlessness underneath the surface of things. There was a civil war going on, the government in Peking was extremely shaky, and the country tragically divided. However, it was obvious that politics was not their concern as much as the social and cultural changes they were hopeful of bringing about. Since most of them were returned students from abroad, they were convinced that Western ideas must replace the old Chinese traditions. Many of them, like the students, were vehemently opposed to Confucianism and wanted to make a complete break with the past—to do away with filial duty, the old family system, the worship of ancestors.

Others like P. C. and Hu Shih were more cautious. They believed it was these factors and the Confucian ethics which had given cohesion to the Chinese people and had enabled them to resist conquest and maintain an unbroken history for 4,000 years. They agreed that the cult of Confucianism must be destroyed and Confucius put back into history along with the other great Chinese philosophers in order to recover the essence of their teaching, the bedrock of their civilization. But it would be tragic, they thought, for a nation with a glorious past and a distinctive civilization of its own to take on a new civilization forced upon it by the necessities of national survival. They hoped that the best of Western civilization could be assimilated, not totally adopted.

I was amazed that, despite all of the political chaos they discussed, those intellectuals had such an unquenchable optimism and vivacity. They believed a new spirit was abroad, and they were filled with idealism and faith that their country could be united and modernized. They saw a great future for China.

A Gathering Storm

Coming events cast their shadows
before them.

THOMAS CAMPBELL

EVER SINCE THE REVOLUTION OF 1911, there had been political turmoil
and unrest in China. Civil war between ambitious warlords in the
north and dissension between the conservative and liberal elements in
the Kuomingtang (Sun Yat-sen's National People's Party) in the
south echoed over the whole country. In Peking the central government had been dominated by a succession of rival warlords who were
corrupt and ineffective. They gave little thought to the ideals and
goals of the revolution. With few exceptions, the only incentive for
public office was personal aggrandizement and wealth. Banditry was
on the increase because of the poverty and misery in the countryside.

The foreigners in Peking for the most part lived above all this dissension. In the Legation Quarter Chinese political problems had little
effect on the social life. Dinner parties took place as usual at the various legations. There was dancing at the hotels, swimming and tennis
at the clubs, polo at the race course, and delightful houseparties at the
temples in the Western Hills. For nearly a year I lived at the T'ung
Fu totally unconcerned with political affairs. I was enchanted with
Chinese culture, absorbed in my work, and enjoying a fascinating
social life. Foreigners lived a charmed life. A visiting writer was not
far wrong when she said, "In the quiet subdued magnificence and
artistic wealth of Peking, the foreigners live in a sort of rarified atmosphere—everything had come true, they had achieved bliss."

But as I gradually became aware of the conditions of life for most of
the Chinese people, I was eager to know the reason for the political
turbulence which was causing so much misery and distress. And why
had the revolution failed so hopelessly to achieve its goal of a China
united in a strong republic? The answer, my Chinese friends told me,
was to be found in the great currents of history that swept over their
country in the nineteenth century when she was least prepared to cope
with them. As they tried to weave for me the complicated tapestry of
their history they always began with the Manchu dynasty. The Man-

chus, I learned, were an alien people from Manchuria who finally broke through the Great Wall in 1644 at the end of the last Chinese dynasty. Once in Peking, they refused to leave and assumed the Mandate of Heaven. The Emperor was brought from Mukden, and Peking remained the center of the Imperial administration until the Revolution in 1911.

Because of China's superior civilization, the Manchus finally lost touch with their own culture. They adopted the Confucian way of government. They promoted the study of the Chinese classics and veneration of ancestors; they extolled the Confucian virtues accepting the idea that the ruler ruled by virtue of moral goodness. There were no major economic or social changes. To maintain their racial purity, it was agreed that no Chinese women were to be taken into the palace, although the first and second emperors had Chinese concubines. Chinese men were required to shave their heads and wear queues, also to adopt Manchu clothes. Chinese women were forbidden to bind their feet although this regulation was almost impossible to enforce. In order to draw into their service the most able and promising Chinese, the "first" in the civil examinations, which for centuries had been the means of selecting officials, was never to be awarded to a Manchu. Thus by various means, the alien rulers of China maintained their racial and social identity, preserved their administrative control, yet gave prestige and opportunity to Chinese of talent. More important to the Chinese than dynasties or races was "the way of government." It mattered little who governed so long as he governed in the proper fashion. Much would be forgiven any government that did not interfere with the people. There is an old peasant song that goes:

> I plough my ground and eat
> I dig my well and drink.
> For King or Emperor what use have I?

China still believed herself to be the center of the universe surrounded by barbarians. She was the Middle Kingdom whose Emperor was the Son of Heaven, ruling by the Mandate of Heaven. She owed her greatness, she believed, to the principles of social order formulated by Confucius and her other great sages, and adminis-

tered by a learned elite. If the barbarians who lived beyond her boundaries wished to trade or bring tribute to the Emperor, they were required to perform the kowtow in token of humble submission. The
kowtow—"three kneelings and nine prostrations"—were a series of
three separate kneelings, each one leading to three prostrations, nose
upon the floor. That left no doubt who was superior and who inferior. It mattered little how they felt about this, for the kowtow was
part of the Chinese ceremonial life. The Emperor kowtowed to
Heaven and his parents, and the highest officials to the Emperor.

The first 150 years of the Manchu dynasty were among the most
glorious in the history of China. In wealth it probably surpassed any
other country. Literature and art flourished. It maintained power for
as long as any Chinese dynasty. More than half the period was included in the reigns of two of the ablest monarchs China ever had—
K'ang-hsi (1661–1722) and Ch'ien-lung (1736–1796) who gave their
country a century and a half of peace. Ch'ien-lung, a contemporary of
George Washington, reflected the attitude of his country in his famous edict to King George III whose envoy had come seeking trade.
"Our celestial empire possesses all things in prolific abundance and
lacks no product within its borders. There is, therefore, no need to
import the manufactures of outside barbarians."

After all, among many other things, China had made silk and
paper, printed books, made elaborate clocks, steered by compass, and
used gunpowder centuries before Europe. Chinese silk had been taken
westward in Caesar's lifetime; and it was not until about A.D. 560,
when a group of crafty monks smuggled silkworm eggs across Asia
to Byzantium hidden in sections of bamboo, that the six hundred
year Chinese monopoly came to an end. The Roman legions were
still in Britain when the Chinese were using wheelbarrows—something which did not appear in Europe for nearly a thousand years.
And it was not until the sixteenth century, when the Portuguese exported it from China, that the English began to drink tea.

During this period of relative tranquility, the population increased
more rapidly than ever before. From approximately 150 million in
1700 it more than doubled in 1794 (in 1700 the population of all western Europe was estimated at only 54 million). This increase in population resulted not only from the cessation of war and internal strife, but

from the development of commerce. The Portuguese in 1514 and the British in 1637 had opened the China trade. Also between the thirteenth and seventeenth centuries hardy and drought-resistant crops had been introduced into China: corn, sweet potatoes, peanuts, and tobacco. But another plant introduced during this period was to have far-reaching and devastating results. This was the opium poppy which the Portuguese had exported from India to China early in the sixteenth century. Then in turn the Dutch, English, and Americans (after 1810) found it to be their most lucrative trade. But it spoiled great areas of land, ruined millions of homes, and fattened the purses of corrupt officials. The story of Western commerce with the Chinese is one of which we cannot be proud.

By the end of the eighteenth century, when the American republic was just getting started, it was the misfortune of China that the throne passed into the hands of weak and incompetent monarchs. In the most crucial years of its long history, the authority of its rulers was challenged within and without. For this was the time when Western ships and merchants were reaching the Orient. In this meeting of East and West, China was to be shaken as never before. From this time on she was to suffer nearly two hundred years of humiliation and exploitation.

In the past the most dangerous invaders were the barbarous hordes from the north. Now barbarian invaders were arriving by sea in the south. The oceans had at last been spanned and, for the first time, the world was one. Unable to understand the new tide breaking upon its shores, the imperial court and its advisers tried to hold to a policy of isolation. There was a Chinese proverb to the effect that "There is no need to fear ghosts and spirits, but a foreigner who speaks Chinese, that's frightening." To keep these barbarians from destroying the stability of Confucian society, the Emperor decreed the death penalty for any one who taught foreigners "the language of civilization." Also, Canton was made the only port of entry for foreigners and a monopoly on trade was given to a very small association of brokers. Even so the trade with the West grew. There was great demand in England and America for Chinese tea, silk, cotton, and porcelain; but there was little that China wanted from the foreigners except opium.

Although the trade became illegal, the demand for the drug grew rapidly and fortunes were made by foreigners and Chinese alike.

As early as 1727 opium-smoking had become so widespread that the sale of the drug had been prohibited in 1800. In spite of this ban, by 1821 five thousand chests annually were entering Canton, most of it on British vessels but part of it, I am sorry to say, on American ships as well. When in the late 1830s the annual imports amounted to thirty thousand chests, the Manchu government finally intervened and burned a huge consignment belonging to the British. In the Opium War that followed (1840–42), the Chinese musketeers and banner-decked war junks were no match for the British armed frigates.

As a result of the war, Great Britain demanded Hongkong as a crown colony and the opening of five Chinese ports. Other Western powers followed later demanding eleven other ports, extraterritorial rights for their nationals, the opening of legations at the Capital, legalization of opium imports, tolerance for Catholic and Protestant missionary activities, and formal permission to travel inland and to study the Chinese language. Thus began the exploitation of China by the civilized and Christian nations of the West. As one Chinese put it "Westerners came with opium in one hand and a cross in the other."

In addition to these foreign infringements of their sovereign rights, the Manchus were faced with great unrest among the Chinese people. Within the high red walls and gold-tiled roofs of the palace was imperial splendor: the eunuchs, the concubines, court attendants, palace guards, formal audiences, and the kowtow. But internal affairs were deteriorating rapidly. Contemporary writers tell of the decadence and corruption of the Manchus, and of the administrative incompetence in the provinces as well as at the capital. Favorites robbed the imperial treasury. According to John Fairbanks, the favorite minister of Ch'ien-lung when tried for corruption in 1799 was found to have an estate worth (in our money of that time) more than one billion dollars. Another high Manchu at the time of the Opium War was found to have an estate of 425,000 acres of land and $30,000,000 worth of gold, silver, and precious stones.

This corruption, the exorbitant taxes of absentee landlords, natural disasters, and the growing imbalance between population and food supply (by 1850 the population was approaching 400,000,000) all fanned resentment into flames. Many rebellions occurred throughout the century crushed by the imperial armies with foreign help. Provinces were laid waste. Invaluable and irreplaceable books, manuscripts, paintings, and monuments were destroyed. The terrible Taiping Rebellion of 1850, a Chinese revolt against the Manchu government, lasted fourteen years and took 20,000,000 lives. The Manchu ruler at the time was the famous, and infamous, Empress Dowager, Tz'u-hsi, who had risen from being an Imperial concubine to being Empress herself. The Boxer Rebellion of 1900, a revolt against the hated foreigner, brought not only widespread death and destruction but saddled the country with a huge indemnity amounting to $700,000,000 in American currency.

Unlike China, Japan had been an apt pupil of the West. Fifty years after the United States had forced open its ports, Japan had changed from a feudal society to a modern nation—something that in Europe had taken five hundred years. By 1895, she had succeeded in humiliating China by driving her from Korea, by annexing the important Liaotung Peninsula on which Port Arthur was situated, and by acquiring for their nationals in China all the privileges enjoyed by Westerners. Western Powers, convinced that this vast empire was about to disintegrate, struggled for more privileges; Germany, Russia, France, and Great Britain acquired leases on strategic ports. Spheres of influence were marked out and concessions were obtained for lending money at high interest rates to build railroads.

Because China's independence seemed threatened, reforms were quickly undertaken. An imperial edict encouraged education by directing the creation of new schools and the introduction of Western subjects into the curricula. The National Peking University was established by imperial order. Thus began a remarkable expansion of education by both the government and the foreign missionary groups. In 1905 the Emperor abolished the ancient classical examination system begun in the first century, B.C. The "new learning" now became the road to a political or scholarly career. But the reforms came too late.

In the past, invaders and conquerors had adopted from China most of what civilization they possessed and always preserved the native institutions. An old proverb says: "China is a sea that salts all the rivers that flow into it." Ideas had come from abroad but the structure of Chinese life was very little changed. Now invaders were coming who possessed a high degree of civilization, a civilization very different from that of China. Far from adopting Chinese civilization they regarded China as backward and semibarbarous. The admiration of the Middle Kingdom which was once strong in Europe now was gone. In the eighteenth century, French philosophers such as Voltaire hailed Confucian China as the model of the truly rational state. Toward contemporary China there was mostly irritation and condescension. The conflict became one of civilizations; in China, in this clash, the institutions of 2,000 years began to crumble.

Chinese students had been permitted to study abroad as early as 1867. But now they went abroad in increasing numbers. Japan became the gathering place for the young nationalists who were beginning to think along revolutionary lines. Their leader, Sun Yat-sen, a remarkable man born of peasant stock near Canton in 1866, received a Western schooling in Honolulu and western medical training in Hong-kong. When he was barely twenty he became interested in national reform. In 1894 he embarked on a revolutionary career. He had already organized a secret society, the *Hsuig Chung Hui* ("Revise China Society"). Its purpose was to overthrow the Manchus and to save China by improving the livelihood of the people through education and the use of modern methods in agriculture and in industry. Farmers and artisans who made up 85 percent of the people were still using tools in effect centuries before; the wheelbarrow was still a means of transportation.

The original revolutionary slogan was "Down with the Manchus." They were foreigners and their dynasty an alien one. Between 1907 and 1911 there were ten unsuccessful uprisings. On October 10, 1911, now celebrated as the Birthday of the Republic, the revolution erupted and brought to an end the empire which had begun during the third century B.C.

The Manchu Emperor, then six years old, formally abdicated February 12, 1912. His regent instructed Yuan Shih-k'ai, once Imperial

Commissioner in charge of all China's armed forces, to establish a republic. It was agreed that the emperor was to retain his title for life, was to receive a large annuity, and was to keep his private property and the use of the palace.

At a national council representing the revolutionists assembled at Nanking, Yuan was eventually elected Provincial President of the Republic. He succeeded in keeping the capital at Peking and his government was recognized by the foreign powers. By a joint resolution of the United States Congress, China was welcomed as a republic: "Whereas the Chinese Nation has successfully asserted that sovereignty resides in the people" and whereas the American people are "inherently and by tradition sympathetic to all efforts to adopt representative government," therefore the United States "congratulates the people of China on their assumption of the powers, duties and responsibilities of self government . . . the happiness of the Chinese people will be secure and the progress of the country insured."

But it was not to be so. The people of China were far from ready for self-government.

In accepting this new post, Yuan was to work with a parliament and cabinet under the terms of a new constitution. But parliament when elected was dominated by the radicals who had brought about the revolution. Yuan Shih-k'ai was the most powerful military figure in the country, a leader who represented the old style in China's politics, a man capable of taking full responsibility for his regime. Gradually he strengthened his position, put his own men into the cabinet, disregarded the spirit of the constitution, attacked Sun Yat-sen's new political party, the Kuomintang, and eventually dissolved parliament in an attempt to become emperor. The attempt failed. Yuan Shih-k'ai, frustrated in his life's ambition and made ill by shame and anger, died on June 6, 1916. In 1916 Woodrow Wilson was president of the United States, and the war in Europe had begun.

After Yuan's death, China broke up into feudal warlord areas although the government at Peking continued to receive international recognition. Each warlord had his own army, each army its district. The great warlords governed entire provinces and fought each other as they sought to control Peking and win the Mandate of Heaven. They waxed fat on opium trade, extorted taxes from peasants years in advance, and wrung land from original owners to add to their own estates. Of the five leading warlords, one had begun life as a peddler, another a fiddler, two rose from the rank of private, and one had been a bandit.

In the meantime at Canton there was organized the Chinese National Military government. In September 1917, Sun Yat-sen formally assumed the headship of the new regime and declared it to be the only constitutional government of China. So China was divided between the warlord government at Peking and the revolutionary regime in the south.

When I arrived in Peking in September 1923, Ts'ao K'un, a former military aide to Yuan Shih-k'ai, had just become president with the help of two powerful warlords: Wu P'ei-fu, a mandarin who had passed the classical examinations, and Feng Yu-hsiang, a peasant who had been converted to Christianity and was known as the "Christian General." However, when it later became known that Ts'ao had bought the votes of some five hundred members of Parliament, opposition built up against him. On September 18, 1924, Sun Yat-sen declared his opposition to President Ts'ao and threatened the launching of a Northern Expedition to overthrow the warlords and the foreign imperialists who supported them. Chang Tso-lin, an ex-bandit who had been born in poverty but who had become Lord of Manchuria, also announced his opposition to Ts'ao.

By the beginning of October, fighting had broken out between the forces of Chang and the forces of Wu at the eastern end of the Great Wall, north of Peking. Feng Yu-hsiang was defending a strategic pass in the Great Wall in support of Wu. When the fighting was heaviest, in mid-October, Feng abandoned his defense position and his support of Wu. He moved swiftly on Peking, took the city, and closed the city gates.

At the T'ung Fu we were involved very little in all of this turmoil. The following letter describes the first direct contact I had with political activities.

T'ung Fu
October 24, 1924

Dear Father;

The city gates are to be opened this morning to let a mail car go through, so I can't resist sending off some word to you. It was yesterday at four o'clock in the morning that the troops of Feng Yu-hsiang, the Christian General, took over the city.

Here at the T'ung Fu we knew nothing of what was happening until eleven o'clock when word came from the legation that we must not venture north of Teng Shih K'ou nor west of Morrison, a street not more than five minutes walk from the college. The city was under military authority, the city gates closed, telephone communications cut off, and every street and corner guarded by soldiers. I had classes all morning so I didn't realize what had happened until tiffin time. Can you imagine my amazement to learn that General Feng and three other generals had formed a provisional government in Peking, that Ts'ao K'un had abdicated, that 30,000 troops had entered the city without a single foreign legation knowing it, and that General Munther's troops (the foreign guard of Peking) had been ordered into their quarters and kept behind sealed gates.

I had ordered my pony for two o'clock because I was expected out at Hatien (a small village beyond the west gate of the city) for tea. It was impossible to go into the west city, but I got on my pony anyway to have a look at what was happening. On the street north of Teng Shih K'ou hundreds of soldiers were camping. Tents were in the streets and soldiers still had their blanket rolls thrown over their shoulders and their tea pots tied around their waists. Though no one could go farther than their encampment, there was no disorder anywhere. On the p'ai-lou, not far from the encampment, the heads of two soldiers had been hung as a warning against looting. These two men had attempted to steal from an old woman and had been killed in order to show other soldiers that looting would not be tolerated.

Going south one would never have guessed that anything out of the ordinary was happening. There were soldiers scattered here and there, but shops were open and the streets were filled as usual with rickshas, carts, and automobiles. I was out for an hour altogether and saw nothing to make me think there was to be the slightest danger. However, later in the afternoon I went out calling. When I came back to the T'ung Fu after dark, the streets were practically deserted. An order had been sent out from all legations for foreigners to stay off the streets after six o'clock.

It was interesting to hear the various explanations that were given for Feng's move. No one knew last night what had happened—whether Feng had deserted Wu Pei-fu, whether he wanted to be president, or whether Chang Tso-lin had defeated the government troops. It seems clear, now, that General Feng is determined to bring about peace in the most effective way. He has declared that there will be no fighting in Peking, and that no one has any reason to be afraid. However, the government has been completely revolutionized and for a while there will be only a dictatorship over the city. There has been no disturbance so far. There was not a sound last night and this morning everything is going on as usual. It is said that Feng's soldiers came into the city after hours of marching singing a song to the tune of "Hark, the Herald Angels Sing." There is a rumor that he baptizes all his soldiers with a hose.

When I think of the quiet, unassuming man whom I met at dinner last spring I can hardly believe it is the same man who has surprised the whole of China. His wife is a Yenching girl and I met him here with her. Faculty members who know him well say his soldiers study the Bible and are admonished by such slogans as "Honor thy Father and Mother, We must not smoke nor drink, We must not gamble nor visit whores." Because they are well fed and well paid they do not desert him.

T'ung Fu
October 28, 1924

Dear Family:

I wish you knew how safe I am sitting in front of a glowing fire as happy as can be. I fear for what the papers have been publishing about the capture of the city. I should have cabled yesterday when telegraph communications were resumed, but the legation sent out official notices that a wireless message had been sent to Washington assuring them that all was safe within the city walls.

A notice came to us in the morning saying a van would be allowed to pass through the gates to take mail to Tientsin in time to catch the Siberian steamer. At that time we were not quite sure what was going to happen, and that night we were all uneasy. I came back from a rehearsal at the Men's College about eight o'clock. The streets were dark—against the blackness one could see only the shadowy form of a soldier carrying a gun with fixed bayonet. Periodically one would stop me to ask who I was and demanding that I go home directly. A curfew was to be rung at nine o'clock and anyone on the street after that time would be arrested. The stillness and the darkness seemed ominous.

It is to me a miracle that such an event could have taken place with no disturbance of any kind. There have been no riots. People have been about their business as usual. If it were not for the encampments of soldiers here and there, one would never guess that anything had happened. The legations and the Chinese themselves have been taken so by surprise that only rumors fly about. Whether C. T. Wang and W. W. Yen, Minister of Foreign Affairs, are the brains behind the move is uncertain. Of course, people are divided in their opinion of Feng's move; on the whole it seems that no one wholly trusts him even though he is a Christian general. Yet it is hoped he will prove strong enough to complete his plans of stopping the war and uniting the country.

Yesterday telephone communications were resumed and last night all forebodings were gone. I went out to dinner at the bank and didn't get home until after midnight. We were not stopped once. Apparently, everything is over and Feng is only waiting for Tuan Chi Jui to arrive in Peking to become Provisional Chief Executive. He was Premier under Yuan Chi-kai.

This morning there is a rumor that Feng Yu-hsiang has driven the little Emperor and his wife from the palace. Evidently they were found selling some of the palace treasures. It is believed they have fled to Tientsin and have taken refuge in the Japanese Concession.

You cannot imagine how strong the feeling is against the Japanese. Last week a meeting of our faculty was called to decide whether or not to accept as a student the daughter of a Japanese Christian minister. There was no question among the foreign members. We expressed a unanimous opinion in favor of accepting her. But Dr. T. T. Lew, head of our theology department, a graduate of Yale University and Columbia Graduate School, said very simply that such a thing was impossible. He explained that ever since Japan had made its notorious Twenty-one Demands in 1915, China had considered herself at war with the country. For those who did not know about these demands he explained that they were designed to put Japan in administrative and economic control of China. Among other things, they required that China confirm Japan's seizure of Germany's leased territory in the strategic Shantung peninsula; concede trade, rail, and industrial concessions in Manchuria, and agree not to contract concessions or loans with other powers without Japan's consent. The Chinese faculty members were as unanimous against admitting the student as we had been for admitting her. Needless to say she was not admitted.

I am busy as usual, so I am not accepting any evening invitations except for Saturday night. One of the bank men, George Johnston, is being very attentive this fall and I am getting fond of him. I met him shortly after I arrived in Peking—at my first houseparty in the Western Hills. His charming manner impressed me at the time; and as I watched him ask another girl to go to a concert, I secretly hoped he would ask me to go with him somewhere, sometime. As a matter of fact, I have seen little of him until lately. He enjoys literature and art so we have much in common. It was he who invited me to the bank Saturday night. There were only six of us. After dinner we sat before the fire listening to his beautiful records until very late. One of the guests was Mrs. Powell-Clayton of Washington, a cousin of Lady Astor's. She is charming. I thought her the most beautiful woman I had ever met.

P.S. You will be interested to know that George's bank is The International Banking Corporation founded by General Thomas H. Hubbard, a Bowdoin graduate in the class of 1857. He was born in Hallowell, Maine, and George tells me that he was a well-known military figure during the Civil War. The president of the bank now is Charles Bennett who grew up in Yarmouth, Maine. What a small world this is! All the bank officers have apartments on the upper floors of the huge bank building. George has a spacious one, beautifully furnished. He has collected Chinese rugs, rare pieces of porcelain, scrolls, an exquisite pair of jade trees, and a few pieces of Chinese carved furniture. The dinner he gave was done to perfection.

Iolanthe and a Basket of Flowers

W HEN MY CLASSES WERE WELL UNDERWAY, when the little Chinese play was over, and before the troops of Feng Yu-hsiang had disturbed the peace of Peking, I began to plan for the Gilbert and Sullivan operetta which I had promised the Peking Players I would produce for them in the month of December. *Iolanthe* had been chosen not only because I had seen it produced at the Bennett School, but because I knew the wealth of musical talent in Peking, especially at Yenching. I saw a perfect Iolanthe in the stately wife of a chemistry professor at the Men's College who had a gorgeous voice. And I felt that the incomparable and charming head of our philosophy department would be the hit of the show as my Lord High Chancellor—and he was.

All went well from the beginning. Many members of the "Players" volunteered for parts and stage jobs. The conductor of the White Russian orchestra agreed to provide the music, and an extremely able cast was assembled. Rehearsals did not always go smoothly for periodically the temperamental Russian conductor resigned, convinced that the performance would never take place. I had to spend precious hours with him just to keep things going.

But the performance did take place. Every seat in the house was sold as soon as the production was announced, with all boxes reserved for the ministers of the various legations. It was a gala occasion, to be repeated at the request of some Chinese at their moving picture theater where we packed the biggest auditorium in Peking! The proceeds kept the Peking Players going for years. An interesting aftermath was the performance of *Pinafore* given by members of the British colony. They were not going to be outdone by the Americans in producing a Gilbert and Sullivan operetta—and who could blame them?

A magnificent basket of flowers was presented to me at the final curtain of *Iolanthe* with a card "from George." We became close friends after that, exchanging our books, going to concerts, and just getting to know each other. On beautiful winter days when the sun was bright and warm we loved to ride our ponies far into the hills.

The beauty of China seemed to us beyond words, there was no end to it.

George's unexpected transfer to the Hongkong office of the bank brought things to a head. He asked to call one evening. As this was something unusual I had a feeling that I knew what was to happen. I asked Chu Pu, our number one boy, not to bank the fire in the living room that night because I was to have a guest. Chu Pu must have peeked through the door as we sat in front of the fire, for the next morning the news was spread all over the campus: "Chai Chao-shih (my Chinese name) is going to be married soon." And so it was that our engagement was prematurely announced; George left for Hongkong a week later.

A long letter to my sister Carolyn about all of this ended:

Mother probably wrote you about the cable I sent giving the date of the formal announcement, a cable that cost me $15. Since the announcement there has been a flood of notes because all of our friends are delighted and surprised about our engagement. It had all happened so suddenly that we were able to keep a secret in this city where news usually flies on wings.

The very first note I opened came from Mrs. Henry Luce. Her son has just started a new magazine called *Time*—do you know it? She wrote "I liked Mr. Johnston a great deal because his sincerity and high-mindedness appealed to me from the first. Besides, his kindness of heart and charm of manner proved him to be the gentleman that he really is—a rare combination of virtues it seems to me."

Everyone in Peking likes and respects George—you will, too! We have no plans for a wedding because I have another year at the college and George's furlough won't begin probably until early in 1926.

My students were elated over my engagement. I gathered from them that nothing was more important to the Chinese than mating. In the old days and even among the conservative families when I was there, mating was controlled by family prudence—a girl's marriage was arranged and not for love. Often engagements were made early in life and couples did not see each other until the wedding day. Even then they did not set up separate households but entered the husband's father's household and became a part of the family system.

But in the 1920s marriage customs were beginning to change; some young people were being allowed to choose their own mates. As a result nothing pleased them more than a happy ending to a romance.

My students now had a romance at hand. They inundated me with gifts. The student body presented me with a pair of scrolls with handsome black calligraphy on vermillion paper (the color of joy) and wished me the five blessings: prosperity, tranquility, health, long life and many children. I was especially touched when one girl brought me a piece of family jewelry—a gold pin with three short chains, each chain tipped with a jade symbol of fertility. She told me if I would wear this after I was married, it would bring me a son! From Jui T'ang came an elegant pair of ceremonial tea cups, each with a cover and base of silver, beautifully displayed in a large glass box.

Almost at once my "embroidery man" appeared at the T'ung Fu not only to present me with a little gift, but to show me a lovely seventeenth century scroll which he said had come recently from the palace. It was exquisite embroidery and painting on cream-colored silk of a gentleman, dressed in a light blue gown, sitting in meditation under a high mountain; his horse and servant waited nearby. Because it reflected the serenity of so many Chinese paintings I fell in love with it. I bought it at once together with a lovely piece of tribute silk —eight yards of robin's egg blue brocade woven with a rose pattern of gold thread—for now I was to have a home of my very own to furnish some day!

All of these things, the gifts as well as my purchases, I have and still treasure today—happy memories of "the June of my life."

* * *

Life in Peking during the winter of 1924–1925 was as glamourous as ever—but for me there was a difference. I was in love. I could not get George out of my mind. He was there when I woke up in the morning and when I went to sleep at night. It troubled me that so often thoughts of him came into my mind even in my classroom. His letters were read over and over again. Hongkong seemed worlds away. It would be a year before we could be together again. Yet I knew that somehow I had to keep going.

I was thankful that I had a heavy schedule of classes which kept me busy. I assigned extra work which meant extra conferences. Because the winter was bitter cold and my classroom was almost unbearable, I had all conferences at the Women's College in my study. The girls loved to come to my little house. After we had discussed their work, they usually stayed on just to visit and to sit by the fire. I enjoyed these times as much as they did, and I think I came to know them as well as any Westerner can ever know an Oriental. They loved to tell me stories about their families and about the queer ideas some of their parents had about the "foreigners." An old story which delighted us all told of a father, a Confucianist, asking his son one Sunday, "Where were you this morning?"

"I was at church of the Christians," answered the boy.

"Christians? What are they?"

"They are people who have done what they should not have done and have left undone what they should have done. That is what they say of themselves, openly, and in unison."

I was impressed by their beautiful manners—an art in China, the result of centuries of training. I found them far less sophisticated than my American students, yet beneath their childlike simplicity there was a depth of feeling, an amazing knowledge of life, and a real sense of values. This quality of simplicity was characteristic of all the Chinese with whom I came into contact—from my amah to distinguished scholars like Chang Poling. To me it was utterly appealing.

Most of my students were very sensitive. I had learned early not to criticize their work in the classroom nor to ask a girl to go on the stage the night of a dress rehearsal without a proper costume. These things they considered an affront to their personal dignity. By some thoughtless word it was easy to wound their self respect—a wound that was hard to heal. This was all a matter of oriental "face"—something I understand no longer exists in China, at least to the extent that I knew it. All of my students were intelligent; some were extremely able and gifted. For me they typified the vitality of their great race. Others shared this feeling. Bertrand Russell had said in an interview when he was in China in 1923 while the horrors of World War I were still in our minds:

I have come to realize that the white race isn't as important as I used to think it was. If Europe and America kill themselves off in war it will not necessarily mean the destruction of the human species, nor even an end to civilization. There will still be a considerable number of Chinese left; and in many ways China is the greatest country I have ever seen. It is not only the greatest numerically and the greatest culturally, but it seems to me the greatest intellectually. I know of no other civilization where there is such open-mindedness, such realism, such a willingness to face the facts as they are.

Probably the most outstanding characteristic of my students both at the Men's College and the Women's College was their unquenchable zeal for learning. This was something deeply embedded in their civilization, for throughout their history most advancement had come through intellectual attainments. In the China that I knew, the scholar was at the top of the social scale, then came the farmer; the tradesman and the soldier were at the bottom. There was an old Chinese saying that "Good iron is not used to make a nail nor a good man to make a soldier."

At the Men's College that winter I began to sense more than the traditional reason for their zeal. Toward the end of the term after all required work had been completed, the men asked to use the class time for speeches. They loved to speak; at times it was difficult to stop them. From their discussions I thought I caught the "new spirit" which P. C. and Hu Shih had talked about.

It was obvious that the foreign exploitation of their country was very much on their minds and that they were deeply disturbed by it. They knew about the treaty-port system with its foreign-controlled residential areas, about foreign "dollar diplomacy" that forced loans on China for construction of railroads at high interest rates, about the gunboats on the Yangtze and the foreign navigational rights on all of China's inland waterways. Wherever they looked they saw part of their country's sovereignty in the hands of foreigners. Foreign banks financed industry and trade; foreign courts administered extraterritorial law, and foreign post offices distributed foreign mail. They realized that they and all young men of their generation must catch the scientific spirit. They must learn something about modern governments; they must become engineers so that they could open their mines, lay roads, and build railroads to unify their vast country. They knew that if they did not do these things for themselves, the Western Powers would continue to do it for them. This sense of responsibility was developing in them an intense feeling of nationalism.

My own sympathies had been aroused early against the humiliating terms of foreign treaties and the unfair privileges enjoyed by all foreigners. But what concerned all of us at Yenching was the feeling that this nationalism was being aggravated by agents of Soviet Russia who were stirring up a strong antiforeign feeling all over the north. There was a rumor, later confirmed, that two of our Yenching students were in the pay of these agents.

In March my students were all greatly saddened by the death of Sun Yat-sen whom they held in deep veneration. I had gone with some of them to greet him on his arrival in Peking. He had come north two months before to collaborate with the Peking Government in the hope of unifying this divided and troubled land. One of the men students brought me a copy of his will which had just been published.

I devoted my life to my country in a futile attempt to raise our nation again to a state of good internal government and a place of independence among world nations. My experience has absolutely convinced me that to attain this goal we must enlist the support of the great mass of our people at home and abroad to work in cooperation with those nations (like Russia) that treat us on a basis of equality.

The revolutionary movement has not succeeded. It therefore is imperative that all my fellow workers should do their utmost in order to realize my "Reconstruction Plan," my "Outlines of Reconstructive Policies," and my "Three Principles of the People." Fight on, my fellow workers, with renewed vigor, to bring about a People's Convention for the solution of our national problems and to abolish the unequal treaties with foreign nations. These things must be done in the shortest time.

The spring term began uneasily.

Russia and the Kuomintang

> "To know nothing of the past is
> to understand little of the present
> and to have no conception of the
> future."

FROM THE VANTAGE POINT of the 1970s when the nations of the world are only hours apart and television brings instant news, it is difficult to realize how far apart they were only fifty years ago. In the 1920s it took a month to reach China, yet from the clipper ship days, it had seemed a fascinating, alluring, and highly civilized part of the world. Russia, on the other hand, although a part of Europe, seemed to me distant and remote. I always pictured it in winter and thought of the people bundled up in furs riding in their troikas. The Russian Revolution took place when I was in college, and although I sensed that it was an important event of history, it seemed far removed from my life. The news of the assassinations, the bloodshed, the terror, and the misery horrified me, but somehow it did not touch me. The very word "Bolshevik" sounded uncivilized. Russia and China in the 1920s seemed to me worlds apart.

Therefore when the Washington Conference took place in 1921, it did not surprise me that the Bolsheviks were not invited. China had been invited, for China was part of what the conference was all about. Secretary of State Charles Evans Hughes, a promoter of the conference, was the father of one of my college friends. (At Wellesley on the night of November 7, 1916, we went to bed believing that he had been elected President of the United States; but Woodrow Wilson had defeated him.) Mr. Hughes was for me the epitome of an American gentleman and diplomat. With the conference in his hands everything seemed safe.

Not until I found myself in China did certain pieces of history begin to mesh. By 1925 the legation life had lost much of its glamour; not only was I engaged to be married but I had begun to be more deeply involved with my students and colleagues at Yenching as well as with friends at the Chinese universities.

I had travelled enough in the Chinese countryside to know about the poverty and misery of the peasants. I saw in the streets of Peking not only the fascinating pageantry but the filth, disease, and plight of many of the people. I could understand why China had to change, why the impact of the West in the nineteenth century, although inevitable, had caused such a convulsion that the effects were still being felt and would continue to be felt for a long, long time to come. It had brought about more profound changes in a century than China had experienced in 1,000 years. It was as if the Renaissance, the Reformation, and the Industrial Revolution had all happened in one generation. No longer would it be possible to bask in its glorious past; China must now look to the future.

I began to understand more perceptively what the Cultural Revolution had meant to this proud country isolated for so long from the Western World. I could understand and sympathize too, with the growing antiforeign feeling and the surge of nationalism. But what deeply disturbed me was my growing awareness that something sinister was happening with regard to the Russians who recently had been coming into the country and who were getting increasingly involved with the Kuomintang.

What had happened to make possible this present detente between the Kuomintang and the Communists? Sun Yat-sen, the nominal head of the Kuomintang, rejected the Soviet's idea that social progress must come by way of class war. He believed the modern era had been determined not by the clash but by the cooperation of capital, machinery, and labor. For him the fight in China was against illiteracy of the masses, ignorance about science, backwardness of the economy and sanitation, individual selfishness, and disunity of the nation. Why then was he now allying himself with this Communist country? The answer was simple and tragic. The United States and the other Western Powers whom he and his followers wished to emulate rejected their cries for help. Russia, on the other hand, was eager and ready to respond.

The intellectual ferment which resulted in part from the substitution of the vernacular for the written classical language was centered in Peking University. Dr. Stuart, our Yenching president, often referred to this university as "the intellectual dynamo of the nation." In 1917 the chancellor, a courageous advocate of freedom of thought and expression, had invited Ch'en Tu-hsui to serve as dean of letters and Hu Shih to lecture as a professor of philosophy. Mao Tse-tung at the time was a student of Hu Shih's and an assistant librarian. Ch'en Tu-hsui, the son of a wealthy family, had absorbed in France the tradition of the French Revolution and had returned to China in 1915, to found a magazine called *The New Youth*. In his first issue Ch'en, who deplored the antiquated and decadent elements he saw in Chinese society, wrote:

We indeed do not know which of our traditional institutions may be fit for survival in the modern world. I would rather see the ruin of our "national quintessence" than have our race of the present and future extinguished because of its unfitness for survival. Alas, the Babylonians are gone; of what use is their civilization to them now? The world continually progresses and will not stop. All those who cannot change themselves and keep pace with it are unfit for survival and will be eliminated by the process of natural selection.

Many other periodicals followed in which the scholars of this revolutionary generation discussed in *pai-hua* the application of Western ideas to China's ancient culture.

When World War I ended in 1918 the Chinese were jubilant believing that the Allied victory was one of democracy over tyranny and the rule of law over militarism. Wilson's promise of a just peace and self-determination had not only lifted the spirits of the world, it had fired the hopes of these ardent young Chinese. Peking University became the center of Chinese nationalism.

Then on May 4, 1919, the decisions of the Paris Peace Conference became known. Not only had the conference confirmed Japan as successor to all German concessions in Shantung, but China's plea for the cancellation of the "unequal treaties" had been ignored. Many conservatives who knew the West well and had come to admire its culture began to think that perhaps China's culture was, after all, the better way. Yen Fu, who had been educated at the University of Edinburgh and was a pioneer in translating Western philosophical works into Chinese wrote:

Western culture, after this European War, has been corrupted utterly.... Formerly, when I heard our scholars of the old school say that there would come a day when the teachings of Confucius would be practiced by all mankind, I thought they were talking nonsense. But now I find that some of the most enlightened men in Europe seem to be coming gradually to a like opinion.... It seems to me that in three centuries of progress the peoples of the West have achieved four principles: to be selfish, to kill others, to have little integrity, and to feel little shame. How different are the principles of Confucius and Mencius, as broad and deep as Heaven and Earth, designed to benefit all men everywhere.

Profoundly disillusioned with the Western Powers and greatly impressed by the effective mass action of the students and the Chinese people in the May 4 demonstrations, several leading intellectuals including Ch'en Tu-hsiu and some young men, including Mao Tse-tung and Chou En-lai, became increasingly interested in the revolutionary experience of the Bolsheviks which had recently taken place in Russia. To counteract this incipient Bolshevik influence, Hu Shih and the more conservative intellectuals invited the American philosopher John Dewey and the British philosopher Bertrand Russell to visit China and present other points of view. John Dewey, who was still in China when I arrived, lectured to enormous and enthusiastic audiences; and among the middle-of-the-road liberals there were many adherents to his plea for a rule of rationalism and liberal humanism. But his beliefs suffered from association with the West. The left wing was unmoved.

In May during the student demonstrations, *The New Youth* dedicated a special issue of the magazine to Marxism. By December a Society for the Study of Socialism appeared on the campus of the University with Ch'en Tu-hsiu, Mao Tse-tung, and some one hundred other professors and students among its members.

What finally led Ch'en Tu-hsiu and his associates to accept Marxism and eventually to organize a Chinese Communist Party were the friendly overtures of Soviet Russia. In contrast to the Western Powers' continued policy of exploitation, the Soviet government announced its intention to return to the Chinese people the Chinese Eastern Railroad and all privileges and concessions seized by the Tsarist regime. The Soviet government also promised support of the Chinese people in their struggle for complete freedom from the Western Powers. When this declaration became publicly known in China, the Society for the Study of Marxist Theory was initiated and the full text of the Communist Manifesto was published for the first time in the Chinese language.

The Bolsheviks undertook to press their advantage further. Three members of the Party arrived in China and sought to give added organization and purpose to the rising tide of Chinese nationalism. As a result, in May 1920 at Shanghai, the first revolutionary Marxist cell was formed. It comprised seven members of the intelligentsia, with Ch'en Tu-hsiu as its leader, and was to become the nucleus of the future Chinese Communist Party. A second cell was established in Peking. Mao Tse-tung, teaching at an elementary school in his native Hunan Province, set up another cell in Changsha. On November 7, 1920, the third anniversary of the Bolshevik Revolution in Russia, the first number of the magazine *Communist* appeared in Shanghai. More cells were formed in Tientsin, Hangchow, Canton as well as among Chinese students studying in France. Many members of the French group, in Paris for advanced education, were to hold high positions in the Communist regime, among them Chou En-lai, a man with a brilliant mind and great personal charm.

Toward the end of June 1921, twelve delegates representing some fifty-seven Chinese Marxists gathered in the French Concession in Shanghai to organize a national Communist Party; among them was Mao Tse-tung. The group was nearly caught by the French Concession police so the meeting place was shifted to a lake in Chekiang Province about fifty miles south of Shanghai. There on July 1, 1921, posing as a group of vacationing sightseers they rented a boat, took a picnic lunch, finished their deliberations, and formally established the Chinese Communist Party.

It was during that winter that China was the focus of international attention as a result of the Washington Conference convened to discuss Far Eastern questions. Secretary of State Charles Evans Hughes and former Secretary Elihu Root (winner of the Nobel Peace Prize in 1912) wanted America to exhibit responsibility in world affairs and expiate the rejection of the League of Nations. Among the countries invited to attend the conference in addition to the major powers were

Italy, Belgium, Portugal, and the Warlord government in Peking. Russia, with more than half its territory in Asia and bordering on both China and the Pacific, was not invited. Instead, the convening powers declared that they would themselves "take into consideration the interests of Russia, without the latter's representation, and reserve the right of inviting eventually a new Russian Government which should replace the present one." Russia considered this offer to a counter-revolutionary government as "a hostile act." They warned: "A policy tending to leave Russia outside the collective decisions of various powers on questions concerning her, far from conducing to the settlement of conflicts at present disturbing the world, can only render them more acute and more complicated." This protest was ignored as was a new note sent to the United States, Britain, France, Italy, and Japan.

What China wanted from the conference as proof of her independence was cancellation of the unequal treaties. American public opinion supported this aim but Secretary Hughes and his policy makers were not prepared to go that far. However, Hughes insisted that China should at least regain the province of Shantung. It took thirty-six meetings to reach a settlement by which Japan agreed by treaty to return this leased territory.

The chief result of the conference which lasted from November 1921 to February 1922, was the Nine Power Treaty. In part it pledged the contracting parties: (1) "To respect the Sovereignty, independence and territorial and administrative integrity of China; (2) To provide the fullest and most unembarrassed opportunity to China to develop and maintain for herself an effective and stable government"; and (3) To refrain from taking advantage of conditions in China "to seek special rights or privileges" which would abridge the rights of citizens of friendly states.

Not being represented, Moscow was not committed. In fact, while the Washington Conference was still in session, Russia held a conference of its own. The Comintern, an international organization of Communist parties, inscribed on its banner "World Revolution" and made it known that the European revolution was only a fraction of the world revolution. They stated that victory would not come until the Far Eastern questions had been resolved. The manifesto adopted by the Congress was addressed to the people of the Far East and ended: "We declare war to the death on the Japanese, American, British, French, and all other world plunderers. We declare war to the death on the warlords and lackeys of our oppressors in China. . . . We declare war to the death on the hypocritical American imperialism and the greedy British usurpers. Out with them from China, Korea, The Pacific Islands, Indo-China, and the Dutch Indies!"

Late in June 1922, Sun Yat-sen was approached by a delegate of the Communist Youth International with a proposal for an alliance between the Kuomintang and the Chinese Communist Party. Sun rejected the offer but agreed to let members of the Party join as individuals. After all there were only 300 Communists in China in 1922, whereas the Kuomintang numbered 150,000. Desperately in need of foreign support and rebuffed by the Western Powers, Sun was hoping by working with individual Communists to secure Soviet assistance for his party and enable it to undertake the arduous task of eliminating the warlords and reconstructing the country. Six months later Adolph Joffe, Lenin's envoy, met with Sun Yat-sen and a foundation was laid for a broad measure of collaboration between the U.S.S.R. and the Kuomintang.

Shortly after Joffe's arrival, the American Minister Jacob Gould Schurman visited Canton. Sun Yat-sen took this opportunity to make one final approach to the West. He called upon the American minister and proposed that the United States pursuade other foreign powers to undertake a joint intervention in China for a period of five years. His plan was to have the Western Powers help with the rehabilitation of both national and local governments. Eventually elections would be held and the foreign administrators would train Chinese personnel to succeed them. The proposition was not viewed favorably as is seen by the instruction given to all American Consular officers in China.

The Department of State believes that foreign nations should stand as far as possible aloof from internal dissensions in China and accordingly desires that officials of the United States in China adhere to strict impartiality. . . .

In August therefore in furtherance of the new relationship with

Russia, Sun Yat-sen sent a mission to Moscow led by Chiang Kai-shek. The Soviets in return sent to Canton, as a personal adviser to Sun, Michael Borodin, an able organizer who had lived in the United States and had taught school in Chicago. As Borodin arrived in Canton, a new Soviet envoy, Karakhan, arrived in Peking—just one week before I arrived at Yenching.

Chiang Kai-Shek returned from Moscow in time to see a display of foreign military power. Sun's Canton government had demanded that Canton and not Peking should receive the southern provinces' share of the maritime customs surplus. The request was ignored but Canton was not to be denied. Whereupon Secretary of State Hughes reported to President Coolidge, "The local Canton government under the leadership of Sun Yat-sen and in professed independence of the recognized government of China is threatening to seize the Canton Customs House and to collect on its own behalf the Customs revenue of that port." He added that the representatives in Peking recommend "a concentration of the available naval units of the powers having war vessels on the China stations in order to deter the Canton government from its threatened course of action." President Coolidge concurred.

The United States joined Britain, France, Japan, Italy, and Portugal in the naval demonstration at Canton, and the integrity of the Chinese Maritime Customs was preserved. Sun Yat-sen's answer was: "We no longer look to the Western Powers. Our faces are turned toward Russia." It was two years after the Western Powers had convened in Washington to settle the problems of the Pacific.

On Borodin's advice, work on reorganization of the Kuomintang was begun. When Chiang returned from Moscow and gave his support to this reform project, the Kuomintang was remodeled on the pattern of the Communist Party of the Soviet Union. The platform comprised three major policies: (1) alliance with the Soviet Union in foreign affairs; (2) collaboration with the Chinese Communist party in domestic affairs; and (3) creation of a base among the workers and peasants. Not only were Communists accepted for individual membership in the Kuomintang but three were elected to the party's new

Central Executive Committee. (Mao Tse-tung was one of six Communists elected as reserve members.)

The Russian advisers together with Russian arms and other Russian support produced a profound change in Kuomintang affairs. Sun Yat-sen was told that the first requirement of a revolution was an indoctrinated armed force. Accordingly a Military Academy with thirty Russian instructors under the direction of a Soviet General was founded at Whampoa. Chiang Kai-shek was appointed head of the academy, and because of the control of the Revolutionary Army which went with the Whampoa post he eventually became the dominant figure of the Kuomintang. The able young French-educated Communist Chou En-lai was Chiang's deputy political commissar.

Sun was also taught the value of propaganda. He was told that the people cannot be aroused by a vague ideal of national unity; an oppressor must be found responsible for the deplorable condition of misery, poverty, and want. China seemed to have no oppressors like the Russian Czar and his favorites, but "the foreigner" was found to be the cause of all the trouble. Since the Chinese had always been distrustful of the foreigner—not without reason—it would not be difficult to fan this feeling into a flame at the appropriate moment. This also pleased the Russians who saw an easy way to pay off old scores for not being admitted into the comity of nations. Antiforeignism, unequal treaties, and foreign exploitation were the slogans on which the national movement surged forward.

The Soviet government continued to deal with the Peking government and the warlords in North China, but the Comintern in the meantime worked for revolution. Soviet propaganda concentrated upon British "imperialism" believing that "Great Britain is the most powerful of all nations and if she falls, the entire structure of foreign rights and privileges in China will fall."

It was not long before trouble began to brew between the radical and the more conservative elements of the Kuomintang. Sun Yat-sen made a desperate effort to unite the party. Finally despairing of unity in the group at Canton, he came north to rally Peking to an understanding of the need to establish a strong national party. (Borodin on his way to Urga accompanied him incognito.) Worn out by conferences and interviews he was hospitalized at the Peking Union Medical College and died of cancer March 12, 1925. Three days after his death, Chiang Kai-shek, leader of the right wing, led a movement to oust the Communists and prevent Borodin from returning. His three months in Russia in 1923 had left him aware of Soviet methods and suspicious of Communist aims. He and his associates wanted national sovereignty. The Communist-left coalition were concentrating on social revolution.

But Borodin did return. He seized control of the Central Executive Committee of the Kuomintang and expelled over one hundred conservatives. Holding the Central Committee in his hands he forced through a resolution giving greater freedom to the army being created by the Russian advisers. He also made peace with Chiang by assuring him that Russia was friend not foe. He announced the goal of a "Northern Expedition" to eliminate the warlords and unite the country.

In Peking rumors persisted that Soviet agents were working among the students in the north to stir up trouble. There was a suspicion that the Russians were working to use the Chinese people as tools of the World Revolution. What would be the spark, we all wondered, that would ignite this volatile situation. The answer came all too quickly.

T'ung Fu
June 2, 1925

Dear Family,

Yesterday morning when I went to meet my eight o'clock class I found my classroom empty and the courtyard deserted. Only one girl was in sight. When I approached her to ask what had happened, this usually docile and seemingly friendly student said curtly, "All classes have been cancelled, and we have been called to a student rally." She turned and walked hurriedly away without giving a word of explanation.

But the explanation was not long in coming. The day before, a group of students in Shanghai had joined some workers in a demonstration outside the International Settlement against the inhuman conditions in a Japanese textile mill where Chinese laborers were working twelve hours a day, seven days a week. Usually when such demonstrations seem to be getting out of hand, the police disperse them with a hose. This time the Shanghai

International police under command of a British officer gave the order to "fire." Twelve students were killed and several more wounded.

Word of this incident spread like wildfire to the universities all over the country and has resulted in what may well become the most violent student movement of recent years. A nation-wide strike has been called and Yenching along with other universities has been closed. Already students have been organized into groups and have gone into the cities and outlying districts trying to urge the people to a national awakening. They are proclaiming that all of China's woes are due to foreign imperialism and the time has come for foreign domination to cease. One of the Soviet advisers, known to be very anti-British, has been quoted as saying "we did not make May 30th; it was made for us." However, most people believe he instigated the whole thing.

I went to the British Legation for dinner last night and naturally was deeply concerned about what had happened at Yenching. When I asked one of the British guests what he thought would happen as a result of this Shanghai incident, he looked at me rather scornfully and said, "Why nothing, of course." This morning I was almost glad when I learned that a general strike had been called against the British. The Hongkong–Shanghai Bank has been forced to close and every servant in a British home or hotel forced to leave on threat of death. I am terribly worried about George in Hongkong.

Demonstrations continued as hatred of the foreigners grew and spread all over China. Dr. Ferguson, who had come to China in 1887, told me that there had not been such bitterness since the Boxer outburst. The whole country was roused. Elements which usually were at each other's throats now had common cause in their rage against the West. Strikes occurred in almost every city of the land. A paralyzing boycott of the British in Hongkong was to last for more than a year. Servants deserted, goods and services were withheld. It was a warning to foreigners of the bitter hatred seething beneath the surface.

This "May 30 Incident" was the beginning of the end as far as old Shanghai was concerned. It had given birth to a Communist-dominated General Federation of Labor which helped to organize a record number of strikes. For a whole year there was a boycott of both Japanese and British goods, and for the rest of 1925 Shanghai was strikebound—a condition that spread to other port cities. Funds poured in for the strikers from all over the country and from Russia. A friend who was in the city at the time said that a fever of antiforeign feeling, nationalism, and a general fury broke out. Li Li-san, a Communist who had studied in Paris with Chou En-lai and was a leading figure among the Chinese, could stir up a crowd into a frenzy. Nationalism was an intoxicating subject and the Marxist slogans were irresistible. There were many who thought that the Communists could not have gained their widespread support if the capitalistic system in its "colonial" form had not failed so lamentably in justice and humanity.

Most labor leaders at this time had no idea that they were casting their lot in with a movement which was Communist inspired and organized, and which was part of a great Russian plan. But soon, Shanghai (like Portugal in 1974) became inundated with propaganda posters, leaflets, and Communist paraphernalia.

The Comintern which was very active and successful at this time was fully aware of what was going on in Shanghai. Many important Communists came to the city from all over the world. Among them were Thomas Mann, M. N. Roy, and Earl Browder. In Canton, where Communist influence was at a peak, Andre Malraux worked to organize their giant strikes. His revolutionary novel *Man's Fate*, which won the Goncourt Prize in 1933, tells of China's bitter struggle at this time. (Years later Malraux became de Gaulle's Minister of Youth, Culture, and Scientific Affairs and redecorated the Paris Opera.)

On July 1, just one month after the May 30 Incident, the military government of Canton was formally transformed into the National Government of China. Its armed forces became the National Revolutionary Army, and aroused people shouted approval of the Northern Expedition to "smash both feudalism and foreign imperialism." It was at this time that Mao Tse-Tung took charge of the Peasants' Institute in Canton. He was building for the Communist Party a network of peasant cadres for mass mobilization. Among his lecturers was Chou En-lai.

The Communist Party which numbered only 400 members when I arrived in China in 1923 and only 1,000 in January of 1925, by November had grown to 10,000 and by 1927 to 60,000.

T'ai Shan, the holy mountain with its
10,000 steps of climbing.

Being taken up by chair coolies.

The ancient town of Ch'u-fu, the birthplace of Confucius.

A typical street scene.

The Confucian temple. Note the carved spirit-walk.

The grave of Confucius.

A scroll from the author's collection showing man
in relation to the mountains and streams.

A Glimpse of Ancient China

The long unmeasured pulse of time moves everything.
There is nothing that it cannot bring to life.
Nothing once known that may not become unknown.
SOPHOCLES

SINCE THERE WAS NO CHANCE of Yenching reopening for the final examinations after the Shanghai Incident, a few of us at the T'ung Fu decided to make the trip to T'ai Shan, a sacred mountain in Shantung Province, and then to visit the ancient town of Ch'u-fu, the birthplace of Confucius.

The spring of 1925 was unusually lovely with warm sunshine and the soft air carrying the fragrance of spring flowers. We arrived at the foot of T'ai Shan in brilliant sunshine and made the steep ascent ("10,000 steps of climbing") in chairs carried on poles by coolies. The spectacular scenery reminded me of the Chinese landscape paintings with steep rugged mountains, a waterfall tumbling over massive rocks, and as always the breathtaking vista of plain and hills.

T'ai Shan was the most famous of the five holy mountains where the emperors for centuries used to offer sacrifices to *Shang Ti,* Heaven, whose mandate they held. What especially interested me at the top of the mountain was the stone monument which Dr. Ferguson had said was one of four such monuments attributed to the Ch'in dynasty (221–207 B.C.) It was believed to have been set there by Shih Huang-ti who, as a young and exceedingly vigorous prince of T'sin, the most powerful feudal state, had put his armies in the field and by 222 had vanquished the last of the rival feudal states.

He promptly created The First Empire of China, assumed the title of First Emperor, and established a system of government that was to last for more than two thousand years—until the little Manchu Emperor Pu-yi abdicated in 1912. This Chinese Empire, as Barbara Ward a noted English historian has said, was to become one of the most remarkable institutions in the whole history of mankind. "It held together a vast mass of mankind living with every kind of climate and geography, and including a broad range of tribal loyalties and historical traditions. It also maintained its unity in diversity over a longer

167

period than any other system we have known. The interesting point about the Chinese imperial structure was that it touched very few things. It defended the frontiers and dealt directly with the punishment of violence, in other words, external or internal aggression; it concerned itself with the maintenance of the very elaborate irrigation system which was necessary to ensure Chinese food supplies. It was also charged with countering disaster and famine and undertook the control of foodstuffs in times of shortage. Thus the imperial government performed what one might call the minimum task of keeping order. It dealt with aggressive crimes. It attempted to keep some sort of overall economic balance of stability. Within that framework, the provinces, the family, the clans, the provincial organizations, the lawyers, the merchants—all enjoyed a high degree of autonomy and were strongly encouraged to settle most of their internal affairs by mediation and agreement."

The reign of Shih Huang-ti (a contemporary of Hannibal) was a period of amazing activity. In order to hold at bay the Huns who occupied Mongolia, sections of the wall were connected to make "The Great Wall" settling the boundary between China and the "barbarians" to the north; broad tree-lined streets were built, a long connecting highway constructed, and a twenty-mile waterway called the "Marvelous Canal" connected two rivers making water transportation possible. Shih Huang-ti's palace built in 212 B.C. was considered one of the wonders of the world; it is said to have accommodated 10,000 people. Other imperial residences within a radius of some fifty miles were "connected by covered roads ... roads bordered by walls and furnished with tents, canopies, bells, drums, and beautiful women." Mules, donkeys, and camels which had been domesticated in middle Asia were now used in China. These animals were to assume great importance in everyday life, especially the camels, for they were to take the precious silk across the deserts to the rich markets beyond the Pamirs during the centuries before the birth of Jesus.

Although the First Empire was short-lived (221–207 B.C.) its founding was an event of great importance in world history. It put into practice for the first time the idea of uniting all people "within the wall," an idea never to be lost sight of even during long periods of imperial breakdown. The feudalism of ancient China had at last given way to a centralized government charged with responsibility not only for law and order but for public works, coinage, and the upholding of the rights of the common man. Not only customs and laws, weights and measures, but even the axles of the wheels had to be unified. The many styles of writing in different parts of the country were reduced to one. Nobility was based on gifts and services to the state rather than on birth. The first contact with the islands of Japan was made at this time. It is no wonder that the name "China" is said to be derived from the Ch'in who exerted much influence on the peoples across Asia.

However, to insure peace and unity and to suppress criticism of his rule, Shang Huang-ti opposed the literati and the principles of Confucius. In 215 he ordered the destruction of most of the old books and records. The books which were not burned were secreted at the peril of the lives of those who saved them. Some five hundred of these were said to have been buried alive while thousands were sent to work on the building of "The Great Wall." Although this was an act of political significance it earned him the enmity of the Chinese scholars for it put an end during his reign to the freedom of thought of the previous eras. Escarra has pointed out that this act of Shih Huang-ti was the first of the many revolts of the Chinese against the fetters of the past. The turbulence of the last revolt under Mao Tse-tung is still reverberating in China today.

Our descent from T'ai Shan was terrifying. No sooner had our chair coolies reached the "10,000 steps" than they began to run. We were being taken down backwards according to custom. We knew that the steps skirted sheer cliffs and a bad slip meant falling over the precipice. We shut our eyes in terror. But we soon learned that chair coolies do not make slips—their feet are poised on the steps at exactly the right angle and they move as lightly as birds. Our coolies never stopped once until they had deposited us safe, but breathless, at the foot of the mountain.

We left T'ai Shan on a local night train and by dawn reached a station where we secured donkeys for the ride to Ch'u Fu. In the loveliest spring weather, our donkey boys tagging behind us, we clipped across neat fields passing white-walled farmsteads with generous manure heaps and well made pens for pigs, cows, and oxen. Fruit orchards, a mass of pink and white blossoms, filled the air with their fragrance. A night shower had washed clean the entire countryside accentuating the charm of this beautiful province. All the while we were travelling still further back in time, for Confucius was born in 551 B.C., 300 years before Shih Huang-ti. This going back in time is not difficult in China for the past always seemed to be intimately woven into the present.

The tranquility and peace of Ch'u Fu with its slow moving ox carts, its people strolling leisurely under the shade of great trees, and its vendors sitting patiently on the street by their wares, were just what we had expected of the birthplace of Confucius. Not far from the inn where we were to spend the night was the palace of the dukes of his family line. In China titles of nobility did not last forever; they were diminished by one degree with each succeeding generation until they gradually extinguished themselves. But the reverence for Confucius was such that in his case an exception was made; in each generation the eldest of the family remained a duke. We soon discovered that nearly everyone in town was apparently named K'ung, the family name of Confucius. After all, in over twenty-five centuries it was not surprising that the family had expanded beyond belief. At the inn we talked with a man who could trace his ancestry through seventy-three generations. Smiling he asked "where else in the world would a grave be tended by a member of the family for over twenty-five hundred years?"

The beautiful temple to Confucius could never have been lovelier than in the spring. Slender lilacs were blooming even in the spacious enclosures to the main building shaded by huge cypress trees. One's mind was stirred to deep reflection in this tranquil spot—"a very tender, ancient and benevolent China."

Confucius had lived when China was divided into a number of independent feudal states which were trying to coexist. Although it was a time of great social unrest and political upheaval, it was also one of great creativity. To the Chinese this was their classical age, the age not only of Confucius but of Lao Tze, Mo Ti, Mencius, and Chuang-tzi. It set the main pattern of Chinese thought of all subsequent ages—

until the Revolution. Hu Shih called it one of the most important and most glorious epochs in the history of human thought: "Its vigor and originality, its richness and its far-reaching significance entitles it to a place in the history of philosophy comparable only with the place occupied by the Greek philosophers." It was a time when laws were written and some of the most memorable poetry and prose; market places increased and money appeared. Science as well as philosophy took a great leap forward. By 444 B.C. the year was calculated by the Chinese as having 364¼ days. Moderately accurate astronomical data on the planetary movements of Jupiter and Saturn had been calculated by 350. Halley's comet was observed in 240 B.C. after which there was an unbroken succession of thirty observations down to 1910 (the year I saw the comet in Portland, Maine). Ideas began to seep through the land barriers to the West. Chinese society was far from static.

Interestingly enough, this classical age of China coincided with the classical age of Greece. While Confucius was writing and teaching in Ch'u Fu, Aeschylus and Sophocles were writing their great dramas in Athens; Socrates and Plato were soon to appear; the Jews were returning from Babylon and Buddha was teaching in India. These ancient civilizations, although they had had no contact, in a way resembled each other. In China, India, and the Mediterranean world, the three centers of these contemporary civilizations, there was for the first time a reaching out for new concepts in philosophy and religion. Before this time, man had approached religion through animism, the belief that all natural forces were in some way expressions of divine power; and he worshipped this power in its natural forms —earth, sea, sky, mountains. This idea of giving nature mysterious and magical powers was man's first attempt to solve the "why" and the "how" of the universe. By 500 B.C. when contact between these civilizations was about to begin, men of great insight and character appeared who were responsible for new concepts. In place of many gods there was one God, and then there came the idea of a religion of the spirit which man must practice in his heart. Gradually there emerged the idea of man sharing in the Divine purpose with the capacity to choose or reject the law of God which would give abundant life. In the East, this spiritual revolution was brought about by such men as Confucius, Lao Tze, Buddha, and the author of the Hindu Vedas; in the West by the Greek philosophers and the Jewish prophets. This spiritual change was probably for mankind one of the most significant of all revolutions.

At this same time in Persia, Cyrus the Great had already begun his conquests. Babylon had fallen to him and he had extended his rule to the Aegean in the West and to the deserts of Arabia in the South. When Darius succeeded Cyrus (Confucius was thirty-four) and brought his mighty imperial army to attack Greece, these two civilizations, the East and the West, were to come into full contact with each other for the first time. Because they met in hostility, the conflict was one of the most momentous in the world's history. "Marathon" and "Thermopylae" are words that still ring across the ages. Twenty-two centuries later there would be another momentous conflict between the East and the West. This time, at the end of the fifteenth century when the Portuguese opened the sea route to India around the cape, China would be involved. Toynbee had said of this second conflict that "it was the first step towards the unification of mankind into one single society."

Meanwhile behind their formidable geographic barriers of deserts, mountains, and ocean, the Chinese were oblivious to all that was happening in the West. Their civilization had already been in existence for nearly 2,000 years. Their pottery and bronze were almost as old as the pyramids; the silk culture had started; there was a calendar of sorts important to a people engaged in agriculture. There was ancient writing on bronzes and stone. The wisdom of their ancient sages had filtered through the centuries in myths, legends, and songs handed down and collected much as were the psalms of David and the sayings of Socrates and Jesus.

The earliest people of which there is record were called the Shangs (1523–1122 B.C.) The earliest writing comes from the capital of the Shang kings around 1400 B.C. Cities had been erected as early as 1300 which contained government buildings, palaces, temples, and mausoleums. (This ancient China has come alive to thousands and thousands of Westeners today as the marvelous archaeological treasures of the

People's Republic of China have been exhibited in Paris, London, Toronto, and Washington.) These highly cultured Shang people were conquered in 1122 B.C. by rude tribesmen from Western China, led by a group known as the Chou. They were to establish the famous Chou dynasty (1122–256 B.C.), the longest dynasty in the history of China. These hardy warriors who knew how to take territory had difficulty at first establishing a well-ordered government. When the king died a few years after the conquest, Chou K'ung, the Duke of Chou, brother of the king, declared himself regent and ruled with a firm hand. Confucius, whose Chinese name was K'ung Fu Tzy, claimed him as an ancestor. (The first Jesuit missionaries latinized his name to Confucius). Although the Duke lived many centuries before Confucius, he has been considered by some the founder of the Confucian tradition. It was during his rule that certain ideas emerged which were to affect Chinese thinking ever since. For instance, to explain and justify the Shang conquest he proclaimed to the Shang people in the name of the king:

I announce and declare to you ... it was not that Heaven desired to do away with the sovereign of Shang. But your ruler ... was extremely dissolute, and despised the commands of Heaven ... he was lazy and slothful, slighted the labors of government, and did not make pure sacrifices, so that Heaven sent down this ruin on him. ...

Heaven then sought among your many regions ... for one who might be attentive to its commands, but there was none able to do so. There was, however, our Chou king, who treated the multitudes well and was virtuous, and presided carefully over the sacrifices to the spirits and to Heaven. Heaven, therefore, chose us and gave us the mandate of Shang, to rule over your many regions.

Thus the pattern was set for rebels to claim possession of the "Mandate of Heaven," a pattern that was to persist through the centuries. Even the revolutionary party of Sun Yat-sen was at one time called "The Association for Changing the Mandate." More important still, the principle was established that rulers existed for the sake of the people and that they held their power in trust subject to revocation if they did not use it well.

Also in this early period the importance of the family was stressed.

In all succeeding generations down to the present, China was to be the stronghold of the family system. Another important aspect of Chinese life established before Confucius was ancestor worship. The founder of the Chou kings was believed to be descended from an ancestor called Fou Hsih, which means "Millet Ruler" undoubtedly an agricultural deity. From an ancient classic we learn that he was miraculously conceived when his mother stepped in a footprint made by the principal deity. Like Romulus and Remus he was abandoned but miraculously escaped harm. A poem says:

> He was laid in a narrow lane,
> But sheep and oxen protected him tenderly.
> He was placed in a large forest,
> But woodcutters found him there.
> He was laid on the cold ice,
> But birds covered him with their wings.

Not only this founder of the Chou family but all its ancestors were thought to be responsible for its power. After death, they were believed to live in the heavens where they supervised the destiny of their posterity giving them victory in war and prosperity in peace. In return for these favors they expected from their descendants the usual sacrifice and rituals.

Thus it was that at the dawn of history customs and institutions were established that were to last for nearly 4,000 years—institutions and customs which Fairbanks has called "the oldest and most persistent social phenomena in the world."

The glorious years of the Chous lasted four hundred years. Then because of weak and decadent rulers, history repeated itself. The vigorous barbarian tribes on their periphery always alert to signs of weakness, invaded and overpowered some of the vassal states. Peasant serfs were overloaded with ever heavier taxes and herded into the nobles' armies. Lords of vanquished states were degraded, peasants' sons and even slaves occasionally became ministers of states; ministers became so powerful as to overshadow princes and replace ruling houses. Merchants, the lowest class of all freemen, began to play an important part in the political life. Everywhere it was a period of political and social upheaval. A soldier tells of the suffering caused by frequent wars and expeditions:

> How freely are the wild geese on their wings,
> And the rest they find on the bushy yu trees!
> But we, ceaseless toilers in the king's service,
> Cannot even plant our millet and rice.
> What will our parents have to rely on?
> O thou distant and azure Heaven!
> When shall all this end?

Social unrest, political disintegration, and moral disorder continued down to the time of Confucius. It is no wonder that his great concern was to bring order out of the chaos of the warring states. Although he had aristocratic forebears he was brought up in poverty because his father died when he was an infant. As a young man he speaks of himself as "in humble circumstances and without rank." He earned his living doing menial tasks. Although he studied he was mostly self-taught. Very early in life he became interested in the ancient books, in the legends and folklore of ancient times. He once said, "I for my part am not one of those who have innate knowledge. I am simply one who loves the past and who is diligent in investigating it."

Confucius became a great teacher and attracted students from the lowest to the highest social strata. "In education," he said, "there should be no class distinction. I have never refused to teach anyone, even though he came on foot with nothing more to offer as tuition than a package of dried meat." He praised one of his disciples for being able "though wearing a tattered hemp-quilted gown to stand beside those wearing costly furs without the slightest embarrassment." His aim was the common good, the end of strife and selfishness. He believed that mankind did not need to live in perpetual discord. To him virtue and intelligence were the cardinal points which should be stressed in government, and he ardently wished that rulers would appoint men of good will to administer their kingdoms. "Advance the upright," he urged, "set aside the crooked. Then the people will acquiesce." He wanted people to work hard and use their intelligence. Because he was serious about preparing his students to go out into the world to work for his principles of good government, he was strict in his requirements about their intellectual abilities. He said, "I point out the way only to the student who has first looked for it himself. If when I give the student one corner of the subject, he cannot find the other three I do not repeat my lesson."

His chief concern was to teach his students about *li*, the proper way to behave, one's moral duty in social relations. According to Confucius there are five basic relationships each with a particular moral quality: loyalty between rulers and ruled; love and respect between father and child; affection between husband and wife; humility between juniors and elders, and honesty between friends.

Duke Ai once asked Confucius "Why don't the princes of today practice *li?*"

Confucius replied: "The princes of today are greedy in their search after material goods. They indulge themselves in pleasure and neglect their duties and carry themselves with a proud air. They take all they can from the people, and invade the territory of good rulers against the will of the people, and they go out to get what they want without regard for what is right. This is the way of the modern rulers."

One way to begin making things right, he said, was by "giving things their right names—that is giving moral qualities their true colors, not glorifying arrogance with the name of dignity nor deceit with the name of prudence, nor weak compliance with the name of good fellowship." To Confucius, that fundamental truthfulness was the beginning of all righteousness.

Confucius often spoke of the "gentleman" and the "superior" man. What he had in mind was something more than a man of good breeding or high courtesy; it had to do with character, with self-control, and honor. "The first thing is to be loyal and trustworthy.... The superior man is ashamed if his words outrun his actions.... The superior man makes demands on himself; the inferior man makes demands on others. Wealth and office are objects of desire; but if they cannot be had in the right way they must be relinquished.... That whereby a man differs from the lower animals a little most people throw it away. The superior man preserves it."

Characteristic of classic China is the opening paragraph of *The Great Learning:*

Striving to bring about world order, men must first govern their own states well. Striving to govern their states, they must first create harmony in their families. Striving to create harmony in the family, they must first develop their own characters. Striving to do this, they must first put right their own minds; and to do this, make their purposes honest.

Confucius was once asked by Tzu Kung, what he considered the essentials of government. The master replied: "Sufficient food, sufficient forces, and the confidence of the people."

"Suppose," rejoined Tzu Kung, "I were compelled to dispense with one, which of these three should I forgo first?"

"Forgo the forces," was the reply.

"Suppose," said Tzu Kung "I were compelled to eliminate another, which of the other two should I forgo?"

"The food," was the reply, "for from old, death has been the lot of all men, but a people without faith cannot stand."

More than anything else Confucius wanted an important official position in order to put his beliefs into practice. Finally in middle age a place was found for him in his native state, but the position proved to be of little importance politically. Discontented with the slow progress of his doctrines in the land of Lu, he spent ten years with some of his disciples travelling from state to state seeking a ruler who would give his philosophy a chance. He never found one. Instead he was treated with scorn; he and his disciples were often in want of food. He learned the age-old truth that to know the good is not necessarily to want the good. He had been eager to reform society but it was as difficult then as now. Finally he was encouraged to return to his native state where he once again became a teacher.

During these last years he edited and thereby preserved the ancient books which came to be known as the Confucian Classics. One of these, the *Book of Odes,* gives an amazing picture of the life of the eighth and seventh centuries B.C. Men sang of courtship and marriage, women of their errant lovers, soldiers of their misery, princes of their unworthiness. These Classics and the "Four Books" (the *Analects of Confucius,* the *Book of Mencius,* the *Doctrine of the Mean,* and the *Great Learning*) eventually became a kind of Bible (like the Thoughts of Mao Tse-tung today) which served as a textbook for every statesman and school child for more than 2,000 years. It was selections from these books which the children were reciting in unison when I visited the little school on my way to Miao Feng Shan. The object of studying these classics was of supreme national importance for it was based on the assumption that a moral foundation was essential to the cohesion and permanence of the empire. Therefore, nothing could be more important for the empire than the human behavior within it.

Although at the end of his life Confucius was disappointed, he was not bitter. "The good man, he said, "does not grieve that other people do not recognize his merits. His only anxiety is lest he should fail to recognize theirs." His joy of life, his enthusiasm, and his love of teaching are reflected in what he said of himself. "I am the man so intent upon enlightening the eager that he forgets his hunger, so happy in doing so that he forgets the bitterness of his lot and does not realize old age is at hand. As being a Divine Sage or even a good man, far be it from me to make any such claim. As for unwearing effort to learn and unflagging patience in teaching others, those are merits that I do not hesitate to claim. At fifteen I set my heart on learning. At thirty I stood firm. At forty I was free from doubts. At fifty I understood the laws of Heaven. At sixty I could follow the desires of my heart without transgressing the right."

Once when he was so ill that he became unconscious some of his disciples dressed themselves in court robes and stood by his bed as if they were the ministers he would have had if he had realized his ambition of being a high official. When he regained consciousness and saw them he smiled and said, "By making this pretense of having ministers when in fact I have none, whom do you think I am going to deceive? Heaven? And is it not better that I should die in the hands of you, my friends, than in the hands of ministers?"

As I stood by the grave of this ancient sage, I marvelled that his thoughts had been kept alive through the centuries to mold and shape this great civilization and that his terse sayings had become one of the most influential doctrines in human history. It was far from his intention to found a religion, yet Confucianism became a cult in the twelfth century and temples to Confucius were built in all great cities as well as in his birthplace. This cult eventually became a kind of strait jacket which prevented freedom of thought and the progress China needed so desperately—something Confucius would have deplored for it had twisted his teachings into a system of ceremonies.

Confucius' great concern was with human life, human conduct, human society. When he was asked how to serve the gods and spirits, he answered: "We have not learned how to serve man, how can we serve the gods and spirits?" When asked "What is death," he said, "We do not know life, how can we know death? A gentleman has no fears nor worries. He searches himself and is not ashamed. A moral life in this world of man is sufficiently an end in itself."

He believed with Shu-sun Pao, an ancient sage of Lu who said, "There are three kinds of immortality: the highest is the immortality of virtue and character; the next is the immortality of achievement; the third is the immortality of the spoken or written word. These do not perish with the length of time."

China was freeing itself from the Confucian cult when I was there. Those who wanted a complete break with the past tried to empty China of Confucian thought. Confucius had been rejected at the revolution in 1911 and was burned in effigy at Changsha in 1926 because he was the friend of emperors and preached loyalty to them. But most of all the cult was considered a cog in the wheels of progress and was blamed for preventing the acceptance of Western scientific thought.

Today Confucius is held up to scorn; he has even been the butt of a comic strip. But can the memory of a nation ever be completely erased? Is it not possible that in time the Chinese may find that the essence of Confucius' teaching is the heart of their nation, its spiritual unity? And if the China of tomorrow is to be the great China of the ages, will it not be in part because of the moral inheritance handed down by their great sages?

In talking with Hu Shih about Confucius after my return to Peking he impressed upon me how important it was in understanding China to realize that the most influential leader of Chinese national life, the idol of millions of Chinese youth and school children throughout the ages, was not a great military hero nor a great religious messiah nor savior, but a school master—one who remained the idol of millions of people even down to Hu Shih's own boyhood. In fact he considered the most valuable and characteristic heritage bequeathed to China from Confucius and the classical period was the importance of education, learning, and thinking.

"Seek the truth and do not compromise" was a motto Hu Shih learned as a young boy. By his father he was encouraged to approach every subject in a spirit of doubt. He was told if he could doubt at points where other people felt no impulse to doubt, then he could know he was making progress. (How often I heard Mary Calkins, the great teacher of philosophy at Wellesley College say, "Philosophy begins when we learn to doubt our cherished beliefs.")

Hu Shih and I talked at length about the three immortalities. These, he said, had satisfied many a Chinese scholar in the last twenty-five centuries for they had taken the place of the idea of human survival after death. They had given a sense of assurance that although death ends one's physical life—the effect of one's individual worth, one's work, and one's thoughts lives on. He believed that every individual, however humble, leaves something behind him for good or evil, for better or for worse. He lives on in a greater self called Society or Humanity. This is immortal. "Today humanity is what it is by the wisdom and folly of our fathers. We shall be judged by what humanity will be when we shall have played our part."

Summer and Autumn 1925

THE SUMMER OF 1925 was hot and humid. After returning from Ch'u Fu, I spent as much time as possible in the Western Hills before the rains began. Then heavy sheets of rain poured down continually day after day. At the T'ung Fu wooden planks were placed across the courtyards, but there was nothing that could keep our feet dry. Everyone was depressed. Among the foreigners there was a saying that when the heat is on and the rains begin there is nothing that so becomes the capital as the leaving of it.

I was too happy for words when an invitation came from the Fergusons to spend August with them at their summer home in Peitaiho, a seaside resort popular with foreigners on the Laio Tung Gulf just opposite Port Arthur. Their daughter Florence was to spend the summer with them and I would be a companion for her. They could not possibly imagine with what pleasure I accepted their invitation. As I sat down at my desk to write to them I heard a crash above the pounding of the rain—then desperate human cries. A house half built of mud had collapsed in a nearby *hutung*—and there was nothing that I could do to help. I could hardly wait to leave Peking!

A letter to my mother tells about this:

Peking
July 28, 1925

You have no idea what this season is like. In two days everything is covered with mold. There isn't a dry thing or space to be found. Actually, my hair has been wet for two weeks. Peking is now a river—fourteen inches of rain in three days! I am praying that my linens and the few wedding things I have will survive the summer. Chinese houses are frightfully damp because of the paper windows and stone floors.

Hongkong must be worse than Peking from what George writes. He has to air everything in his trunks once a week. All of his books have had to be varnished to keep away the white ants. It is the combination of dampness and heat that makes it so very bad. How are my books at home? They are my most precious possession, so please look after them for me. If George and I have nothing else, we ought to have a superb library between us. We are

181

having great fun planning for our home. Won't it be wonderful to have you come to visit us? You will love George, I know, for he has a marvelous sense of humor and is great fun.

Clothes are a problem. Will you please send me some fashion sheets so I shall know what people are wearing now-a-days? There is an excellent French dressmaker here in Peking who has promised to make my wedding outfit—something I can wear for best on our trip. From the tourists who have been arriving recently I know that everything I have is out-of-date. Skirts are evidently much shorter (mine are all ankle length) and they are wearing light colored stockings. Since I have only black stockings you will have to send me whatever is fashionable.

Tell Carolyn that I have been greatly honored. Sophie Hart (a Wellesley professor beloved by my generation) has sent me an advanced copy of *The Winged Soul* so that I should be the first alumna to receive a copy of it. That, because I sent her a little package of tea for Christmas! Did she go up for the celebration at the college? I hear it was lovely.

I hope you are having a happy summer at the island; I am wishing it for you. By the time this letter reaches you the goldenrod will be in bloom, the tides will be running high again, and flocks of birds will be arriving on their way south. The west wind will be blowing across the sparkling bay and across our porch in the afternoon. The afterglow of the setting sun will fill the sky and the evening star will be low over Portland. I think I am a little homesick tonight.

The Ferguson's house was built on a bluff with a large veranda looking out to sea. Like most of the houses in Peitaiho it was foreign in style. I loved to sit on the railing of the veranda and look down to the beach with its miles of golden sand stretching along the gulf, to watch the waves on a windy day curl over one another, and to follow the fishing boats with their gray sails as they moved toward the horizon and disappeared. (Mao Tse-tung knows this beach well. A portrait of him with his back to the waves, the wind whipping a corner of his long overcoat, is a favorite in China).

The month at Peitaiho was a quiet, relaxing time. Every morning Florence and I went to the beach for a long swim and then lay on the sand for hours letting our bodies soak in the warm sunshine. Florence is a lovely sensitive person with a delicate beauty; she was a little older than I but we had much in common for we were both in love. The

At Peitaiho with the Fergusons, looking out toward the fishing fleet departing in the morning.

One of the boats anchored for the night.

year before she had been divorced but she expected soon to be married again.

As I look back from our society today when one out of every three marriages ends in divorce, it seems almost incredible that she was the first person I had ever known who had been divorced. In those days when one took the marriage vow one made a commitment for life— for better or for worse. Divorce in my family was looked upon as a disgrace. But as I listened to Florence tell her story, divorce seemed the most natural thing in the world. When two people no longer loved each other how could they stay married? In my naivety, I assumed that all the married people I knew loved each other. There were my father and mother, my aunts and uncles, the fathers and mothers of my friends. It never occurred to me to wonder whether or not they were happy in their marriages. Perhaps because people then rarely showed their emotions. There was a saying: you don't wear your heart on your sleeve.

Yet there was my own broken engagement which I confided to Florence; it was something I found difficult to talk about. A Bowdoin college senior had fallen in love with me when I was a sophomore in college and urged me to marry him. He was a handsome Cuban whose family had spent a summer on Little Diamond Island. The family fascinated me. His father owned a sugar plantation near Havana and had exciting stories to tell; his mother was a charming, regal Spanish woman. The family was large like my own and we had good times together. I was nineteen. Already many of my friends were engaged, some were even married for this was the time of the "Great War." Somehow I felt that marriage to him was my fate although I had no idea what marriage meant. I had certainly not "fallen in love." In Portland in the teens, it was not proper for young people to be affectionate with one another. Even holding hands was considered being "forward." A girl who let a boy kiss her was "bold." New England when I was young was not unlike China today in this respect.

It was my father who made me realize that we were not suited for each other, although when I returned the ring which he had given me, I thought my heart was broken. "Very probably if we had married," I told Florence, "I would be divorced today." We were both sure now that we had found the right one. I looked forward to my marriage with George; and I knew that when I took the marriage vow I would be making a lifetime commitment.

At Peitaiho there were lovely walks to take in the afternoon and shops to explore which for me were all too tempting. The evenings were a great joy for we would sit on the veranda for hours reading or talking about China. Dr. and Mrs. Ferguson had a wealth of stories to tell for they had lived through the Boxer Rebellion and the Revolution.

Then just before it was time for me to leave Peitaiho, the news reached us that the National government in Canton had threatened a northern expedition to smash the warlords and the foreign imperialists who supported them. In the north the warlords—Chang Tso-ling, Feng Yu-hsiang, and Wu Pei-fu—continued to struggle for control of Peking, the government still recognized by the Western Powers. All over the country the antiforeign feeling was spreading.

Dr. Ferguson began to be apprehensive about being so far from Peking, so it was decided that we would all leave Peitaiho together; orders to pack were given at once to the servants. It was a sad day when we left that beautiful spot by the sea to board the train for Peking. But when the 170 mile journey was over and our train ran under the Tartar Wall near Ch'ien Men, the high gate which leads to the Forbidden City, we all felt a new surge of life. It was one of those clear autumn days of North China; it was good, after all, to be back again in this ravishingly beautiful city.

*   *   *

It is strange that under the shadow of threatening events, ordinary life goes on as usual. In 1925 there was no real government in Peking. Yet the camels were still bringing in coal from the hills, squealing pigs were still being taken to market. There were the wedding and funeral processions, the children playing shuttlecock and flying their kites, the silken-gowned gentlemen still riding comfortably in their polished rickshas, and the fortune and the storytellers were drawing their curious crowds.

There was a no man's land between Peking and Tientsin where the warlords were fighting; yet the city gates were still open and through them passed a steady stream of Peking carts, pedestrians, rickshas, and all the other types of Peking traffic. No one mentioned the tragic Shanghai Incident yet one who had a sensitive ear could hear the vibration of the antiforeign feeling.

And so, on a beautiful day early in October, Yenching University reopened as if nothing had happened. We all assembled as usual at the great hall of the Men's College and marched in our academic gowns according to rank and service. I had advanced three places. As I reached my place on the platform and turned to face the student body, there was the American flag flying gently against a soft blue sky. I looked lovingly at my flag. But now I was used to living in a foreign land. China seemed like a second home to me.

When my classes began, I found my students as earnest and as hard working as ever. One class of seniors gave promise of being one of the most brilliant and creative classes I ever had; they had great ideas for the coming year and were eager to share them with me. As classes were getting underway, a letter came from George. His furlough was to begin in November.

After the Shanghai Incident in the spring, I had secretly hoped that I might find a substitute so that I would be free to leave Peking at the end of the fall term. Now I was determined to do so. I talked at once with Mrs. Frame, our dean, whose friendship was one of the deep satisfactions of my life at the T'ung Fu. She was, as I had hoped, not only understanding but encouraging. "Of course, this is what you must do," she said. "It is exactly what I would do if I were in your place."

I wanted my good friend Eleanor Holgate to take over my work, but she confided to me that she and Owen Lattimore were to be married soon. They were to travel to Europe by the overland route taken by Marco Polo—a fascinating but extremely hazardous way to spend a honeymoon, I thought. Dorothy Rowe, a free lance writer whom I knew, was glad to join the Yenching faculty; and to my great relief she was more than acceptable to Mrs. Frame and Dr. Stewart.

George was delighted with this news and began at once to plan our trip back to the States. Since he was to have a six-months' furlough, he suggested a leisurely trip "because," as he wrote, "we might never have such an opportunity again—do you agree?"

We would go by way of India, Egypt, and Greece; of course I must

go to Athens to see the beautiful Greek theater where *Antigone* had
first been performed, to Mycene where Agamemnon left for Troy,
and on to Epidaurus. Then we would sail up the Dardenelles to Con-
stantinople and up the Golden Horn. We would go through the
Bosphorus and cross the Black Sea to the Romanian port of Constantsa
where Livy had been exiled. By way of Bucharest we would go to the
beautiful city of Budapest, built on either sides of the "blue Danube"
—then to Vienna for the opera. We must have a month in Italy to see
Venice, Florence, Rome, Naples, and Pompeii. Then to France to see
Paris and the great French cathedrals; and to England to see London,
Canterbury, and the lovely English countryside. George had taken
most of this trip before. For me, it was another impossible dream that
came true.

It was agreed that I could leave Peking as soon as the mid-term
examinations were over, so our wedding was planned for January. We
both wanted to be married quietly in Hongkong. During the inter-
vening months, George decided to travel in French Indo-China and
Siam. He had long wanted to visit the city of Bangkok.

The remaining months for me were taken up with wedding an-
nouncements, last minute shopping, and the inumerable things that
had to be done as I prepared to leave Peking, to get ready for a wedding and a six month's trip half way around the world. Clothes were
still a problem for much had to come from the States. I had little
money and most of what I had was spent for embroidered linens and
silk underwear—both irresistible in Peking for a prospective bride of
those days. Mails were slow and my family never seemed to realize
that it took at least a month for anything to reach me. "Shoes and
gloves," I wrote my mother, "I shall buy in Europe" (she had always
impressed upon me that a lady was known by her shoes and gloves).
"Clothes are cheap in Paris, I understand, so I shall buy one good outfit there in order not to disgrace you when I get off the boat in New
York." Boat schedules were studied and to my delight I found the
ship that was to take me to Hongkong would be the S.S. *President
Madison*.

There were the "showers" and the farewell parties given by very
dear friends. And there were, of course, the things to do for the last

time; I wanted to become deeply conscious of everything in my life there. So once more Jui T'ang and I went to the Chinese opera to see Mei Lan-fang. Never was I more impressed with his grace and genius. He epitomized the willow waisted, swaying, slender, delicate Chinese maiden. His every gesture was the essence of what movement should be—whether moving his long-fingered hands, arranging his robes, or opening a fan. As always he did not walk so much as glide, float, sway. (Mei Lan-fang never took part in politics, but the day he died in 1961 was a day of national mourning throughout China; and in Peking, the Communist government decreed a state funeral for him.)

There was the last feast of Peking duck with jolly friends at my favorite restaurant in the Old Chinese City—and one last walk on the Peking Wall. Once more I stood before the magnificence of the For- bidden City and gazed on the great expanse of white carved marble; each column of the balustrades carved with some traditional design: the dragon, the phoenix, the waves of the sea, or the cloud pattern. Carved, too, were the spirit ramps which divide the wide low flights of stairs over which the Emperor's sedan chair was carried and which were, otherwise, for the convenience of spirits only.

I wanted also to say good-bye to the tea merchants and the other Chinese gentlemen who had been so kind to me. Of course there was one last weekend in the Western Hills when the moon was full. I wanted to return to Ta Chieh Ssu, but some friends insisted that I should not leave Peking without seeing Chieh Tai Ssu, one of the two most famous of all the monasteries. It was very old, built in the T'ang dynasty (seventh century), restored by the Mings, and was the favorite resort of Ch'ien Lung. It was very large with many monks in residence, for this was a center of Buddhist faith and learning. More than a hundred monks still attended the daily services when we were there.

Chieh T'ai Ssu has a dramatic location well up a mountain slope, on a cliff. Built on terraces, the most imposing of which is four hun- dred feet long, it commands a magnificent view over the plain. Out from these terraces lean curious twisted white pines; one spreading over a balustrade is called The Nest of the Phoenix, another close to the ground, The Sleeping Dragon. There are impressive halls with beautiful roofs of colored tile and painted eaves, paved courts, and pavilions. Thousands of stone steps lead from the great entrance *p'ai lou* to its heights.

This is a place of immense importance to the Buddhists because it was here that priests were ordained, the ordinands coming from as far as the Yangtze. The ceremonies took place high on the hill at the Ordaining Platform where there is a huge square marble altar. The ordinands took their vows having come all the way up the steps from the entrance *p'ai lou* while on their shaven heads were sticks of incense which burned right down to their skulls—thus marking them priests for life.

It astonished me to learn that in the 1930s Alan Priest was ordained here. At his own expense candles burned on every step all the way from the entrance, as well as along the balustrades of the terraces. Alan was a graduate of Harvard in the class of 1920. He came to Peking in 1924 as a member of the Fogg Museum Expedition to China and while in the Orient was awarded Carnegie and Sachs fellowships to continue his studies. In 1927 he was appointed an assistant professor at Harvard but went instead to New York as curator of the Department of Far Eastern Art at the Metropolitan Museum of Art. In 1954, when my husband and I met him at the Museum, he gave us a copy of his delightful book *Aspects of Chinese Painting,* a collection of essays which he wrote for the Metropolitan Bulletin.

Those were hectic, exciting, and swift-flying months—months during which my students and Yenching played a very significant part. Jui T'ang came often to see me. One day she asked for the negatives of the pictures I had taken in China which meant the most to me. These she had enlarged and put in a book with wooden covers. On the top cover four Chinese characters were delicately carved. When she presented the book to me she said "Here are some memories of your life in my country" and she explained that the characters on the cover meant "the footprints of the pheasant in the snow"—for her a poetic expression for memories.

Typical of a landscape with palaces and temples. By Yuan Yao, 1712.
Courtesy of the Museum of Fine Arts, Boston.

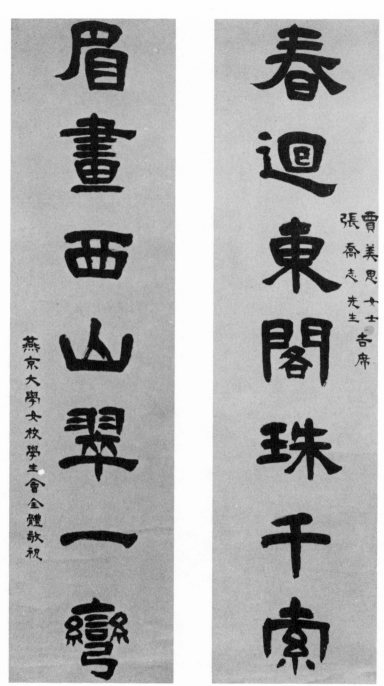

The marriage scrolls presented to me by the students of Yenching.

Last Days in China

What's past is prologue.

SHAKESPEARE

IT WAS DURING THAT WINTER of 1925 when things began to be different in China. The traditional good form in the conduct of war was over. Now there was more bloodshed; the wounded poured into the cities, and the countryside was strewn with dead. Roads swarmed with soldiers of one side or another and with uniformed bandits. Foreigners who ventured outside the city carried supplies of cigarettes and calling cards which usually let them get by. Railroad transportation all over North China was paralyzed. For weeks no train ran between Peking and Tientsin although, according to the 1900 Protocol after the Boxer War, the foreign powers had the right to maintain communication from the capital to the sea.

I wrote to my family:

December 27, 1925

I wonder if you realize what a critical condition Peking has been in for the last two weeks. Probably one of the fiercest battles ever fought here has been raging just outside the city. Until yesterday no trains were running. Even telephone and telegraph communications have been cut. Not a letter has come into the city in all that time! But the day before yesterday Feng Yu-hsiang took Tientsin so communications have opened once again. For awhile I worried for fear I would not be able to leave the city in time to reach George for the wedding day.

Beside the civil war, there was a serious threat made by the anti-Christians that Yenching was to be burned on Christmas Day. The Chinese communists in league with the Red Russians are ready to do most anything. Poor China! One's heart aches for her.

Nothing has come yet from the States; probably everything will arrive this week now that the mails are coming through. I know that George will appreciate seeing me in some new clothes. But even though nothing arrives I can get along—the clothes I have had made over have come out very well and will do for travelling.

We have decided to have a very simple wedding. So I shall be married in an afternoon dress, a soft blue crepe de chine made by the French dressmaker. I can hardly wait to see the hats you have sent. I do hope that the check will come for I now have only just enough money to get me to Hong-kong!

The days are going very fast and I am radiant at the thought of being with George. I can hardly wait for you to know him and love him.

History never seems like history when you are living through it. It just seems confusing and disrupting. Somehow, in spite of the tensions and the turmoil, I managed to get my examinations corrected and my trunks and suitcases packed. Wha T'ing was a godsend—as he had been ever since I was first put in his care on the day of my arrival at the T'ung Fu. He had already taken upon himself to pack, crate, and ship all of the Chinese treasures that I was taking with me to the States. He picked up my tickets at the steamship company and delivered innumerable chits. He kept watch for the packages and mail that I was expecting from the States. Each day he would greet me with an encouraging smile: "Today they come," he would say. But day after day they did not come. How does one thank a Wha T'ing?

At last on New Year's Day he came toward me waving a letter and a little package. Although these were not what I was expecting, he knew that they would delight me because they came from George. The little package contained his Christmas present—a magnificent string of Japanese crystals which to me were as beautiful as diamonds. I wore them on my wedding day. His letter had been written just as the report reached him of the serious fighting around Peking and he was worried. "I do hope that you have decided to make the journey to Shanghai by boat because the railway journey is far too dangerous and there is the possibility of your missing the *President Madison* at Shanghai. I have written Chet Leaber at the bank and he will be glad to help you as you pass through Shanghai."

His description of Bangkok delighted me because it brought back memories of Uncle Heyward. He had been at the Hayes Memorial Library and was told there that Dr. Hayes became one of the most respected men in Siam.

Bangkok, Siam
Christmas Day, 1925

Bangkok is a city which grows on one. At the end of the second day I decided that there was a good reason why few tourists came here—that it was a city of little interest and charm. The more that I saw of it I commenced to alter my ideas and now I think that next to Peking it is the most interesting city in the Far East. Just now the weather is ideal—not too warm and not too cool. The nights are a little chilly and one needs blankets. The sky is a soft blue and the courtyard of the hotel is filled with palms and other tropical plants. The hotel faces the river and it is pleasant to sit on the veranda and watch the native boats go by. Each one is a complete household with cats, chickens, even caged birds and potted plants on board. Everyone is doing something; the husband steers, young boys push oars, and the wife hangs the washing on a bamboo pole or sits fanning the coals in a brazier where the rice is cooking.

The temples are most alluring. At first I thought them cheap and tawdry and in some respects they are—but in the soft evening twilight when their sharply pitched roofs are seen against the pale yellows and pinks of a tropical sunset they suggest an old world charm and calm that is indefinable. The walls of the temples are usually white but the roofs and gables are lavishly decorated with colored tiles or lacquered wood-carvings. In some of the courtyards, there are dozens of peculiar cone-shaped pagodas that give the general effect of a formal garden of neatly trimmed poplar trees. I like the informality—the democracy of these sacred enclosures. The yellow-robed priests are not disturbed by the small boys who use the courtyards as playgrounds or the little pig that rambles about looking for a frugal tiffin. Dogs of strange breeds bask in the sun and discuss the few problems of dog life in Siam. Ancient dames sit on the pavements—chew betel nut and gossip.

The small boy of Siam is very much like the small boy of America. At first he will have none of you. Gradually he becomes interested in your Kodak and he wants to look through the finder. After a while he is quite willing to stand up like a soldier and have his picture taken. Up to the age of five or so, he dresses with distinguished simplicity—simply a silver anklet or silver necklace. The older boys wear sarongs—or black trousers and white shirts.

Tomorrow I leave at noon for Ream. From Ream, I go by motor to Ankor Wat, an ancient city which the French have uncovered from the jungle. I expect to remain for three or four days, then sail down the Mekong river on my way home.

Well, darling, my heart is full of happiness because our wedding day is so near. It is still difficult to understand that soon all my days of solitude will be over and that you will be with me always. After all, life is sweet and in the warm shelter of our mutual love, I know that we shall find happiness.

This letter, with all that it promised for the future, made it easier when the moment finally came for me to leave my little Chinese house. I stood for a while in my courtyard. I thought of the roses that would be blooming in the spring—and the lilacs with the little yellow butterflies flying about them. There was the wisteria arbor where Tagore had had lunch with me and my students. I thought of the nights when I stood in the moon gate listening to the distant calls of the vendors. And I thought too of all the wonderful friends who had been woven with my life during these precious years. I walked slowly through the moon gate, through the many courtyards to the huge outer gate where my ricksha boy was waiting for me. There were the last affectionate farewells before I climbed into my ricksha and rode away from my beautiful old T'ung Fu—forever, as it turned out. (For three years I have been trying to return to China. But letters to Peking are never answered and the Wellesley College group, as well as other groups on which I was to be a delegate, was turned down at the last moment by the People's Republic.)

On the little steamer which took me to Shanghai I wrote of those last hectic days:

> En route to Shanghai
> S.S. *Sientien*—January 11, 1926

Dear Mother and father,

At last I am on my way—most of which, so far, I have slept. I left Peking early Friday morning on the International train and left Tientsin by boat Sunday morning. The trains between Tientsin and Peking had been running only three days when I left! Our train was stopped by Chinese soldiers who tried to board the car I was in, but fortunately the foreign soldiers on board prevented any trouble. So you see what conditions are in North China! And you can imagine the state of my mind for the past month, wondering each day whether I could get out of Peking!

The package containing the dresses arrived on the 5th. The two packages with the hats on the 6th, the letter with the check on the 7th—and I left on the morning of the 8th! I love all the things, and the check saved my life For everything my heartiest thanks!

The manager of the bank wants us to have a noon wedding so that he can have a wedding breakfast for us. I think George would like this because he has made some good friends there, but it can't mean very much to me. All that I want is to be with him again and nothing else matters. I think it is well that we are having three days together before we are married; we have been apart so long that it will seem like getting acquainted all over again.

The last week in Peking was hectic. I got frightfully tired, and if it had not been for the Fergusons I know I should have been ill. They insisted upon my sleeping at their house so that I could get away from the mess in my rooms. Their amah took care of me; she rubbed me every night, washed my hair, brought in my breakfasts—and so I kept going. I feel much better now, although I sleep all the time.

In Shanghai I boarded the *President Madison*. The officers and staff who had been on the boat when I had sailed before, greeted me like an old friend. Because most of the passengers had debarked at Shanghai, the purser was able to give me a beautiful large stateroom with a private bath—"for a third less than the regular price," I wrote my father. So for three days I relaxed and lived in the lap of luxury; and I enjoyed every minute of it.

We were to reach Hongkong at dawn on the morning of the twentieth. I was too excited to sleep; so I was up, dressed, and on deck as we sailed into that magnificent harbor in the early morning light. There were at least twenty large ocean-going vessels in port, besides warships and cruisers; Chinese junks and sampans swarmed around the ships. I counted eight foreign flags on the vessels—besides British and American, there were French, Italian, German, Dutch, Portuguese, and Japanese. Of course East of Suez, in those days, the British flag predominated everywhere.

As I looked about the harbor, I thought of Sun Yat-sen who once said that it was here in his student days that he first got his revolutionary ideas. When he realized that it was foreigners—Englishmen —who, in less than a century, had transformed this barren island into one of the busiest shipping centers of the world, something that China had not done in 4,000 years, he knew that his country had to be shaken out of its lethargy. He returned to his home in Heung Shan, only fifty miles away, and tried to persuade the village elders to start making roads to the next village—to begin to make Heung Shan a little Hongkong. But there was no interest in changing things as they were. It was then he made up his mind that there had to be a revolution. A revolution there was, but his dream of a republic of the people, by the people, and for the people was never fulfilled, although his dream lived on in the hearts of the young Chinese whom I knew.

Life began to stir on the wharf as our ship eased into its berth. Almost at once baggage was being hoisted on board and passengers en route to America began to come aboard. In the crowd I caught sight of George and ran to the lower deck to greet him. As he took me in his arms, I vowed that never again would we be separated.

The days before the wedding were not long enough to do all the things which he had planned. Besides the visits to the consulate and the church, there were the beautiful drives to take around the island, the tram to take to the summit of the Peak for the famous view—one of the most spectacular panoramas in the world! We took the little ferry that runs from the island to the mainland to get a view of the Peak with the flights of stone steps which mount the hillside instead of streets, to see the junks, the sampans, and the floating city of boatmen for which Hongkong was famous. Whole families lived on these boats. It fascinated me to watch the boatmen propel their crafts with a great sweep of the oar at the back. With a turn of the wrist they could maneuver into any position. Canton, which I had hoped to see, was closed to all foreigners from Hongkong because of the strike after the Shanghai Incident.

I stayed at the home of some bank people, a young couple who did everything to make things pleasant for me. He was George's best man and she was my attendant. The wedding took place at noon in a small chapel—a very quiet wedding with a simple service. A wedding breakfast at the home of the bank manager on the Peak was gay and friendly—and it lasted until late afternoon. George and I went at once to beautiful Repulse Bay (of *Love is a Many Splendored Thing* fame) and had three blissful days there swimming in that wonderful phosphorous water and taking lovely walks. At that time of year the air was soft, flowers were blooming everywhere—yellow poppies by the hotel, poinsettias and hibiscus growing wild on the hills. Brilliant birds fluttered about—kingfishers dove into the water to catch their fish. At night we loved to walk on the beach watching the fishermen put out to sea with their lights low and splashing the water to attract the fish. We danced each night at the hotel. It was an idyllic time.

Back in Hongkong there was a day of shopping and consular visits before it was time to board the S.S. *Esquilino*. Then once again a gangplank was lifted, and we waved good-bye to the kind friends who had come to see us off. The ship moved slowly out of that great harbor, out into the open ocean. We had each other now, and that was all that mattered. Regardless of what life had in store for us (the great depression was ahead), we knew that our love would be our strength. We knew, too, that our days together would always be the richer because of the happy memories we shared of our life in that fabulous city of Peking.

EPILOGUE

The Northern Expedition

As long as one is only a
man of one's time, one is
less than a man.

NICHOLAI BERDYAEV

By THE END OF JUNE 1926, just after George and I had arrived in the
States and were experiencing the joy of being reunited with our families and of sharing with them the highlights of our travels, the stage
was being set in China for the military unification of the country
under the united front of the Kuomintang and the Communist party.
The armies, drilled and trained by Russian officers, were clad in well-
tailored uniforms. They were well controlled and well paid so there
would be no need to loot, to mutiny, or to desert as had happened with
soldiers in the past.

Finally on July 9 Chiang Kai-shek, as commander in chief of the
armies, led the long awaited Northern Expedition out of Canton with
the three great cities of the Yangtze valley—Hankow, Nanking,
and Shanghai—as the first objectives. Newly trained propagandists,
many of whom were eager Western-educated Chinese, preceded the
armies with Russian aid and Russian advisers. It was not by force
alone that the Nationalists were to conquer the country. Just before
the Expedition started Chou En-lai slipped into Shanghai and took
the lead in organizing the trade unions who would eventually help
take that city. Mao Tse-tung worked with the peasants organizing
rent strikes and antilandlord demonstrations. He predicted that the
peasantry rather than the industrial proletariat would provide the
main strength for the revolution in China.

The Northern Expedition advanced in two columns, reflecting the
rift in the Nationalist Movement. The left faction advanced into
Hunan toward Hankow, while Chiang Kai-shek took the more east-
erly route through Kiangsi toward Shanghai. The soldiers, following
the revolutionary doctrine of not molesting or preying upon the people, swept forward in a series of triumphs. Hankow was taken in
October and the Nationalist Government was transferred there from

Canton in December. Hankow, now proclaimed the new National capital, soon became the gathering place for radicals from all over China. Here were collected among other leaders Madam Sun Yat-sen, Eugene Chen, the antiforeign foreign minister, and Borodin, the chief adviser on revolution. They settled down in "a fervent atmosphere of international revolution."

With the support of the more conservative leaders of the Kuomintang, Chiang Kai-shek aimed for the rich, strategic Shanghai-Nanking region. He had close connections with the moneyed interests in Shanghai and was able eventually to arrange substantial loans which were to free him from further reliance upon the Soviet Union. As he entered Hangchow, only one hundred miles from Shanghai, thousands of spectators lined the streets, smiling as they watched the well-equipped troops parade through the city. Seldom had the people of China ever welcomed soldiers before. A future chancellor of Peking University who was in the crowd said "my heart thumped against my ribs in ecstasy as the good name of a modern army in China was established." Their reception confirmed the Nationalists' assertion that the war would be won 30 percent by fighting and 70 percent by propaganda. (One is reminded of Lisbon in 1974 when crowds lined the streets cheering the revolutionary soldiers and giving them red carnations.)

As Chiang's troops advanced on Shanghai, their battle was fought for them. The revolutionists led by Chou En-lai called a general strike which closed all the industries of the city. They first seized the police station, next the arsenal, then the garrison. They armed 5,000 workers and created six battalions of revolutionary troops. A citizens' government was proclaimed.

The Western Powers fearful of a revolution had frenzied consultations and a state of emergency was declared. Foreign residents prepared for a seige. At the height of the crisis, 5,000 American Marines arrived in Shanghai led by General Smedley Butler.

Two days later the Nationalist troops, whose behavior up to that time had been exemplary, moved on to Nanking and let loose a day of terror against the foreigners. Troops rampaged through the city yelling and looting, attacking foreigners, and burning foreign homes. Six foreigners were killed including the vice president of Nanking

University. Many foreigners took refuge on Socony Hill, the Standard Oil property from which they escaped over a wall to American and British gunboats in the river. Thousands took refuge in other concessions; many left the country. In the Treaty Ports there was an outcry at this Nanking outrage. No one knew for sure where to place the blame—on the local commander known to be anti-Chiang, on the Nationalist command, or on the Communists and radicals of Hankow. The startling events that followed led to the belief that it had been Communist inspired in order to embroil Chiang with the foreigners.

On April 6 in Peking, with the approval of the dean of the foreign diplomatic corps, Chang Tso-lin's police entered the Russian Embassy compound and searched the office of the Military Attaché. They made off with a large quantity of documents and twenty Chinese revolutionists who were found on the premises. These Chinese were strangled when the documents gave evidence that Russia had seized a directing control of the Nationalist Movement and that the Internationale was working through Hankow.

When this news reached Chiang Kai-shek, his troops returned to Shanghai and launched a massive attack on the labor unions and the workers' organizations. About three hundred Communists, labor leaders, and radicals were killed, among them important Communist leaders. Chou En-lai was captured but later escaped to begin his life as a fugitive from Kuomintang assassins and as a leader of the revolution. The longing for revenge for this "white terror" never ended; the event was neither forgotten nor forgiven. When the Communists took the country in 1949, they exacted the last drop of blood from every individual they could find who had taken part in chasing them from Shanghai twenty years earlier. On April 18 in a counter revolution Chiang Kai-shek established his own government and set up his capital at Nanking.

At this same time, 600 miles up the river in Hankow, the Communist party received new instructions from Stalin directing that the confiscation of the landlords' land should proceed immediately, that the unreliable generals should be destroyed, and that within the Kuomintang Army, Red Army forces should be created that could suddenly surface and take over. Borodin made the mistake of showing these instructions to Eugene Chen who immediately recognized Moscow's cynical game of supporting the Kuomintang with the expectancy of taking over everything for itself and the Communists, once the country had been won. When the Kuomintang-left learned what had been planned for them, the Hankow Government was shattered; and the Kuomintang-Communist coalition ended abruptly. Many of the Communist leaders fled to Moscow as did Borodin. Stalin removed him from any connection with Chinese affairs and ultimately arrested him. He died in a Stalinist concentration camp in 1953.

The new Nationalist Government in Nanking expelled the Chinese Communists from its ranks; and Chiang, urged on by his capitalist supporters, began a nationwide effort to suppress the Communist revolution. Persecution of Communist leaders, labor organizers, peasant leaders and leftists in general lasted nearly a year. Probably a quarter of a million persons lost their lives in this "purification movement."

Chiang Kai-shek strengthened his position by marrying Mai-ling Soong, sister of the wealthy banker T. V. Soong. The marriage was made possible when he disposed of his first wife as well as the Japanese mother of his son, and, at the insistence of Madame Soong, became a Christian. On December 1, 1927, following a private Christian ceremony in the Soong home, a civic wedding took place in the Majestic Hotel. More than a thousand guests attended the wedding including Admiral Bristol of the American Asiatic Fleet. In January Chiang was designated Generalissimo of the Nationalist Army, chairman of the Central Executive Committee and, as such, chief of the reorganized Nationalistic Government at Nanking—a one-party dictatorship. Financially its strength lay in the Chinese mercantile and financial circles which centered in the Industrial Settlement at Shanghai. T. V. Soong became minister of finance.

The following spring, Chiang led a further expedition from the Yangtze to Peking which was occupied in June. In Peking at last the Northern Expedition had reached its goal. Then on October 10, 1928, the seventeenth anniversary of Sun Yat-sen's revolution, the National Government was formally established at Nanking (Southern Capital). Peking (Northern Capital) was renamed Peiping (Northern Peace). One by one the foreign powers made treaties with it and so gave the Nationalist revolution international recognition. But the civil war which began in 1927 was to last for twenty-two more years —and it was a battle to the death.

"Out of order and disorder, perpetually clashing and reclashing, came the worlds."

The Long March

Crystals grow under fantastic pressures in the deep
crevices and confines of the earth.
They grow by fires, by water trickling slowly in
strange solutions from the walls of caverns.
They form cubes, rectangles, and may have their
own peculiar axes and molecular arrangements.
But they, like life, like men are twisted by the places
into which they come.   LOREN EISELEY

HUNTED AND DECIMATED by Chiang's forces, the remnants of the Communists went underground or retreated into the mountainous regions of southeast Kiangsi to gain what foothold they could to survive. By October Mao Tse-tung with a small band of followers settled in the almost impregnable mountain fortress of Chingkangshan. Here in April he was joined by the ragged forces of Chu Teh, a reformed warlord and ex-opium addict.

Chingkangshan was eventually turned into a small soviet base area. When the various units which gathered there joined forces, the Red Army came into being. Chu Teh was later to be the commander in chief and Mao his political commissar. Mao and Chu remained loyal to each other through the early leadership crisis. Mao's ascendency came slowly for in the process of expansion he came into conflict with the various factions of the Communist party, among them Li Li-san and the Returned Student group. They opposed his emphasis on agrarian reform and criticized the peasant excesses. He retorted by saying that what Sun Yat-sen had not been able to accomplish in the thirty years which he devoted to revolution, the Hunan peasants had accomplished in a few months. And he reminded them that:

Revolution is not a dinner party.... It cannot be done "gently, kindly, politely, and moderately" (quoting Confucius). Revolution is insurrection, the violent action of one class overthrowing the power of another. An agrarian revolution is a revolution by the peasantry to overthrow the forces of the feudal landlord class. If the peasants do not apply great force, the power of the landlords, consolidated over thousands of years, can never be uprooted.

Mao's position strengthened as the old city leaders and officials were killed or fled to Moscow (as Li Li-san did in 1931) or were forced to take refuge with him and agree to his ideas. Because Mao worked with the peasants, they soon provided him with recruits for the Red Army, and when it was necessary hid, spied, and fought with the soldiers. Because of this peasant support, Mao and Chu worked out guerilla tactics which enabled them to survive four massive major offenses of Chiang Kai-shek. Between 1930 and 1932 hundreds of thousands of Nationalist troops were hurled against them. Mao explained his tactics by saying "When the enemy advances, I withdraw; when the enemy halts, I harass. When the enemy avoids battle, I attack; when the enemy retreats, I pursue." It has been said that modern guerilla warfare and "Chinese Communism" were born twins and both survived.

Eventually Mao and Chu left Chingkangshan to create a new and larger base at Juichin on the southern fringe of Kiangsi. Other Red units coalesced with a number of widely scattered soviets, with Juichin as the capital. The way was soon clear for the proclamation of the Chinese Soviet Republic. At Juichin on November 7, 1931, delegates from some fifteen soviet areas assembled and adopted a Constitution. Mao Tse-tung was elected Chairman of the Republic and Chu Teh was confirmed in his position of overall commander in chief of the Red Army.

The fifth campaign which Chiang Kai-shek launched against the Communists in 1933 was based on a new strategy conceived by him and his German advisers. Instead of rushing troops into the Communist stronghold, Chiang threw a tight blockade around the entire Central Soviet District depriving the Communists of vital supplies.

The combined pressure of the Kuomintang economic blockade and military attacks was so effective that by the summer of 1934 the size of the Soviet district was greatly reduced. With mounting casualties the Communist position became increasingly precarious. Faced with the prospect of being completely annihilated, the Communist leaders made the agonizing decision to evacuate their remaining forces. In October 1934 after a year's resistance they broke out of their Kiangsi stronghold. Then moving swiftly by night, they began their epic Long March—a march which was to take them a year and cover some six thousand miles (more than twice the greatest distance across our country). About 90,000 men and women set out on their gruelling journey; only 20,000 survived at the end.

Constantly harassed, the guerillas crossed eighteen mountain ranges and twenty-four rivers, fighting at least one action every day. They faced such daunting hazards as the bridge over the Tatu River in the far west. The Nationalists had removed half the wooden floorboards of this bridge which was more than three hundred feet long and suspended on sixteen iron chains. The bridge had to be crossed for the river was in roaring flood, so the soldiers swung themselves hand over hand across the chains which still hung above the river gorge. The pass over the Great Snowy Mountains farther to the North was 16,000 feet high, and the army had no warm clothes. Many of them were barefoot. Speaking of this pass afterwards, Mao said: "We seemed to be climbing up vertical sheets of ice, and I have no idea how I survived. Some fell down the mountainside and perished from the cold. Sometimes in the plains it was just as bad, for we were surrounded by mystery and horror. We did not know where we were. We had no maps. There were places where no one had ever been before, places so solitary we thought we had reached the end of the world. I don't know where my strength came from, for day after day I remember marching without any sleep. Day after day, endlessly." When asked what was his worst memory of the Long March, he answered "The cold—the terrible cold—and the hunger."

At year's end in spite of their terrible losses, the organization of the Red Army was not broken. Chiang had succeeded in chasing them from their Kiangsi stronghold only to see them establish themselves even more firmly in the caves of Yenan.

A Time of Promise

In great things it is enough to have tried.
ERASMUS

BY 1927 YENCHING UNIVERSITY had moved to its beautiful new buildings at Hatien with great hope for the future. Because of the high quality of its teaching and research, it was recognized as the greatest of the thirteen Protestant educational institutions in China—Topping has called it "Harvard in China." The new campus was exciting and alive—it was one of the centers of liberal Western thought. In less than ten years there had been developed a College of Natural Sciences. There was a College of Public Affairs which took its name from the Princeton School of Public and International Affairs and was largely supported by an association of graduates known as the Princeton–Yenching Foundation. Promising Yenching students often went to Princeton for a doctorate and frequently returned to the Yenching faculty.

There were departments of political science, economics, and sociology—all extremely useful in the modernization of China. Because in the 1920s newspapers were becoming increasingly influential in Chinese life, there was a Department of Journalism. It seemed important to inculcate high standards of editing and ethics at the beginning of a new profession; and from the outset this was one of the popular majors along with economics. Even vocational courses were offered. One, especially promising, was the attempt to revive the ancient Chinese ceramic industry by new scientific methods.

Chinese were given an increasing share in the educational and administration leadership so that in time Yenching could become essentially a Chinese university. President Stuart always hoped that eventually its Western origin would be largely an historic memory. With the help of the Harvard–Yenching Institute, Yenching developed an excellent department of Chinese studies. Dr. Hu Shih in his introduction to Dr. Stuart's book *Fifty Years in China* paid tribute to the Chinese scholars at Yenching, especially to Dr. William Hung who was responsible for building up a superb Chinese library, and for helping to edit and publish the excellent *Yenching Journal of Chinese Studies*.

The study of English was important. It was taken for granted that students, on entering, could take any subject in either Chinese or English. Faculty members were free to use either language or both. Visiting lecturers speaking in English were never interpreted. In talking to the student body, President Stuart often went from one language to the other. Thus students lived in a bilingual environment and those who continued their studies abroad seldom had any language difficulty.

One of Dr. Stuart's great concerns was the crucial need of better international understanding. Universities, he believed, should be centers for generating a cosmopolitan outlook. Yenching already had a start in that direction. Although it was predominately American in origin and support, there was from the beginning a significant British element. This was strengthened by adopting the Oxford Tutorial system with special British sources of support. And almost from the beginning a committee in Switzerland supported two Swiss members on the faculty—Dora Demiere was one of these when I was there. The French government granted a fellowship for graduate study in Paris. The German government made an annual grant to the Department of Western Languages. Italy granted eight fellowships with most of the expenses paid for travel and residence together with the privilege of studying at any recognized university in the country.

The future of Yenching was full of promise. In fact it was a time of promise all over the world for on May 21, 1927, Charles Lindberg had flown the first plane across the Atlantic and had landed in Paris. His jubilant reception in France and his heart-warming welcome in America reflected the feeling everywhere that a momentous event had taken place.

I had recently returned from the Orient. I remember, as I tried to go to sleep that night, that Mongolia came into my mind. I thought of the slow-moving camels that had taken the precious Chinese silk across the deserts to the rich merchants beyond the Pamirs. I could see the long train of camels that came out of the shadow of Hongor Obo and slowly disappeared in the glow of the western sky.

I thought of Vasco da Gama's caravels that had sailed out upon an unknown ocean; they were to discover the sea route to India and make it possible for Portugal to open the China Trade. Each one had brought the world a little closer. In time had come the great ocean liners and I thought wistfully of the *President Madison*. Now the airplane had ushered in a new age and the world was never to be the same again. One of the basic revolutions in history had taken place.

The great promise of Yenching was never to be fulfilled as anticipated. Forces were already at work which would not only affect Yenching but would engulf the world and lead to a second world war—a war in which the airplane would play a devastating part. Hu Shih remarked, "The time has now come in this world of ours when peace as well as war is indivisible."

The Japanese War

> For right and wrong are confused here, there's so much
> war in the world.
> Evil has so many faces, the plough so little
> Honor; the laborers are taken, the field untended
> And the curving sickle is beaten into the sword that yields
> not.
> There the East is in arms, here Germany marches;
> Neighbor cities, breaking their treaties, attack each other;
> The wicked War-god runs amok through the world.
>   THE GEORGICS OF VIRGIL (CIRCA 40 B.C.)

ON SEPTEMBER 18, 1931, five years after Yenching had moved to Ha-tien, the Japanese army on the pretext of a bomb explosion on the Southern Manchurian Railway, seized Mukden in "self-defense" and moved swiftly to a military occupation of Manchuria. This Japanese invasion was the first deliberate attack on the world order which had prevailed for twelve years after the First World War. It was a challenge—a test of the reality and strength of that international order which had been built upon a number of treaties and which we naively believed had at last ushered in a world of brotherhood.

When the news of this incident reached Nanking, Chiang Kai-shek, embroiled with the Communists, instructed Chang Hsueh-liang to avoid any enlargement of the incident. And on September 23 he announced to the nation that China was entrusting its case to the League of Nations. The League was unable to come forward in China's defense but it twice designated time limits for the withdrawal of Japanese troops. Tokyo ignored the League demands. Therefore, in December, the Lytton Commission was appointed by the League to go to Manchuria to investigate. Although their report was phrased in such a way as to hope that Japan would save enough face to accept it, the report did find Japan an aggressor and recommended an autonomous administration under the restored Chinese sovereignty. Again Japan rejected the findings and a month later withdrew from the League. Well do I remember this Mukden incident for I was reminded of what my Swedish friends in Mongolia had prophesied during the summer of 1924.

Secretary of State Stimson was quick to warn Japan that the United States, although not a member of the League, did not intend to recognize "any situation, treaty or agreement which might be brought about by means contrary to the covenant and obligations of the Pact of Paris." However not only did the United States offer no material aid to China but American merchants continued to sell shiploads of scrap iron and steel to Japan.

The fact that the League Powers were unwilling to back their stand by force, military or economic, led to the collapse of Western prestige in the Far East, caused bitter disillusionment in China, and encouraged Japan to move ahead with her imperialistic ambition in Manchuria, Mongolia, and North China.

China had rested her defense on guarantees which the world had provided for just such a situation—not only the League Covenant but the Nine–Powers Treaty, and the Kellogg–Briand Pact signed in Paris in 1928 by which fifteen nations, including Japan, undertook to renounce war as an instrument of national policy and to agree that the settlement of all disputes "shall never be sought other than by peaceful means except in cases of self-defense and vital national interests."

Japan had now tested the powers and was to prove the futility of international words without teeth. In 1934 she gave notice of her intentions to terminate her adherence to the Washington Naval Treaty —her last treaty tie with the West. She had already created in Manchuria the independent state of Manchukuo. Now on March 1 at a replica of Peking's Temple of Heaven, Henry Pu-yi, the last relic of the Manchu dynasty in his twenty-eighth year, made obeisance to Heaven and was enthroned as Emperor K'wang Teh. In 1931, just seven years after he had fled the palace in Peking to take refuge from Feng Yu-hsiang's troops, he had boarded a Japanese steamer to return to the land of his ancestors. As Emperor K'wang Teh he was to be only a front for Japanese imperialism. Manchuria was to become the staging ground for Japan's mainland advance.

The following month in an historic statement called the Amau Doctrine, Japan announced her intention of controlling China. She slammed shut the Open Door and proclaimed a Pacific Monroe Doctrine. The statement proclaimed that Japan's purpose was to act "as guardian of the peace and order of East Asia." As such she claimed the right to oppose loans and any support of other nations to China and denied China's right "to avail herself of the influence of any other country to resist Japan." This Amau Doctrine shocked the world.

But it was a time of economic crisis in Europe. Great Britain, the major Western power in the Far East, was about to go off the gold standard. Europe was on the edge of panic. The United States in the midst of the great depression was not looking for a foreign quarrel. Certainly no one who lived through the 1930s can ever forget the widespread feeling of despair and fear. Although our Secretary of State put America on record as rejecting the Amau Doctrine, the reply was issued, as he said, "in a respectful and friendly spirit."

Not only America but all the other nations, eager to avoid war with a "fanatical Japan," remained quiescent. From then on each successful encroachment was accepted more and more as inevitable and the foreign powers became less and less inclined to demand a halt. As an era of appeasement began, the international horizon began to darken.

Hitler and Mussolini saw the point. Hitler withdrew Germany from the League. In March 1935, he repudiated the Versailles Treaty and declared Germany's intention to rearm. In March 1936 he occupied the Rhineland unopposed. In May Mussolini annexed Ethiopia. I can remember the despair which everyone felt when Halle Selassie in a final appeal for help warned "If they do not come, the West will perish." In July civil war broke out in Spain when a rebellion of the right was supported by the dictators and resistance encouraged by the Communists. The world's growing concern of Fascism focused on Spain, although the democracies took a stand of nonintervention. But even as they looked on, sides were being drawn for the struggle that was soon to come.

Japan's next move came in November 1935 when she issued another ultimatum—this time demanding the declaration of an autonomous North China. The arrogant presence of the Japanese in North China had brought into being an intense nationalism. When this news broke there was a massive student protest in Peking. Crowds applauded, then joined the march defying the police and shouting patriotic slogans. Tens of thousands participated in the Peking–Tientsin area. Reminiscent of other student demonstrations, this one spread to other cities. Students commandeered the train on the Shanghai–Nanking run and urged people along the way to compel the government to stand firm against Japan. A National Salvation League was organized and in the next months some thirty groups and associations were formed for patriotic defense against Japan.

Mao Tse-tung declared that the defeat of Japan took precedence over social revolution. It was necessary first to defeat foreign imperialism and win independence, for only then could the struggle for socialism succeed. He was willing to join forces with the Kuomingtang against the imperialistic enemy. "For a people being deprived of its freedom, the revolutionary task is not immediate. . . . We cannot even discuss Communism if we are robbed of a country in which to practice it. If China wins her freedom, then the world revolution will progress rapidly."

The Chinese joined forces and Japan saw the signal. A China developing a sense of national unity would obstruct her peaceful advance. On July 7, 1937, the Japanese created another faked incident near Peking and on July 28 they took over the city. Dr. Stuart recounts this in his *Fifty Years in China:*

I was awakened soon after dawn that morning by the dropping of Japanese bombs on a military barracks located near our campus; it was my first experience of aerial bombing and a terrifying one. There was panic on the campus and the wildest rumors.

The immediate problem for me was whether to follow other universities in a hasty withdrawal to some spot in Free China or to take the consequences of staying where we were. No one could predict what the Japanese would do. I finally decided to stay. The disrupted entrance examinations were resumed. We flew the American flag for the first time on our high pole. (Previously at Hatien we had flown only the Chinese national flag or our University pennant.)

On August 8, if anyone had been standing on the old Tartar Wall over the Legation Quarter, he would have seen the Japanese forces enter the city of Peking. The old capital had seen many conquerors before—now the oppressive Japanese had come. By September, the long-awaited formal announcement was made that the Kuomintang–Communist united front had been formed. The Chinese war for national survival had begun.

For four years and five months China fought Japan single-handed —a longer period than World War I. In the meantime the war in Europe had begun. Hitler's panzer divisions overran and subjugated Poland, Denmark, Norway, Holland, Belgium, France, Yugoslavia, and Greece. By the summer of 1941 there were only two nations left fighting aggressors—the British Empire fighting in Europe and Africa, and the Republic of China fighting the Japanese in Asia. Not until Germany suddenly attacked Russia, and Japan occupied the whole of French Indo-China, was there a concerted world action.

A few days after Japan's march into French Indo-China, the United States, the British Empire, and the Netherlands East Indies enforced an embargo against Japan. In August President Roosevelt and Prime Minister Churchill met and proclaimed to the world the eight principles of the Atlantic Charter. But these actions were not enough to stop Japan's well-planned attack on the Pacific outposts of the British Empire, and the United States. These attacks came on December 7 and horrified the world. Not only had Pearl Harbor been attacked but Guam, the East Indies, Hongkong, the Philippines, and Malaya. The democratic world was unified at once. On January 2, 1942, a joint declaration of war against Japan, Germany, and Italy was signed and announced in Washington by the representatives of twenty-six United Nations.

What about China in her fight against Japan? In the first fifteen months of the war, China lost all of the important cities on the coast and on the rivers. She lost control of all her modern centers of commerce, industry, and manufacture. With the loss of Canton, she was cut off from direct access to the sea. According to Hu Shih who was our Chinese ambassador at the time, the government had lost over 90 percent of its revenue; tens of millions of people were homeless and penniless; war casualties ran into the millions, and civilian suffering was beyond belief.

The situation was so desperate that many people declared that with the fall of Canton and Hankow the war was over. It was not. With no money, with little modern equipment and with no direct access to the sea, the Chinese fought on for another three and a half years.

How did they do it? First they had great space—a whole continent to move around in. In over four years of fighting, the Japanese were never able to occupy more than 10 percent of the country. Having space gave them time—two ingredients which the small European countries did not have. And they had numbers which gave them a tremendous supply of manpower. China's population at the time was over 400,000,000 as compared with Japan's 80,000,000. They had an enormous army of 3,000,000 men. This numerical superiority prevented Japan, with all of her mechanical superiority, from ever encircling or entrapping that army.

Above all, the Chinese people had an amazing capacity for hard work—a torrential energy unlike any other people. Without modern tools, they built thousands of miles of highways with hand labor. Thousands of tons of equipment and machinery were transported into the interior without a single modern railway; it was transported mostly on human backs and human shoulders. In parts of the famous Burma Road they had to chisel into the side of a mountain with thousands of feet of canyon below. This was done by actually hammering away the rock, for the dynamite and gunpowder had to be saved for the enemy.

Finally when the whole world became involved in the fight against aggression, there was the assistance from abroad for which they had waited so patiently. The financial and economic aid and the embargo against Japan were all invaluable in strengthening China's will to fight on.

In 1942 while speaking of China's fighting strength and morale, Hu Shih said "If there is a moral in this story of the fight of my people for freedom, the moral is a little patience. We must realize that we are now fighting the greatest war in human history ... let us all work together, work hard but with patience, for the coming of that great day when in the words of your President 'The sun will shine down once more upon a world where the weak will be saved and the strong will be just.'"

During most of the Japanese occupation of Peking the Westerners had been unmolested. Life went on very much as usual. However, it was evident that time was running out for those who had lived so comfortably in the shell of Old Peking. There began to be a different tempo, a Western speed. "The long rich tranquil hours" were nearly over. The American flag began to be raised over courtyards on intermittent days of crisis; an American passport assumed new meaning. As American relations with Japan became worse American citizens were more and more the target of Japanese annoyance. There were frequent visits to the embassy to talk over "the situation." Finally those without vital employment were urged to leave so that if things got worse there would be fewer fellow citizens left stranded without ships to take them home.

What about Yenching? For four years the university proved to be a little oasis of freedom against Japanese oppression. There were almost daily incidents, usually minor ones, but always with the possibility of becoming serious. With the protection which the Chinese students enjoyed on an American-owned campus it was understood that they would not take advantage of this to carry on anti-Japanese activities. The Japanese were constantly on the watch for underground hostility and had a horde of secret police and spies whose reports led to cases of student arrest and torture.

Dr. Stuart was questioned about the nature and purpose of the university. The Japanese military mind simply could not conceive of an institution the size and importance of Yenching being on a private basis. Perhaps to trap him, a high official called one day to ask if, in view of financial needs, the university would accept a substantial annual subsidy. When he was told that the university was dependent entirely upon voluntary private gifts, that the American Government had never contributed a dollar nor would they accept any contribution, he was so astonished that he forgot his Japanese manners and left without the usual formalities.

The autumn of 1941 was typical of the clear sparkling weather of North China and the good weather held through November. The Tientsin Alumni had long been asking President Stuart to visit them. After postponing the visit repeatedly for fear that something would "break," he finally decided to go for the weekend of December 7.

Early on Monday morning it was obvious that the Japanese had taken swift control. He was discovered on the train and taken back to Peking by two military police. On arrival he was escorted to the marine barracks in the American Consulate where some two hundred marines were interned. On the third floor where he was taken he found many old friends, among them Dr. Henry Houghton and Trevor Bowen of the Peking Union Medical College.

There were all kinds of rumors about the outbreak of war; at first they refused to believe the devastating news about Pearl Harbor, the sinking of the British ships off the Malayan coast, and all the other appalling calamities. Dr. Stuart once said:

After my first shock I began to feel an unholy satisfaction over the dastardly attack on our navy. For years I had been sending highly confidential reports to our Yenching Trustees about the Japanese menace and the advisability of our doing something to stop this before too late. These were circulated among a carefully selected list of leaders in Washington. It was discouraging to observe how unheeded were all such warnings. It came over me that some such disaster as this was needed to arouse our people to action. The Japanese were woefully deficient in their understanding of the American temper. This was probably the most costly victory in all history when—as a Chinese adage has it—the clever failed because of their cleverness.

After Pearl Harbor Yenching University was closed. The campus was taken over by the Japanese forces in the Peking area. Dr. Stuart, Dr. Houghton, and Mr. Bowen were imprisoned in the rear quarters of a compound belonging to a British businessman. They had seven guards who occupied the front residence including the only bathroom. By an underground route they were assured that they would be repatriated by the S.S. *Gripsholm* sailing from Shanghai in June. However the ship sailed without them; for some mysterious reason the local Japanese military authorities refused to release them. These quarters were to be their home for three years and eight months.

As long as Americans and other foreign friends were at large they received letters, flowers, birthday and other remembrances. When these were repatriated or imprisoned, there was loneliness and a haunting fear of what was to happen.

But there were occasional breaks. The famous bones of the "Peking

Man" had been deposited in the Peking Union Medical College after several replicas had been made. Apparently some Japanese scientists felt that the new position of their country in the world entitled them now to have this prehistoric treasure. So Gendarmerie officers called one day to question Dr. Houghton and Mr. Bowen about this. They could say truthfully that they did not know where the bones were. Actually they had been sent to Chingwangtao where an American transport was to pick them up. Whether the bones were delivered to the transport, or scattered on the sands, or met some other fate neither of them knew.

A few days later, Bowen was carried off to headquarters where he was stripped of everything by which he might commit suicide. Then he was forced to crawl on his hands and knees into a cage too small to recline in at length. A soldier stood guard and a leather thong hung nearby. He was unable to eat the food he was given but he drank the little cups of water. After five grueling days, he was questioned once more and sent back. He trembled for days at any sound which might indicate that "they" were coming again. (On February 4, 1973, the *New York Times* carried a story which told of an American tourist in Peking who was asked by his host to help find the "Peking Man." "If you can return him to us," he implored, "you will be a hero to the Chinese people." A $5,000 reward was offered but to this day the whereabouts of the "Peking Man" is still a mystery.)

*   *   *

By 1945, the world situation was complicated and discouraging. War was still raging in Europe. The Japanese war was far from ended. Furthermore, in China, there was the shadow of a dangerous conflict between the Kuomintang and the Communists. And China on the brink of civil war could not fill the vacuum that would be left by the defeat of Japan.

President Roosevelt had been informed by his military advisers that the help of Russia was needed if Japan was to be defeated in Manchuria. They predicted that the Japanese war would last for eighteen months longer with the possibility of a direct invasion of the Japanese islands a necessity. Because this would undoubtedly mean a million American casualties, Roosevelt finally decided to meet with Stalin.

On February 15, by the famous Yalta Agreement, without China's knowledge or consent, the United States made promises which forced upon China a treaty ceding to Russia joint operation of the railways in Manchuria and special commercial and naval rights in Darien and Port Arthur. Edmund Clubb, the last United States Consul General in Peking, declared that seldom in modern times had political horse-trading been based on such scanty rationale or undertaken with less regard for possible long-term consequence. Not only did the United States ride roughshod over China's interests, it neglected its own. "Just as the war was ending, Russian troops entered Manchuria where they brutally slayed Chinese, publicly raped the women, looted their possessions, and plundered the allied nations of two billion dollars worth of industrial machinery." Later they were to make available to the Chinese Communists a stockpile of Japanese military equipment. Russia's appearance in Manchuria sowed seeds that were to be harvested long after the Japanese war was over.

Two months after Yalta, on April 12, Roosevelt was dead. On May 8 war was ended in Europe. On July 16 the atomic bomb was successfully tested in New Mexico. Had this happened five months earlier there might not have been a Yalta, Russia might never have entered the war in China, and the course of history might well have been vastly different.

From July 18 to August 2 Truman and Churchill met with Stalin at the Potsdam Conference and summoned Japan to surrender unconditionally or face "prompt and utter destruction." The ultimatum was rejected by Japan's military rulers although efforts of civilians to reach a negotiated settlement had already begun with the Emperor's consent. On August 6 the atomic bomb was dropped on Hiroshima. On August 9 a second bomb was dropped on Nagasaki. On August 14 after an intense struggle over the status of the Emperor ending in America's agreement to his retention, Japan surrendered.

On August 17 Dr. Stuart, Dr. Houghton, and Mr. Bowen were summoned to Gendarmerie Headquarters. They were driven in automobiles with guards to the Commandant's reception room. The Commandant came out promptly followed by his staff in full regalia. After a short speech, regretting that they had been "inconvenienced," he informed them that they were now at liberty. Why had these three elderly men been imprisoned for more than three years? The theory was that in case the Japanese Army had to surrender, Dr. Stuart would have been used as a mediator for peace with Chiang Kai-shek; Dr. Houghton would have the responsibility of keeping him physically fit; and since they were both the top administrative officers of their respective institutions, Bowen was held as a third hostage.

Anyway, at last the thirty years' nightmare of Japanese subjugation of China was over. As Dr. Stuart said, "Now there was only the agonizing memory of the sufferings and slaughter of millions of Chinese in order that Japan's hideously militaristic ambition might be forever quelled."

The resilience of the human spirit is almost beyond belief. Two days after President Stuart's release, he met with a committee of Chinese faculty members who themselves had suffered the horrors of Japanese imprisonment. Together they began at once to consider the reopening of Yenching. Even though the university campus was being used as a Japanese military hospital and every building had been stripped of equipment, they met there to make their plans.

It was agreed that they would take a freshman class of about four hundred and have the formal opening on October 10, the Chinese Independence Day. The opening ceremony was to have as much of the usual colorful academic procedure as possible.

President Stuart, on October 10, was the principal speaker at the national observance of the formal Japanese surrender. But on that day, old friends and colleagues gathered on the University campus overjoyed at reuniting once again. They packed the auditorium and listened with rapt attention to a stirring address by Dr. William Hung. After four gruesome years, Yenching was reopened. Its nineteenth year began with enthusiasm and hope.

Once again a great world war had come to an end. There was deep relief and much rejoicing; but for those of us who had lived through the First World War there was no longer the assurance that we had fought another war to end war. We were now more aware of human hatreds and human selfishness. We had learned about the "military-industrial complex" and the fortunes that were to be made out of war. The atom bomb had made the world tremble. America, alone, had "the secret" and scientists warned that it must be guarded carefully. But nations do not trust one another; six countries scattered over the face of the earth have now successfully exploded their own bombs. There is even fear that terrorists will acquire the know-how. Today when national hatreds, suspicions, and fears flare up and explode into local wars, we know that all mankind is in peril.

The Chinese Civil War

> Even the finest arms are an instrument
>   of evil, a spread of plague
> And the way for a vital man to go is not the
>   way of a soldier.
> But in time of war men civilized in peace
> Turn from their higher nature
>   to their lower nature.
> Arms are an instrument of evil,
> No measure for thoughtful men
> Until there fail all other choice
> But sad acceptance of it.
>
> LAO-TZU (CIRCA 600 B.C.)

THE JAPANESE WAR HAD ENDED, but China's troubles were far from over. With the common enemy eliminated the struggle between the National Government (the Kuomintang) and the Communists broke into the open once again.

During the war, the National capital had been forced to move from Nanking to Chungking in the Szechwan mountains beyond the Yangtze gorges. Here Generalissimo Chiang Kai-shek established his government which had once been the rallying point for the best talent in modern China. It had attracted men like Hu Shih who was China's ambassador to the United States from 1938–1942 and P. C. Chang who was one of the representatives to the United Nations. But now after eight years of war, the leadership was worn and demoralized.

Since I knew something of the idealism, the vigor, and the efficiency of the early leaders, the evils which had grown up during the war were hard to believe. They were the age-old failings of China's officialdom—profiteering from public funds, red tape, incompetence, and concern for family and friends rather than the cause of the country. Soldiers were as much neglected as in the past and given only the barest provision for their existence. Dr. Stuart went so far as to say that the Kuomintang had become almost as bad as the corrupt bureaucracy it had overthrown. Stilwell, in charge of American operations during the war, had found Generalissimo Chiang Kai-shek impossible to work with—advice was ignored, the officials corrupt and inept beyond belief. His advice to the United States at the end of the war was "to get out now."

It was obvious that the Kuomintang was in danger of losing the support of the people, as was Chiang Kai-shek of losing the Mandate of Heaven. Yet General Douglas MacArthur, as commander of the Allied powers in the Pacific, had no alternative but to designate the Generalissimo as the agency for accepting the Japanese surrender in China, Formosa, and Indo-China. This action supported Chiang's claim that the National Government was the only legitimate government in China. And it was this government which the United States for various and seemingly compelling reasons supported throughout the ensuing civil war.

The Communists were at Yenan in north Shensi province where in 1936 they had settled after the Long March. Here in the arid, sun-baked northwest, halfway between Nanking and the border of Soviet Outer Mongolia, they lived a simple, disciplined life. An American Vice-Consul in Yenan describing what he saw of the Long March wrote of their strong morale and almost fanatical unity of purpose. Though poorly equipped and underfed they were led by men seasoned by hardship, and they showed a dedication not seen in a group in China since the Taipings.

Edgar Snow, the first journalist to visit the Communists, described them as a self-confident, even jovial, band of veteran revolutionists who had a homespun earthiness and were wholeheartedly devoted to the peasants' cause. Other foreign visitors spoke of the optimistic, sunny atmosphere at Yenan in contrast to the frustrations at the capital at Chungking. When Seymour Topping was there in 1946, he said to members of the Central Committee, "you know people in the United States are suspicious of Communists. Why don't you change the name of your party to the Agrarian Reform Party or something like that?" The committee members looked at each other in astonishment and one said gently, "We call ourselves Communists because we are Communists!" Before he left Yenan, Topping began to sense the commitment and fervor of Mao ideology. "Stand up, and be the masters of your own fate," Mao was telling his people. "In the night," Topping wrote, "the sides of the hills were streaked with light as the

people, bearing lanterns, weaved down the narrow path to the meeting hall in the valley where the leaders spoke of the struggle for a
Communist China." Mao, the scholar-poet revolutionary, read
through the night.

The party workers were taught to live in the villages, to work with
the peasants, eat their food, and live their lives. During the war, their
troops were trained to regard themselves as protectors of the people.
That meant paying for their supplies and helping the households that
quartered them. There was a Communist slogan that "the soldiers
are the fish and the people the water."

The expansion of the Communists from Yenan was at first military.
The Red Army was abolished in 1937, put nominally under the order
of the National Government, and named the Eighth Route Army.
By degrees its forces pushed into Shansi province and finally out onto
the plains of North China occupied by the Japanese forces. Because
the Communists fraternized with the people they were able to operate
as guerillas, appearing and disappearing in the populated farmland
behind the Japanese lines.

Local politicians in these areas often went over to the Japanese so
the Communists were able to replace them with their own people. As
they spread out toward the coastal areas, these new leaders were often
teachers from Peiping or other venturesome idealists who became
chairmen of guerilla governments and were later organized into a
network of decentralized government. Into these local situations came
a great influx of young students from Yenching and other universities
who had packed their belongings and joined the guerillas; they were
all fired with the spirit of the May 4 Movement. Living close to nature
and the common people they were emulating the adventurous heroes
of Chinese folklore like Sung Chiang, the Chinese Robin Hood whom
my students loved to write about.

Choral singing was a wartime development in all parts of China.
Fairbanks tells how the Communists made use of this. "It was combined with an ancient type of country dance to create a new art form
called 'seedling song,' an all-talking-singing-dancing poor man's
opera which used simple rhythms, folk tunes, a very simple chain
dance step, and propaganda songs." Like those in the days of the Em-

pire who contended for the Mandate of Heaven, the Communists worked for the support of the people.

By war's end, while the Kuomintang were eroding, the Communists were dynamic and growing. In 1936, the party membership was estimated at 40,000; by 1943, 80,000; by 1945 it had increased to 1,200,000. They were virtually an independent body—a state within a state—with political organization, territorial control, and an army.

Even before the war ended, Mao made it clear that the Communists would not accept a continuation of the Kuomintangs' one-party system nor Chiang Kai-shek's personal dictatorship. He proposed an alternate course—"a coalition government that would unite the country, abolish dictatorship, effect democratic reform . . . and build up a new, independent, free and prosperous China." There was no question that he was appealing to the deepest desires of the Chinese people who wanted peace above everything else. Even so there was never any question about Mao's ultimate goal. On the subject of coalition he stated explicitly "We Communists never conceal nor disguise our political aims. Our future and ultimate program is to advance China into the realm of socialism and communism; this has been settled and cannot be doubted."

The party members on both sides were a mere fraction of the huge, disorganized, inarticulate populace. These were neither Kuomintang nor Communist but merely Chinese wanting only to live their own lives with a minimum of government intervention or oppression. Government had never been important to the Chinese people. It was how they were governed not by whom that was important. In China it was still a time when a regime was measured by its moral worth.

The sanction to determine the final outcome between the two parties lay to a large extent with the Chinese people: the articulate middle group—the intellectuals, students, and writers who shaped public opinion—the petty bourgeoisie, the minor officials of the country's vast bureaucracy, and the peasants. At war's end the issue was still open. But China's middle group, whose shift of allegiance could prove crucial, was war-weary and ready to oppose any party that gave the appearance of being warlike. Already the Democratic League, a combination of the middle-of-the-road parties, strongly supported the Communist proposal of a coalition government.

*   *   *

When the war ended, it was the National Government that was faced with the enormous problem of ensuring the surrender of millions of Japanese in China and Manchuria. There was the overwhelming task of reoccupying the major cities from Canton to Peiping, not to mention Manchuria which Japan had occupied for fifteen years. Since the Kuomintang had neither the organization nor the resources to meet this need, the Generalissimo made an urgent plea for continued American aid. Transportation was China's greatest handicap with 90 percent of railways out of operation, river shipping destroyed, and roads as inadequate as ever. For the ultimate control of the country, the return of government forces to key cities in North China and Manchuria seemed the most urgent concern; the Communists already controlled the North China countryside and had a strong head start in the race for towns.

Thus the United States, just as it was beginning to relax and demobilize, was faced with a dilemma. Should it respond to Chiang's request for aid and undoubtedly become involved in China's civil strife or should it take Stilwell's advice to get out and let things in China take their own course?

The decision to continue aid was determined by a new world alignment. Although Fascism had been defeated, Communism now loomed as a new enemy. Since the wartime alliance with the Soviet Union was ended, fear and hatred of Communism reasserted itself. Russia had already embarked upon a cold war against its former allies. In America this led to a reign of terror imposed by Senator Joe McCarthy. Who does not remember the fear that engulfed us all on the disclosure of the Hiss case and the Fuchs case? One of the casualties of this time was Owen Lattimore who had married my good friend Eleanor Holgate. I agonized as I thought of what they were suffering. America's China policy at the time became the central issue promoted chiefly by the China lobby, agents and supporters of Chiang Kai-shek.

Under these circumstances it was argued that the United States had no alternative but to support Chiang. It quickly air-and-sea lifted 500,000 National forces back to the north and east, and thousands of miles into the principal cities of Manchuria. At the same time, 53,000 United States Marines were landed in North China to hold ports, coal mines, and railway centers until the government forces could take over. To have done otherwise, America believed, would have meant a divided China and the probable resumption of Soviet power in Manchuria.

There were many diplomats both in China and in Washington who believed the decision was futile. Colonel Yeaton, chief of the Military Observer Mission in Yenan, warned that despite the numerical inferiority of the Communists "over a long period of time the Kuomintang cannot hold out against them even with United States help." Furthermore it aligned America in many Chinese eyes with the oppressors, the landlords and tax collectors; it disheartened the liberal forces and violently antagonized Mao Tse-tung and the other Communist leaders. But there had seemed no feasible alternative. To abandon the legal government for the Communists at that time seemed not within the realm of possibility.

The last thing that the United States wanted was to get involved in another war in East Asia. It was made clear that America's aim was to see China a friendly, unified country with a stable government resting as far as possible on the freely expressed support of the Chinese people. In the hope that a political solution could be reached, everything possible was done to keep negotiations open between Chungking and Yenan. It was at the urging of the United States that Chiang finally invited Mao Tse-tung to Chungking to discuss "affairs of state." Mao's reply pointed up the issues:

It is requested that you at once discard one-party government and call a conference of all parties, establish a democratic coalition government, discharge corrupt officials, discard the secret police, recognize all parties and all groups which in the past have been declared illegal by your government, abolish all laws and regulations oppressive of the people's freedom, recognize the popularly elected governments in the liberated areas, release political prisoners, and effect economic reforms.

Assured of United States support, Chiang repeated the invitation. On August 28 just two weeks after the Japanese surrender, Mao Tse-tung and his colleagues including Chou En-lai arrived in Chungking. Although the discussions began with both sides bracing for a civil contest, the gap between them seemed at first negotiable. Neither side wanted a civil war which would only further impoverish the country. Already a spiraling inflation had brought untold misery and threatened an economic collapse. But even as the leaders talked at Chungking, troop movements were being directed northward toward the important areas to be evacuated by the Japanese. Both sides had their eyes on rich, industrialized Manchuria. There was a Nationalist slogan "China will survive or perish with the Northeast." The Communists and the Kuomintang had no illusions about each other and it was not long before Mao and Chou, convinced that Chiang had no intention of considering their demands seriously, returned to Yenan. Already sporadic fighting had taken place as the National forces met and clashed with Communist units.

It was against this background that President Truman asked General George Marshall, a man above politics who commanded national respect, to go to China as his special representative. His mission was to get the two contending parties represented in a coalition government under Chiang; their armies would be merged and reduced, whereupon American aid for reconstruction would be forthcoming.

On Marshall's arrival in January 1946, Chiang convoked the Political Consultation Conference to which all parties were invited, and a political agreement was eventually reached. A cease-fire order was issued by both armies and in February a military merger was agreed to. Fighting practically stopped. This remarkable achievement was a great tribute to General Marshall who remained neutral in China's internal political affairs but at the same time upheld the supremacy of the recognized government.

Unfortunately early in March, Marshall was recalled to Washington and did not return until late April. Immediately upon his departure, the smouldering animosities broke out again. Each side accused the other of violating the agreements; mutual suspicions and hatreds rapidly intensified.

When General Marshall returned in April he at once resumed his meetings with Chiang and Mao, but he became mired in the complexities of Chinese politics. For help he turned to Yenching's president—a man whom he knew to have influence with the Chinese people and great familiarity with the country. So just ten days after his festive seventieth birthday party at Yenching, John Leighton Stuart, at General Marshall's urging, agreed to become Ambassador.

In spite of their combined efforts, the truce—so desperately sought after—threatened to collapse in Manchuria. The National forces had already occupied Mukden and were deployed around the major cities and communication lines. The Communists, too, had arrived, in Manchuria. As the Soviets withdrew from Manchuria westward, the Chinese Communists had quickly occupied the evacuated territory and were deployed throughout the countryside.

The coming struggle for Manchuria was already taking shape. It was evident that unless the Manchurian crisis could be solved, peace would be lost. General Marshall and Ambassador Stuart did everything in their power to explain to the Generalissimo the seriousness of the situation. They urged him to make concessions to the Communists. But the Generalissimo was adamant; he would accept nothing less than the complete National Government sovereignty in Manchuria. There are some conflicts that have to be fought out; they cannot be negotiated. This was one of them. In July, the Communists renamed their military forces the People's Liberation Army, and civil war began in earnest.

*   *   *

From 1946 to 1949 China was involved in one of the great wars of modern times. At the beginning, the Nationalists had every advantage. Their forces totalled 3,000,000, the Communists 1,000,000. General Wedemeyer, Stilwell's successor, with 1,000 American instructors and advisers had trained and equipped thirty-nine divisions. The United States aid after V. J. Day totaled more than two billion dollars in addition to a billion and a half during World War II. But no aid was enough; supplies were hoarded or squandered and used ineffectively. Furthermore corruption, demoralization, and desertion steadily depleted their armies.

The Communists, on the other hand, steadily increased their

strength. They grew in numbers and in armament not only from the Japanese stock but from Nationalist defections, sales, and surrender. In contrast to the Kuomintang they were organized from the grass roots up and received strength from the support of the people.

On October 1, General Marshall notified the Generalissimo whose troops had gone into action in North China, that he would discontinue mediation unless a basis for agreement with the Communists was found without delay. But no concessions were proposed. In December, Marshall warned Chiang in person that the Communists were too strong to be defeated militarily and that negotiation offered the only way to avert the collapse of China's economy. Chiang ignored the advice. That month, just one year after he had arrived in China, Marshall notified President Truman that his mission had failed. In January 1947, he was recalled to Washington and became Secretary of State. When Stilwell learned of the mission's failure he remarked "But what did they expect? The mission was impossible. George Marshall cannot walk on water."

The National cause was deeply affected by the economic collapse which Marshall had anticipated. There was an attempt to stabilize the economy but inflation continued and brought on a creeping paralysis. Prices doubled sixty-seven times in two and a half years. In late 1948, according to Fairbanks, prices rose 85,000 times in six months. Friends who lived in Peking at that time told of the large bags of money they had to carry to pay for a single restaurant meal. Furniture, books, and clothing were sold for food. Student strikes and demonstrations became frequent—always a symptom of discontent. The Nationalists use of force against the liberal intellectuals served only to weaken their position. The public humiliation and beating of demonstrating students who were mostly noncommunist turned them toward the Communists.

Anti-American feeling was deepening because our aid was delaying the Communists' overthrow of a "rotten government." An attempt at economic reform to curb currency speculation, hoarding, and black marketing revealed a Chinese "Watergate." Chiang Chung-kuo, the Generalissimo's son by a former marriage, was put in charge of the reform program in Shanghai and was determined to enforce the regulations rigidly. The Mayor of Shanghai supported him but Chung-kuo soon found himself involved with a notorious leader of the underworld, a member of a secret society whose influence extended to top Government officials. Even Madame Chiang became involved when a huge cache of prohibited goods was uncovered in the warehouses of the Yangtze Development Corporation controlled by H. H. Kung, the banker husband of Madame Chiang's elder sister. Chung-kuo raided the warehouses and threatened to arrest David Kung, the banker's son who was in charge. But Madame Chiang quickly flew to Shanghai and David Kung soon departed for the United States. T. V. Soong, the brother of Madame Chiang, was another member of the family whose participation in government and private business manipulations linked him with the bureaucratic capitalism.

Madame Sun Yat-sen, the second sister of Madame Chiang and widow of the father of the Chinese Revolution was, on the other hand, above reproach in this respect. As head of the China Welfare Institute, she helped distribute medicine and other relief supplies to many organizations in both Nationalist and Communist areas. When the Communist government was founded in 1949, she became one of the vice-presidents of the Government Council. She had long been estranged from Chiang Kai-shek.

*　　*　　*

After three years of uninterrupted conflict, the civil war had become a National rout. Disaster followed disaster as Nationalist-held cities began to topple. In the far north Lin Piao's crack red columns had swept victoriously through Manchuria and had taken Mukden, the great industrial center of the region.

By the end of 1948, the fate of North China had been decided. The disciplined and magnificently led Communist forces were aided by defection from the ranks of the enemy. Peking and Tientsen were taken peacefully, thanks to the reputation of the People's Liberation Army.

As one city fell after another, the Nationalist Air Force transports flew into Nanking bringing generals with their personal loot. According to Topping, for weeks the transports were flying in from the north "evacuating the families, concubines, gold bars, furniture and other personal belongings of senior Nationalist officials." Because he had been with the Mukden garrison toward the end of the siege of that great city, he swore as he thought of what the transports might have done for the thousands of Nationalist troops who died trapped in the Communist encirclement on the frozen Manchurian plain.

Almost immediately after the Manchurian debacle, one of the great battles of modern history took place in central China—the decisive battle of Hsuchow upon which would turn the fate of Nanking and Shanghai. The battle began with 600,000 troops deployed on each side. The Nationalists were better equipped with tanks and artillery and had unchallenged control of the air. Against them, the Communists used the same strategy as in Manchuria cutting communications around the vast battlefield and chopping the defending forces into segments to be dispatched piecemeal.

After two months of fighting, the 130,000 survivors of the Hsuchow garrison were surrounded by 300,000 Communist troops. Supplies dropped from the air could not begin to aid the garrison adequately. Topping, describing the misery in Hsuchow, wrote that horses were slaughtered for food. "The soldiers scrounged for bark and roots in the fields. Women and children froze to death in the crowded village huts which had no fuel. Communist loudspeakers began to offer the Nationalists troops food and safety if they would surrender. Before the final artillery barrage opened fire, the loudspeakers boomed 'There is no escape!' Panic spread among the Nationalist troops as one group after another surrendered."

When the sixty-five day battle ended the Communists had won a total victory. The Nationalists had lost 550,000 men including the last of the thirty-nine American trained and equipped divisions. The Communists had taken 325,000 prisoners and won enormous booty. The way was now open for the crossing of the Yangtze and the advance into Nanking.

General David Barr, reporting to Washington on his mission to the National Government wrote: "No battle has been lost since my arrival due to lack of ammunition or equipment. The Nationalists' military debacles in my opinion can all be attributed to the world's worst leadership and many other morale destroying factors ... the complete ineptness of high military leaders and the widespread corruption and dishonesty throughout the Armed Forces."

Nanking in the winter of 1949 was shrouded in hopelessness and despair. Ambassador Stuart describing his feelings during that harrowing time wrote: "My heart ached for the nation in its exhaustion from the gigantic struggle and for the people of all classes who were suffering the consequences." Hundreds of Nationalist soldiers in their padded dishevelled uniforms wandered aimlessly in the streets. They were stragglers and deserters from defeated armies in the north. Refugees squattered on sidewalks, huddled against buildings for shelter from the cold. Every morning, the city sanitation trucks came through the central districts picking up the bodies of those who had died of hunger or cold in the night.

Before the Communists arrived at Nanking, the National Government officials had hurriedly fled from the city along with the National garrison and the municipal police. The army which had been ordered into the city never arrived. Looting had already begun. Mobs of Chinese were raiding the palatial residences of the Nationalist officials. From upper floor windows they were hurling sofas, carpets, and bedding. The goods were being hauled away in peasant carts and on the backs of excited men, women, and children. The Mayor tried to escape with 300,000,000 yuan from the city treasury but was captured by the Communists on the highway south; the value of the money he had taken was estimated that day on the Nanking market as less than 200 United States dollars.

Many of the exhausted Nationalists soldiers and refugees, fleeing from the Communist artillery fire, had entered the city and were grabbing every vehicle in sight. Even rickshas were commandeered; the ragged ricksha coolies, barefoot or in sandals, were straining as they pulled their soldier passengers with their packs. At the airport there was pandemonium as the planes of the Chinese Air Force and the two Chinese airlines were being loaded for a quick takeoff. Sobbing civilians trying to force their way on board were held back by soldiers swinging their bayonetted rifles so that the families and possessions of senior Nationalist Army officers could be taken aboard.

One Nationalist general was seen shouting orders to load his grand piano and other furniture aboard an air force plane.

The nights were full of horror. In the large American Embassy compound, the young Foreign Service officers patrolled the grounds with flashlights. All but six of the American Marines had been flown to Shanghai to avoid confrontation with the Communists. Those left behind acted as an embassy guard for the two-hundred remaining personnel.

Early in the morning of April 24, the Communist vanguards finally entered the city. Dr. Stuart at the Embassy noted sadly the marked contrast between their disciplined behavior and morale, and the apathetic appearance and disorderly conduct of the government troops.

Students from Nanking University, Ginling, and other colleges came out shouting welcoming slogans and cheering the soldiers. A few weeks earlier these same students, some six thousand of them, had demonstrated against the government demanding that peace be made with the Communists. They had even been attacked violently by government troops and police secret agents; two had been killed, hundreds wounded. Yet these students—middle-class liberals—were ignored and brushed aside by the Communists, for they had chosen to remain in college and work for peace and good government from within rather than to go into the "Liberated Areas" and join in the fight for the Communist cause. They were trapped in the middle, among the thousands of tragic victims of the war.

In May, shortly after the Communist take-over, Huang Hua arrived in Nanking to head the Bureau of Foreign Affairs and to deal with the diplomatic officials and other foreigners. Eventually he was to play an important part in the new Communist government—in 1966 he took over the Cairo Embassy, the key Chinese post in the Middle East; in 1971 he was appointed Ambassador to Canada, and later a permanent representative to the United Nations.

There was evidence that Huang Hua had been sent to Nanking because of his old association with the American ambassador. As Wang Ju-mei he had attended Yenching University and had participated in the big student demonstration protesting the inadequate government resistance to Japanese aggression. For this he had been jailed. Because he continued to be a militant activist he was often in trouble with the Nationalist police; at such times he was befriended by his Yenching professors who hid him in their homes. When in 1935 he became one of the first Yenching graduates to join the Communist Party, he changed his name to Huang Hua, as was common in such cases.

It was not long after his arrival in Nanking that arrangements were made for a meeting with his former Yenching president. Because the Communists had taken a hard anti-American stand and had announced that all diplomatic officials were to them only ordinary citizens, Dr. Stuart wondered what their meeting would be like. It was as friendly as ever and lasted two hours. During their conversation, Huang broached the subject of United States recognition of the Communist regime. Dr. Stuart explained that the foreign countries could not do otherwise than continue to recognize the National government until a new government emerged which had the support of the Chinese people and gave evidence of its willingness and ability to maintain relations with other nations according to international standards. Huang then raised the question of a visit to Peiping saying that he was quite sure that Mao Tse-tung and Chou En-lai would be very glad to see him. "You are an old friend of many in the Communist Party." Huang made it clear, however, that the visit would be a personal one in his capacity as the former president of Yenching. But to the Ambassador it was obvious that the Communist leaders were seeking an opportunity to discuss relations between the two countries. Both men notified their respective capitals of the results of their first contact; Dr. Stuart stressed in his message to Washington the invitation to Peiping.

A month later in Shanghai, Dr. Stuart met with some three hundred members of the Yenching Alumni Association. All of them—Nationalists and Communists alike—urged him to go to Peiping to meet with Mao and Chou; they considered this invitation of momentous importance. But no answer had yet been received from Washington regarding such a visit.

A few days later Mao Tse-tung made an overture for diplomatic relations:

We proclaim to the whole world that what we oppose is exclusively the imperialist system and its plots against the Chinese people. We are willing to discuss with any foreign government the establishment of diplomatic relations on the basis of the principles of equality, mutual benefit and mutual respect for territorial integrity and sovereignty. The Chinese people wish to have friendly cooperation with the people of all countries and to resume and expand international trade in order to develop production and promote economic prosperity.

Huang called a second time on the Ambassador and reassured him of a welcome in Peiping by Mao and Chou. That day Dr. Stuart sent a second dispatch to Washington. Again there was no answer.

On July 1, the twenty-eighth anniversary of the founding of the Chinese Communist Party, Mao Tse-tung made known both his domestic and foreign policy:

Internally, arouse the masses of the people. That is, unite the working class, the peasantry, the urban petty bourgeoisie and the national bourgeoisie, form a domestic united front under the leadership of the working class, and advance from this to the establishment of a state which is a people's democratic dictatorship under the leadership of the working class and based on the alliance of workers and peasants.

Externally, unite in a common struggle with those nations of the world which treat us as equals and unite with the peoples of all countries, that is, ally ourselves with the Soviet Union, with the People's Democracies and with the proletariat and the broad masses of the people in all other countries, and form an international united front.

Dr. Stuart was shocked when he heard this statement and knew that it shattered any hope of an understanding with the United States. He was not surprised when the next day a message was received from the State Department instructing him to decline the invitation to Peiping. He began at once to plan for his departure for Washington. There were weeks of discomfort, frustration, and vexation before matters were cleared with the Communists. It was August 2, 1949, that John Leighton Stuart finally flew out of China—out of the country and away from the people he loved and to whom he had devoted his life. Shortly after his arrival in America, the State Department announced that the United States intended to retain its diplomatic relations with the Nationalist government. Four days later Mao published an article "Farewell Leighton Stuart" in which he described the Ambassador as a symbol of the complete defeat of the United States policy of aggression. All of his former colleagues in Yenching were sad that he had not remained in Peiping where he was so beloved as president of the university.

Dr. Stuart believed that had he been permitted to go to Peiping a way might have been found to keep open a channel of communication between Washington and Peiping. There were many who agreed with him and thought that the Truman administration should have accepted eagerly Mao's invitation. They were convinced that if America had been able to talk with the Communists, many misunderstandings might have been avoided as well as much of the agony in East Asia in the following decades. The refusal of the State Department in 1956 to allow correspondents into China when the Chinese government offered them visas without condition was considered another tragic diplomatic error. As Fairbanks has said "Fear and ignorance led to disaster." Washington cut itself off from relations with a government controlling one-quarter of the world's population.

In the summer of 1949, with the Kuomintang's army in demoralized retreat and Chiang Kai-shek, with American aid, soon to be on his way to Taiwan, the Communists moved their government from the caves of Yenan to the yellow-tiled Forbidden City in Peiping which was renamed Peking. Their government, called the People's Republic of China with Mao Tse-tung as the head and Chou En-lai as premier and foreign minister, was duly constituted on October 1, 1949 and recognized by the U.S.S.R., Great Britain, India, and a number of other nations. When the new Chinese flag was raised in Tien An Men Square a new era in China had begun.

In power, the Communists proceeded with a program of reform. They took land from the landlords and gave it to the tenants. There was a Communist slogan—"Land to those who till it." They began to subject the whole population to courses of indoctrination. They established a system of secret police, of informers, of people's courts.

They "nationalized" all education. They closed in on merchants and shippers both Chinese and foreign. They abused foreign officials. They refused to do business with some of the diplomats even with those from countries which had recognized the Communist regime. They embarked on a series of violent purges in which they liquidated several million of their own people. Their animosity was directed especially against the Chinese who had opposed them politically or who had been "poisoned" by foreign influence.

At first the intellectuals had enthusiastically welcomed the advent of the Communist regime. But as they were forced to attend the re-education courses, they began to sense what this "People's Democracy" was going to mean in their lives. One Chinese professor at Yenching told a friend of mine on returning from such a meeting "This is intellectual suffocation. All of this may be necessary for China but it is my misfortune to have been born at this time."

Foreigners in China, especially those who had roots there, were loath to believe that the Bamboo Curtain was being lowered, that the Communists wanted none of their works inside the Curtain and meant for most of them to leave. They were forced to face the hard facts. They saw their institutions and enterprises destroyed or taken over; they saw their Chinese associates persecuted and imprisoned, their properties confiscated and appropriated for Communist use. They found themselves mistreated, squeezed out, and, in many cases, forcibly deported.

One of the last liquidations of Western-created-and-supported cultural enterprises was the closing of Yenching University and the merging of all the faculty, student body, and facilities into a new National University under the direction of the Communist Ministry of Education.

When most of the foreigners had departed, the Bamboo Curtain was finally dropped. For twenty-five years China was once again (except for the U.S.S.R.) isolated from the West.

A New China

There is a loftier ambition than merely to
stand high in the world. It is to stoop down
and lift mankind a little higher.

HENRY VAN DYKE

WHAT HAD HAPPENED during those twenty-five years? For me who
knew the old China in the turbulent warlord era, a miracle had taken
place.

The country was at last united. Sun Yat-sen had once complained
that getting the Chinese to work together was like trying to make a
rope out of sand. It was independent, freed from the foreign powers
who for a hundred years had dominated, exploited, and humiliated
China. All the poverty and misery which I had seen had completely
disappeared. There were no more pitiful beggars on the streets nor
underfed ragged children. The people—all the people—now had
enough to eat, decent clothes to wear, and a place to live. There were
no more sweating ricksha coolies nor other human beings being used
as beasts of burden.

China was clean; there was no more filth nor refuse in the streets.
There were no more flies such as covered the top of my Peking cart
and swarmed on the *k'angs* of the Chinese inns where I stayed. Disease had been brought under control. There were no more famines,
no more epidemics of cholera, smallpox, plague, nor dysentery. Competent medical care at minimal or no expense was now available in
all but the most remote areas of the land. "Barefoot doctors," mostly
peasants trained as paramedics, were working in the rural areas where
80 percent of the people lived. There were more than a million of
them involved in sanitation activities, health education, and im-
munization programs. They dispensed medicine and provided simple
medical services. The difficult cases were referred to physicians at the
commune or county hospitals. Almost every peasant belonged to a
cooperative health care group and paid low medical insurance fees.
Prescriptions were covered by insurance; contraceptives and im-
munizations were free.

All the antiquated and decadent elements of the old Chinese society had disappeared. Gone were the opium dens and the houses of prostitution. Venereal disease had been practically eradicated, even in Mongolia. No longer were young girls being sold as prostitutes, concubines, or as household slaves; this happened when I was there. Socially the Chinese had developed a cohesive, well-disciplined society in which crime, corruption, and juvenile delinquency were virtually unknown. People were safe anywhere in China—even at night on unlighted streets. Illiteracy had practically disappeared; 80 percent of the people had been illiterate before. And at last all women had now been released from the miseries of a very degrading feudal system. They had equal rights with men—in some cases even equal pay for equal work. Mao said "Women hold up half of heaven."

China had no debt, little or no unemployment. The galloping hyper-inflation which had been raging since 1945 had been brought under control. Prices had not risen in twenty years. Bridges had been built, even one across the great Yangtze river. Hydro-electric plants and huge reservoirs had been constructed as well as irrigation and draining stations. Now there were railroads and highways where once "cracked feet plodded with their burdens." A merchant navy was flying its flag in many ports of the world. A Chinese atomic bomb had been exploded and a Chinese-made satellite had been placed into orbit. "The East Wind is prevailing over the West Wind," Mao declared.

Was this all true? Could this have been accomplished in only a quarter of a century? Old China friends who had been admitted into China during and after the Nixon visit have assured me that most of this was true. They all impressed upon me that the social revolution going on in China was unlike any other in the world. China was experimenting in an incredible way with an overturned and leveled social order; it was the most rapid reordering of society in human history. All traces of the old Chinese society which we knew had disappeared—the society with its privileges and wealth for the very few but demoralizing poverty for the vast majority of the peasants and the Chinese people.

China had "stood up." It had made itself into a largely self-sufficient, growing, fiercely independent country. It now had a place of dignity in the world and by its own strength had accomplished this. Although it was still in a revolutionary and economically developing stage with many grave problems, there was a new spirit in the land—a buoyancy, an excitement, a spirit of confidence, a strength which comes from belief in oneself.

The son of one of my friends who was born in China, had gone to the Peking American School and attended Yenching University, had gone to Peking in the spring of 1971. What had especially impressed him was to find that the reverence for Mao was honest. He had expected snickering when the people sang "We love Mao" but that was not true. He was struck by the cleanliness of everything. Spitting, defecating, and urinating in the streets—commonplace when I was there—had been outlawed; execution on occasion had been used to put the law across. Each person had a certain area of the street to clean and did it proudly—several times a day—every man, woman, and child.

He spent a day at Yenching, now a part of the great Peking University complex, lecturing and speaking to the students. From the students' questions he judged that they were on a low junior college level. At least he was thankful that after the Cultural Revolution young people were studying again. He looked into the stacks at the library and was surprised to find everything intact. He looked up several books he especially remembered and they were still there although the word was that they had been burned.

He talked with the American physician, Dr. George Hatem, known and venerated all over China as Dr. Ma Hai-teh (Virtue from overseas). He was born in Buffalo, New York, educated at the University of North Carolina, and medically trained at the University of Geneva in Switzerland. It was he who was largely responsible for ridding the country of prostitution and V.D. This had been done by closing all brothels in the cities. The girls were sent to rehabilitation centers and told that they were not to blame for what had happened to them. "You are the victims of the old society; you were forced into prostitution for the profit of others. Now there is a new order, a new government, a new society and you are a part of it. If you want a trade you will be taught one." Gradually as their pride and dignity as human beings were restored, they were sent out as nurses, teachers,

and clerks with the assurance that never again would their government permit poverty to drive them or their children to beg, steal, or
prostitute themselves in order to survive. They were told "China has
eliminated the economic roots of prostitution and crime."

Not only had the Chinese government outlawed prostitution, it had
also mobilized an army of dedicated medical and political workers to
find and treat millions of V.D. sufferers. Asked if he thought the Chinese system would work in America, Dr. Ma replied, "No, you have
to devise a social system wherein your masses, your personnel, your
medical people are more intensely motivated than they are at present.
I think it is sad that the United States which has more money, more
doctors, more antibiotics, more of everything than any other country
in the world is unable to conquer its V.D. affliction."

"What of drugs?" he was asked. "I think you will never get rid of
drugs as long as you have a profit system."

He found it hard to believe that the Chinese were really Communists. Like many of us who knew the old China he had thought that
the humanistic traditions of Chinese civilization and the materialism
and dogmatism of Communism would clash. But after more than
twenty years there was no question in his mind that there was great
vitality in Mao's version of Communism. Yet China was by no means
a new heaven and a new earth; like every other country it was made
up of human beings. Serious mistakes had been made and disputes
had occurred at high levels and low. While the Communists could
count great achievements, he saw that they could not deny grave
problems.

In the spring of 1973 the Randolph Sailers, colleagues of mine at
Yenching, spent a month in China. They were married in Peking in
1925 and had lived and breathed Yenching University for nearly
thirty years. Ever since they left the Orient in 1950 they had been
completely out of touch with their Chinese friends.

On their return to this country they were asked: "What did you
get from your visit there?" "Great inspiration," they said, "and what
seems to us fresh insights and deep questions to ponder." They felt a
determination to create a new type of society for a quarter of the people of the world. The central point of contrast to our American society

was not Dictatorship versus Democracy, Regimentation versus Freedom, but the presence in China of one over-riding national purpose and goal as contrasted with our own exaltation of diversity and individuality. What was China's goal? A gradual rising standard of living evenly distributed, a society governed by the principle "from each according to his ability; to each according to his need." This was to be accomplished by preventing the rise of a privileged class, by assigning jobs and educational opportunities, and requiring all who do not work with their hands to spend months each year working in the factories or countryside.

They spent three days on the old Yenching Campus. To them it looked amazingly the same except for the huge statue of Mao Tse-tung opposite the entrance and a great banner "Serve the People" written in Mao's handwriting on the marble boat on the lake. At the University they saw many of the professors whom they had known—most of them teaching, writing, or doing research in their old subjects. They talked with one professor whose son was now a peasant. When asked if this disappointed him, he said: "I hope he will be a good peasant and maybe some day his abilities will be used in another way." A Yenching graduate whom they met had a daughter who was in the country tending sheep. It was where her country needed her. They also saw other friends and former students, some of whom were in places of great responsibility. All were working hard and with apparent enthusiasm for the New China.

Though they found it hard to conceive a society that repudiated individualism, they were convinced that in China something new had come into the world with tremendous possibilities for good. It is too early to know whether or not the great venture will succeed. But whatever the future brings they believe that the world will be much poorer if it does not succeed and infinitely richer if it does.

There were many things to ponder after their visit, like the cultural shock that hit them as they came back to America where the life purpose of "getting ahead" and all that it implied were so widely accepted; the flood of appeals for worthy causes they found in their mail on their return. In China money contributions were declined—sharing meant shared services.

Before they left Peking two couples came to see them. One brought

500 Chinese dollars, the principal and interest of a patriotic bond they had taken out in 1950 and forgotten, the other with a big suitcase and leather bag beautifully packed with some of their Chinese treasures, plus seventy dollars from furniture sold—all left in 1950 for their friends to keep and use. One of the four remarked "you know that the People's Government is very careful about private property."

* * *

I was in London in the spring of 1973 and visited my friend Jui T'ang just after she had returned from two months in China. As we sat talking one night I said to her, "Jui T'ang tell me about Peking."

"There were many things I missed," she said, "like the Peking Wall, my home, the birds, the sound of a solitary flute at night and a hawker's cry. But there was nothing I saw that I did not approve of."

"I can understand," I said, "why the peasants and the workers are happy with China today, but what about men like your father and the Chinese professors at Yenching?"

"I saw many of them," she answered; "they are well taken care of and I did not see one who did not think that what had happened was for the good of China."

"Visitors to China have told me how very drab the women are. Did they seem this way to you?" I asked.

"The Chinese women today are too busy doing what needs to be done for China to think of themselves or of makeup and pretty clothes. Other things are more important to them."

"What about Mao Tse-tung? How do you account for his great hold upon all the people?"

"His common sense" was her quick reply. "He was able to rise from obscurity and lead China to dignity. He is one of the people and his life's work has transformed their lives. Because of this he has become both a symbol and an inspiration."

She wanted me to know about the May 7 Schools, named from the date when Mao suggested setting them up. They are mostly farms in the countryside where professors, Party bureaucrats, engineers—basically everyone who does not work with his hands—are expected to spend several months each year working, holding discussions, and studying. The idea is to remind them of how most Chinese live so that they will identify with the interests and ideas of the workers and peasants. She told of an engineer at one of the schools who spent most of his time tending pigs. He felt it was a valuable experience. "I have always liked pork," he said, "but I never knew how much work goes into raising it."

When she had finished a faraway look came into her eyes and she said thoughtfully: "Only those of us who are Chinese and lived through the agony of the civil war can understand or appreciate China today."

We sat for a few moments in silence. Then in her quiet way she told me that what was happening in China was really not anything new. The Thoughts of Mao Tse-tung in the "little red book" are different from those expressed before because we are living in modern times; but the pattern is not new. During the days of Medieval China when Neo-Confucianism took form, Chu Hsi (1130–1200), the greatest teacher and scholar of that time, devoted himself to compiling the thoughts of his great contemporaries in works which became required reading for every literate Chinese from the fourteenth century on. And his compilations in turn had its roots in the most famous book in Chinese history, the *Analects,* the sayings of Confucius.

So to the Chinese people it is not strange to have Mao telling them to think and act in a certain way. Thought control has long been accepted in China. And, smiling, she reminded me that the great Charles Darwin had once said that the highest possible state of moral culture is when we recognize that we *ought* to control our thoughts.

For awhile we talked of the old China which I had known and loved, of her father, the typical Confucian scholar, of her home and the beautiful old T'ung Fu, of our production of the *Goddess of the Moon* and our visits to the Chinese opera and to the Buddhist temple with the lovely peony trees—all reflections of that old Chinese Civilization which was one of the great achievements of the human spirit. She was glad that I knew something of the old Chinese life; it had disappeared because it was no longer viable in the modern, industrial world. But the basic cast of characters that made China great still exists, and she believed that no revolution could ever uproot all of China's cultural roots. She found Mao's stress on morality in keeping with the traditional Chinese view that good government depends on superior men guided by inner sincerity and ruling by moral example. This to the Chinese had always been more important than rule by impersonal laws and abstract principle. Even many of Mao's reforms are like those of the past, she said.

There was Emperor Wu-ti (140–87 B.C.) one of the great figures of Chinese history who lived in the Han dynasty. He had nationalized the resources of the soil to protect the poor against the rich, extended government control over transport and trade, laid a tax on income and established public works including canals that bound rivers together and irrigated the fields. To prevent rich merchants and shopkeepers from making big profits, prices were regulated throughout the empire. By the end of his reign China was at one of the three high points in its history. But there was no competent successor to Wu-ti. Selfish officials lined their own pockets and unworthy men achieved high office; floods and droughts created tragic shortages which raised prices beyond control. Plagued by the high cost of living, the poor joined the rich calling for a return to the old ways. Reforms were rescinded and gradually forgotten.

A century later when Wang Mang became ruler he at once instituted a series of reforms. He gave land to the peasants, freed male slaves, controlled prices rigidly, started public works with paid labor, took over mortgages from moneylenders, granted government loans, and set up pensions for the old, the sick, and jobless. Even school curricula were reformed—literary subjects reduced and practical subjects emphasized. After awhile those whose profits had been clipped by his legislation united to plot his fall; they were helped by a Yellow River flood. When rebellion broke out practically no one came to his support, and he was cut down by a soldier. Everything was as before; the cycle had started all over again.

A thousand years later, Wang An-shih (1021–1086), the famous prime minister, tried the boldest reforms of all. Land and government loans were given to the peasants, prices controlled, trade and commerce nationalized, and welfare provided for the unemployed, the old, and the sick. Education and the examination system were reformed; books of rhetoric were replaced by primers of history and political economy. These reforms affected not only the officials, the usurers, the landlords, and the merchants but the scholars as well. In spite of the support of the Emperor, Wang's program collapsed. Taxes had to be raised to finance the swelling band of government employees. Corruption in the bureaucracy led the conservatives to argue that human corruptibility and incompetence made governmental control of industry impractical. When another period of floods and droughts coincided with the appearance of a terrifying comet, the Son of Heaven was forced to dismiss Wang An-shih and put an end to his reforms.

"What about Mao's China? Will that change too?" Jui T'ang hesitated a moment and then she said that China was bound to change because its needs and circumstances would change in a rapidly changing world. Just as Mao had brought order out of chaos, had created a new kind of society and given moral leadership to the people, so future leaders must make more use of the Chinese genius in order to develop the technology and administrative skills demanded of a strong modern nation. Now that China had a place of dignity in the world she believed that Chinese Communism would become more flexible, less ideological, and would permit more freedom of thought. This would take time. Then with a twinkle in her eyes she reminded me that the Chinese people are very patient. They see time as eternity broken down into centuries. She hoped that universities would once again attain the distinction of Yenching, for then intellectual and creative personalities would emerge as they had in the past to help shape China's future growth. "Growth needs freedom," she said, "but it needs discipline too." She saw the West plagued by grave social problems because it had stressed freedom without keeping the necessary controls. "Perhaps China will show the way to combine the two," she said.

There were many things to think about when I left Jui T'ang that night. My other Yenching students came to mind—especially those bright, eager, idealistic students who had dreamed of making China a free, united, and great country. Somewhere they were living and working in China. Were they among those who had helped to shape this New China—or had they been among the victims?

Wherever China is being discussed someone is bound to say: "But

China is not free." Can the freedom of a whole society ever be measured objectively? Whose freedom? What freedom? By whose standards shall we judge? In the *London Sunday Times* Richard Hughes once wrote: "I knew Shanghai when it was the gayest city in the Far East—gay, that is, if you were a foreigner or a Chinese millionaire. But there were corpses in the street every night; 20,000 died a year from hunger, cold, and exposure. And there were swarms of beggars. And the childish streetwalkers. And the rickshaw coolies, with a professional life expectancy of eight years if they didn't smoke too much opium. . . . Now no one goes hungry in Shanghai.

"So arises the dilemma. Who can strike the balance between freedom from starvation for the majority against freedom of thought for the minority? The comparison, one must keep repeating, is not the China of today with the Western world of today, but the China of today with the China of yesterday."

Felix Green has pointed out that when a Chinese uses the word "freedom" he is not talking about it in any theoretical sense. He means he is free at last to eat and not to starve; he is free of the landlord and the moneylenders; he is free to exercise talents which he had never been able to develop before; he is free to send his children to school, to have them taken care of when they are ill; he is free to look at the future with hope and not with despair. One has only to talk with farmers in a people's commune, he says, or to watch workers on the many construction projects, or school children trotting along the boulevards of Peking during the morning exercise period to sense a vitality, a tenacity, and an enthusiastic dedication to the development of this New China.

"It is easy for pluralistic America," Ross Terrill wrote in his book *The Real China,* "which has 6 percent of the world population and about 35 percent of its wealth to attack the regimentation of China which has about 25 percent of the world population and 4 percent of its wealth. Easy, too, for America to shake its head at the psychological simplicity of China's nation-building mood and forget that America was itself once in a proud, naive stage of nation-building with a sense of innocence and mission. . . . One has to be in China to see this civilization in its present power in order to sense how much the Chinese people and nation may mean in the pattern of future decades."

Reflections

IT WAS 200 YEARS AGO that America was in this "nation-building"
mood. Our founding fathers, that galaxy of great men, had high
hopes for this new nation. It was to be "a model for all mankind, a
city on a hill, a haven of liberty and reason and justice." Because this
was a little country of 3,000,000 on the edge of a wilderness, the com-
munities in which the people lived were small. Families worked together, relaxed together, and worshipped together. On their coins
was stamped "In God we trust." Although like China today there
were grave problems, here too, among those early patriots, was a new
spirit—a buoyancy, an excitement, a spirit of confidence, a strength
that comes from belief in oneself. In half a century remarkable things
had been accomplished. Europeans began to cross the great expanse
of ocean to see for themselves this new nation, just as today people
from all over the world want to fly to the Orient to see this New
China.

In 1831 when Alexis de Tocqueville came from France, he called
America "a land of wonders, in which everything is in constant motion and every change seems an improvement.... No natural boundary seems to be set to the efforts of man; and in his eyes what is not yet
done is only what he has not yet attempted!" Was he right? A century later America had become the richest and most powerful nation
in the world with the highest standard of living of any people in all
history.

Who would have dreamed that in less than a century, in 1918,
America would have been able to turn the tide of battle in a great

European War? Why had America entered that war? Was it only because her neutral rights had been violated by German submarines? In a book *Too Proud to Fight: Woodrow Wilson's Mentality,* published this year by the Oxford University Press, the author adds another dimension: "that only by entering the war would the United States gain representation at the peace table and only as a belligerent could the President effectively use his influence to promote a better world order. He hoped to change the war from a crime into a crusade and could not but see himself as one who in all humility would lead mankind to a universal dominion of right."

I was in college in 1918. In those days we still believed in the ascendancy of history; the world was going to get better and better. In our innocence we believed that there would be no more wars. Although this was called the "Flapper Age," we had a vision of human greatness. Education was focused on man and his great achievements, just as it had been since the days of Thomas Jefferson and John Adams. We were proud of our technology and excited about all the wonderful things it promised, but we had no idea of radios, television, washing machines, nor electric refrigerators—we thought the "ice-man" was here to stay.

Our great leaders, like Harry Emerson Fosdick, were men of deep convictions—they had a positive and dynamic program of democracy, social and economic justice. Above all they had faith in moral and spiritual values which gave us a sense of purpose and a direction to our lives. In the recess of our college chapel was "God is Love." Our college motto was "Not to be administered unto but to minister." I thought of that motto as I sailed for China.

Also we had a deep love of country. Katherine Lee Bates, one of the great teachers at Wellesley with whom I studied Shakespeare, had written "America the Beautiful" and it had been set to music. We knew every word of it and sang it heartily.

> O beautiful for spacious skies, for amber waves of grain,
> For purple mountains majesties above the fruited plain!
>
> O beautiful for pilgrim feet whose stern unpassioned stress,
> A thoroughfare for freedoms beat across the wilderness!
>   America! America! God mend thy every flaw
> Confirm thy soul in self-control, thy liberty in law.

America! America! May God thy gold refine
Till all success be nobleness and every gain divine.

O beautiful for patriot's dream that sees beyond the years
Thine alabaster cities gleam undimmed by human tears!
America! America! God shed his grace on thee
And crown thy good with brotherhood from sea to shining sea!

These were years of great promise and hope for America. There were still grave problems but we were not overawed by them; they were merely hurdles in our path. We believed we were moving with history, just as the Chinese today believe it is they who are moving with history. But forces were already at work shaping our world—a world that was to become vastly different from what we had dreamed. "Events move at their own pace toward their own far-off ends, no more affected by the shifts of days and decades than the depths of the seas are affected by surface storms or calms."

This is our bicentennial year when "tall ships" and ambassadors from all over the world paid tribute to our founding. Although we are young as nations go, ours is one of the oldest governments in the world today. It intrigues me to think that the new China, with its ancient civilization, still has one of its founding fathers living. This is The Year of the Dragon in China, the year 4674.

We have already crossed the threshold into the last quarter of the twentieth century. Fifty years have gone by since we sang of those "alabaster cities undimmed by human tears"—fifty years since I stood by the railing of the S.S. *President Madison* and thought, as I looked out onto the expanse of ocean, that the time had come when there was to be a brave new world. This was a dream that had stirred the hearts and minds of men and women almost since the dawn of history. Confucius had said "Under Heaven, all are one." St. John nearly two thousand years ago wrote, "And I saw a new heaven and a new earth; for the first heaven and the first earth were passed away." We thought the moment for the fulfillment of that dream had come.

But we were wrong. Within the decade came the great depression which brought misery and tragedy to millions of homes throughout the Western world. Another terrible war erupted engulfing the entire globe—a war more devastating and cruel then could possibly have been imagined. Not only was there the terror of the atomic bomb but the evil leadership of Adolph Hitler with his Dachau and his other Nazi death camps. James Michener has written, "The most profound thing that has happened during my years on earth was neither the hydrogen bomb nor man's walk on the moon; it was the deterioration of Germany, the world's best-educated nation, under the leadership of Adolph Hitler, for this related to man's inherent nature and threw a gloomy shadow over all men. This moral collapse proved that nations cannot survive by intelligence alone; they also require spiritual guidelines, and if these are lacking or inadequate, even the finest nation can descend to barbarism."

In the wake of this war there was a social upheaval in which the old moral code disappeared and no new code came to replace it. Durant suggests that caught in the relaxing interval between one moral code and another, an unmoored generation surrendered itself to luxury, corruption, and a restless disorder of family and morals. Permissiveness loosened all controls and under the guise of "freedom," almost anything was permitted.

Many great countries like France and Italy never fully recovered from these disruptions; they brought an end to the proud British Empire. The United States did recover and became bigger, richer, and more powerful than ever—but material success, competition, and self-interest became the dominating force. Although life became easier, more comfortable, more enjoyable than ever before, a sense of disillusionment gradually crept in. Science, after all, had not ushered in a Utopia. Auden called this "The Age of Anxiety."

Now as I look out onto our society, I see my country faced with staggering problems—social, economic, and political. There is little trace of the buoyancy, the optimism, the vitality and energy, the sense of destiny that fired earlier generations. Instead I sense an uneasiness, a frustration, a bewilderment as if we do not know where we are going. Many people believe that the Western world is slipping into a new "dark age"—they are reminded of the fall of Rome.

Lewis Mumford is a thoughtful, distinguished scholar who has recently finished a visiting professorship at the Massachusetts Institute of Technology. "If I were to add up all the evils that have been increasing over the last half century," he told David Salisbury of the *Christian Science Monitor,* "this would be a horror story. Nonsensical violence, increased crime, drugs, assassinations, the fact that Linda Lovelace (a star in pornographic films) is being invited to give lectures around the country, all signal a fundamental dissolution in the forces that hold society together."

What happened? Did our comforts and conveniences weaken our physical stamina and our moral fiber? Was it our technology that gained control and created a megamachine, a juggernaut that is taking us where we do not want to go—with more and more automobiles on more and more superhighways; and air, earth, and sea polluted by industrial waste? Has the doubling of our population in the last fifty years created such a big, diversified country that it cannot be effectually governed under our system? Abraham Lincoln said "It has long been a grave question whether any government, not too strong for the liberties of the people, can be strong enough to maintain its existence in great emergencies." Or have we entered a new era when all the industrial nations of the world are facing a crisis and we are caught up in the web of issues that crisscross and affect the entire fabric of the Western world?

The questions come easily. The answers are more difficult for events are moving so fast that we can hardly keep abreast of what is happening in this complicated world of ours. Since 1950, seventy new and independent nations have come into being. What is true today is not necessarily true tomorrow. We have discovered that oil is not just something to put in our cars, or to heat our homes, or to feed our factories; it can topple governments and change the world's balance of power. For years the nations of the world have spent billions of dollars on armaments "for defense." Their stock piles could destroy the world. Yet the Arab nations, without firing a gun, were able to challenge their power. This is a new kind of war. Although we have long been warned about overpopulation, we now have to face the fact that very likely our era is the moment in time when population growth may well exceed food growth on this small planet of four billion people.

After two hundred years of industrial expansion, the Western countries may have reached an historic "crunch-point." Continued commitment to physical growth and the reckless, wasteful use of the earth's treasure may only bring disaster. Think of it, the United States expends on air-conditioning alone as much as the total energy used in all of China. This highly technical civilization of the West has benefitted those who live in it, yet this civilization has depended to a large extent on scarce natural resources from the developing world. This system of interdependence which the rich countries have produced is global and the cooperation of the poor countries is needed to survive. "And here," says Maurice Strong, United Nations environmental chief, "morality and self-interest reinforce each other. For the first time we have a situation in which the moral, philosophical, and spiritual insights of the great leaders of the world—concepts of brotherhood, sharing and caring—are preconditions for survival."

For as long as we can see into the future and certainly until the end of this century, there will undoubtedly be problems of scarcity. For us in the "rich" countries it will be a time of testing. I like the way August Heckscher describes the future: "We'll walk a great deal more. More people will plant gardens. More will farm; they will draw power from windmills, from the sunlight, from the falling water. The profligate use of land for suburban developments will be curtailed and central cities will again seem warm and habitable places for living. All animal species will become precious to us; green things will be cherished for what they are and for what they symbolize of nature's being.

"Of course, there will still be a good deal of foolishness. T.V. and radio will continue to urge us to buy useless luxuries. But gradually men and women will come to take them less seriously, and they will listen to other voices—those that speak to them of half-forgotten truths and of neglected virtues. This is not what we dreamed our future would be. It will resemble more the past. Hard work, sacrifice, and self-discipline will be important once again, with love and friendship being the bonds that hold society together."

All agree that we have the intelligence and the technical skills to face up to the dangers. But Toynbee asks, "Have we the wisdom and the resolution?" Many who are studying the long range problems fear that the Western countries may have to impose authoritative controls in order to manage their economies. Robert Heilbroner in *For-*

eign Affairs goes so far as to say: "Central among the changes will be the extension of public control far beyond anything yet experienced in the West, socialist or capitalist. To bring environmental stability, the authority of government must necessarily be expanded to include family size, consumption habits, and the volume of industrial output." Some years ago, Durant in his *The Lessons of History* wrote, "The Western world visibly moves toward the synthesis of capitalism and socialism. East is West and West is East, and soon the twain will meet."

Such changes will not be made quickly, but a beginning must be made. First of all we must realize that the whole chain of life is one; it is wrapped around all of us and we cannot escape even if we try. "In becoming aware of this crucial environment challenge," Mr. Heilbroner says, "we feel within ourselves the first stirring of a new view of the human future and our responsibility for assuring that there will be a human future. This startled recognition can set the stage for more decisive action by generations to follow."

Does China have anything to say to the world as it faces these crises? It is the only country so far that has managed the gigantic feat of organizing a new society that is making maximum use of human resources and minimum use of energy. Unlike the other developing countries, China has not rushed to buy the latest and the best in Western industry and technology. In an article in the *Monitor,* "Managing our Planet," Takashi Oka tells of a friend who knew the desolate Chinese northwest during World War II—a land of treeless plains, a land eroded over the centuries by mud and sand and sudden fierce floods—a land pitted with deep gullies. When he returned a couple of years ago he stood amazed at what he saw. The hills had been leveled, the gullies filled in. Long straight canals brought water, and drainage ditches took it away. Vast belts of trees stretched to the horizon. And all this had been done mostly by human hands and feet.

They are beholden to no one. China has received no gifts of American grain. The Soviet Union abruptly withdrew its aid and its technicians in the late 1950s and no other country has taken its place. Their people are healthy and there is no starvation. They have curbed population growth to less than 2 percent a year; when couples have more than three children, the fourth and every subsequent child is counted as nonexistent for rationing purposes.

It has been suggested that Bangladesh, instead of depending on Western handouts, should go the Chinese way: mobilizing the population for huge projects to dam rivers, build dykes, canals and drainage ditches—in other words, use to the full the only resource which Bangladesh has—its own people. Those who supported the Chinese way lost the argument.

There are many people who contend that the Chinese way is not for export; it works for China because the people have had "four thousand years of being Chinese." Nevertheless, China challenges the West. In China's collective life today there is an ingredient of personal moral concern for one's neighbors that has a lesson for us all.

Ross Terrill hints at this when he writes: "The Chinese people and all the other people of the world are now drastically interlocked together. We shall understand ourselves together and make a livable future together or not at all. We owe it to our common humanity and to the children of this world to turn a critical eye on this land of 800,000,000 people."

Who knows? Perhaps the storm cloud that is looming on the horizon may have a silver lining. Under the surface a new life may be knitting together struggling still to find its way. Camus once said: "great ideas come into the world as gently as doves. If we listen attentively, we shall hear amid the uproar of empires and nations a faint flutter of wings, the great stirring of life and hope." The Chinese use two brush symbols to shape the word "crisis." One stroke means "danger," the other "opportunity," suggesting that we can reduce the danger by seizing the opportunity.

It may be that we are living in one of the great turning points in history as epochal as the evolution from hunting to farming or the advent of the industrial revolution. Some of our world leaders are saying that we are already at the beginning of the evolution from a world of independent nations to a global world and that the great turmoil and disruptions in the world today may be the birthpangs of a new era.

They believe that if we act wisely and with vision, the decades ahead could be in retrospect one of the great periods of human creativity—a time when we took one step nearer to the unity of the human race. All agree that this will take great human resolve and human ability, but they point out that man's future is in his hands for it is people and ideas that make history.

Certainly, if this vision is to be fulfilled it must begin with ourselves. Each one of us must go his own way, but go as one who means to help bring it about; for the world will never be right until we make over ourselves. It has been suggested that we turn off our radios and televisions more, get out of our automobiles and begin talking and listening to one another, start caring more and sharing more. Durant suggests that we listen more to the philosophers and saints who are the only real revolutionaries. Samuel Eliot Morison calls our attention to the Preamble to the Declaration of Independence:

"We hold these Truths to be self-evident, that all men are created equal, that they are endowed by their Creator with certain unalienable Rights, and among them are Life, Liberty, and the Pursuit of happiness."

"These words," he says, "are more revolutionary than anything written by Robespierre, Marx, or Lenin, more explosive than the atom, a constant challenge to ourselves, as well as an inspiration to the oppressed of all the world."

Confucius would say that a new world must rest with people worthy of a new world. And it is a Chinese proverb that reminds us that a journey of a thousand miles begins with one step.